Walter Colton

Ship and Shore in Madeira, Lisbon and the Mediterranean

Walter Colton

Ship and Shore in Madeira, Lisbon and the Mediterranean

ISBN/EAN: 9783337765101

Printed in Europe, USA, Canada, Australia, Japan

Cover: Foto ©Andreas Hilbeck / pixelio.de

More available books at **www.hansebooks.com**

IN

MADEIRA, LISBON, AND THE MEDITERRANEAN.

AND

SEA AND SAILOR.

By REV. WALTER COLTON,
LATE OF THE UNITED STATES NAVY.

BOSTON:
CLEAVES, MACDONALD & CO.,
1886.

Ship and Shore,
and
Sea and Sailor.

PREFACE.

In defiance of a profound maxim of my distant relative —I say distant, because he was so far removed from me on the genealogical tree that even a Yankee peddler in the remote part of the South would not, upon the force of such a relationship, put up his horse and himself for more than six weeks, and that must place him on a very extreme twig, perhaps even its shadow.—By the way—it is a little singular that these fellows of the wooden nutmeg should always know where to find a market for their nuts and notions.— But as I was saying—in defiance of a profound maxim of my distant relative—what a world of tender thoughts and emotions spring up in that one word *relative!*—what beings step from the magic of its circle:—uncles not a few, aunts without number, and cousins a whole ship-load—all taking a warm interest in you if rich, a pride in you if learned or politically great, and never deserting you unless you become poor — blessings on their sweet hearts! — Without them what would a man be, or rather, what would the world be to him?—A garden without a flower, a grove without a bird, an evening sky without one lovely star.—His feelings would break over his desolate heart, like a sunless ocean surging over a dead world.—But as I was saying—in defiance of a profound maxim of my distant relative, the author of—that word *author!*—it never had such a fearful meaning to me before.—It may be my imagination, but it seems like a garment lined with sharp hatchel-teeth to be wrapped around my naked form.—It so agitates my whole system, that my poor bedstead gets into such a shake every night, as to take quite all the next day for it to become tranquil, and even then the tester trembles like an aspen leaf, or a pigeon, in a thunder-storm.—To see others become authors —to see them tried, condemned, and executed, is comparatively nothing; but to be put to the bar yourself—to hear your own sentence—to see the noose tied for your own neck, and to know that among the thousands who are gathering to witness your swinging fidgets, not one heart will throb with pity;—it is this which so agitates and confounds me!— But as I was saying—in defiance of a profound maxim of my distant relative, the author of Lacon—that is a book which only the wise will read, and only the profound can comprehend,—it is an intellectual mine, where every thought is a diamond of the keenest edge, and most brilliant ray, and where giants may work with their pickaxes and still leave it unexplored; and yet he who created this mine had nothing about him in keeping with it—no consistency in morals or money.—He was the most singular of men—dining on a herring, and keeping the most splendid coach in London— wearing a hat soiled and rent with years, and trowsers that betrayed at the bottoms of their legs the gnawing despair of some famishing rat, and carrying at the same time in the top of his snuff-box a diamond that was itself an independent fortune,—preaching a part of the year to his English parishioners, and gambling out the rest in the French metropolis.—But as I was saying—in defiance of a profound maxim of my distant relative, the author of Lacon—who, I am sorry to say, committed suicide—committed it too, after having penned against the act an aphorism that might well have fallen from the lips of an angel;—an aphorism numbered in his manuscripts C C C, which express not only its numerical relation, but the initials of his own name, as if he had unknowingly addressed it to himself.—If there be not something more than mere coincidence in this, then there is no truth in my grandmother's manual on auguries. —And yet he committed the act;—but such is ever the inconsistency of one who has broken the balance-wheel in his moral nature.—He is like a ship that has lost her helm— with which the winds for a time disport, then dash it on the rocks!—But as I was saying—in defiance of a profound maxim of my distant relative, the author of Lacon, which says——there! I have forgotten now what it says—this is a hard case—for I was just making port—all ready to let go anchor—and I am now out at sea again in a fog:—this dirty, thick weather always comes on as you near a coast —it has been the cause of more shipwrecks than all the tempests put together.—Most people think the nearer the shore the safer the ship:—directly the reverse—a whale is never stranded at sea, nor is a ship—unless an island comes bobbing up out of the water like Venus—a debut which I think was in extremely bad taste.—But—the fog begins to break away—and now, as I was saying, in defiance of a profound maxim of my distant relative, the author of Lacon, which says,—" a writer who cannot throw fire into his works ought to throw his works into the fire "—I publish this book. rather, I allow it to escape.

>Go, little book, I *will* not burn thee,
>Wander at will the country o'er,
>And tell to all who do not spurn thee
>Thy simple tale of Ship and Shore.

AUTHOR.

CONTENTS.

CHAPTER I.

The Light-House—Pleasures and Pains of Memory—Unaccountable Presentiment—Loss of Companions—Ship Discipline—Ladies on board a Man-of-War—Ward-Room Officers and Midshipmen—Traits of a Sailor—The Setting Sun—Tribute to Woman—Funeral at Sea—Welcome to a lost Bird........................ 17

CHAPTER II.

First Sight of Land—Peak of Pico—Terceira—City of Angra—Visit to the Shore—Appearance of the Inhabitants—Cathedral—Vespers—Convent—Nuns—Gardens Singular Monument—Shaving the Hog—A Gale and Wreck... 34

CHAPTER III.

Madeira—First Appearance—Glories of Sunset—Ride into the Interior—Ponies and Burroqueros—Deep Ravines—Peasantry—A Madeiran Beauty—An English Lady—Dinner and Dancing 46

CHAPTER IV.

Madeira continued—Excursion—Villa of an English Bachelor—Tragical Death of George Canning—Wild Ravine—Singular Waterfall—Lady of the Mount—Superstition—The Dying Mother's Request—Star of Bethlehem—Visit to the Convent of Santa Clara—Introduction to a beautiful Nun—Her involuntary Confinement—Personal Attractions—Mental Accomplishments—Proposed scheme of Escape 57

CHAPTER V.

A singular Marriage—Cathedral—Clergy—Weighing a Protestant—The proscribed Fidalgo—Camancha Villa—Its Lady—The Ribeiro—A sleeping Sentinel—Force of human Sympathy—Mystery of Sleep—Joy of Morning—Matins of Maria—Ride to the Curral—Stupendous Scenery—Quiet Hamlet—Force of Habit—Saint's Day—Homage of Gunpowder—Recollections of Home—Twilight—The Vesper-Bell 74

CHAPTER VI.

Sketches of Madeira—Physical Features—Wines—Climate—City of Funchal—Priests—Society—Morals—Peasantry—Merchants—Political Opinions—Habits of the Ladies—Courtships—Our Parting and Farewell....... 92

CHAPTER VII.

Passage from Madeira to Lisbon—Sea-sickness as a Purgatorial state—Situation of a Member of Congress and Officer of the Navy compared—Rock of Lisbon—Pilot—Tagus—Cheering—Rockets—Don Miguel—City of Lisbon—Cabriolets—Postillion—Madam Julia's Hotel—A partisan Merchant—Alcantra Aqueduct—Church of St. Roque—Mosaics—Queen Maria First—Church of St. Domingo—Statue of King Joseph—The Earthquake—Inquisition.............................. 104

CHAPTER VIII.

Excursion to Cintra—Scenery—Marialva Villa—Peter's Prison—Penha Convent—Royal Palace—Visit to Mafra Castle—Its Extent—Richness—Singular Origin—Return to Lisbon—Its Streets and Dogs—Don Miguel—Habits of the Females—Friars and Monks—Perils of Night-walking—Impositions on Strangers—A Blind Musician—Political Disasters.................... 127

CHAPTER IX.

Passage from Lisbon to Gibraltar—Diversions of the Sailor—His Tact at Telling Stories—Love of the Song—Fondness for Dancing—Unhappy Propensities—Duty of the Government towards him—Gibraltar—A befitting Emblem of British power—Romance of its History—

Fortifications—Troops—Motley Population—Summit of the Rock—St. Michael's Cave—The Five Hundred—Monboddo's Originals—Pleasure Party—Music and a Mermaid 152

CHAPTER X.

Malaga—Coming to Anchor—Cathedral—Tomb of Moliana—Fiddles and Organs in Churches—Castle of the Moors—Hours of a Malaguena—Traits of a singular Bandit—A Spanish Lady—Twilight and the Promenade—A Funeral 172

CHAPTER XI.

Passage from Malaga to Mahon—Tedious Calms—Relieving Incidents—Vist of a Bird—Capture of an ominous Shark—Intrusions of a Ghost—Unfair taking off of a Black Cat—Petted Hedge-hog—Morgan's Spectre at Niagara—Mahon—Harbor—Fort St. Philip—Admiral Byng—Lazaretto—Navy-Yard—Habits of the Mahonees—Effects of a certain vice on Man—Grand Organ—Sailors on Shore—Jack and the Opera—Entertainments 187

CHAPTER XII.

Passage from Mahon to Naples—Life at Sea—Chest of a Sailor—Power of a Poet—Track of the Ship—Naples from the Harbor—Unreasonable Quarantine—Grievous

Disappointment—Premature Departure—Ebullition of Spleen—Passage from Naples to Messina—Volcano of Stromboli—Dead Calms—Utility of Whales—Pastimes in Calms—Faro di Messina—Charybdis and Scylla—Ancient Whirlpool—Curiosities of the Sea—Messina from the Strait 214

CHAPTER XIII.

Excursion to Mount Etna—Sleeping in a Corn-field—Incidents of the Ascent—Storm at Night—View from the Summit—Descent—Catania—Gayety of the Living above the Dead—Museum of the Prince of Biscari—Franciscan Monk—Passage from Messina to Milo—Murat and Ney—Tides of the Strait—Island of Candia—Island of Cerigo—Aspect of Milo—Historic Incidents—Greek Pilot—Medicinal Springs—Natural Grottoes—Ancient Tombs 235

CHAPTER XIV.

Town of Milo—Steepness of the Streets—Advice to Distillers—Statue of Venus—View from the Town—Greek Wedding—Dress and Person of the Bride—Fickleness of Fashions in Dress—Anecdote of Franklin—Passage from Milo to Smyrna—Cape Colonna—Temple of Minerva—Profession of Pirates—Island of Ipsara—Aspect of Scio—Massacre of the Inhabitants—Conduct of the Allies—Gulf of Smyrna—Ancient Clazomenæ—Traits of the Sailor 258

CHAPTER XV.

Smyrna—Its Seamen—Motley Population—The Tartar Janizary—Modern Warfare—Encounters in threading the Streets—Fruit Market—Bazars—Greek Girls—Turkish Burial-Ground—The Child unacquainted with Death—Smyrna continued—Religious Sects—Visit to Governor—His Palace—Pipes—Horses—Troops—Coffee-House Scene—Prayers of the Mussulmen—Martyrdom of Polycarp—Birth-place of Homer—Parting with the Reader 283

SHIP AND SHORE.

CHAPTER I.

A SAILOR ever loves to be in motion,
  Roaming about, he scarce knows where or why;
He looks upon the dim and shadowy ocean
  As home—abhors the land; and e'en the sky,
Boundless and beautiful, has naught to please,
Except some clouds, which promise him a breeze.

THE LIGHT-HOUSE—PLEASURES AND PAINS OF MEMORY—UNACCOUNTABLE PRESENTIMENT—LOSS OF COMPANIONS—SHIP DISCIPLINE—LADIES ON BOARD A MAN-OF-WAR—WARD-ROOM OFFICERS AND MIDSHIPMEN—TRAITS OF A SAILOR—THE SETTING SUN—TRIBUTE TO WOMAN—FUNERAL AT SEA—WELCOME TO A LOST BIRD.

IT is now seven days since we weighed anchor in Hampton Roads, and took our parting leave of the land. The last object that vanished from my steadfast eye, was the old Light-house on Cape Henry. I watched that as it sunk slowly in the horizon, and felt, when it was gone, as one that has parted with a venerable, attached friend. Never before did a light-house appear to me an object of such beauty, fidelity, and affectionate regard. It seemed as if it had come forth from the thousand objects of the heart's yearning remembrances, to take its position on that promontory, where it might look its last farewell, and express its kindest wishes.

During the seven days that we have been at sea, I have lived but in the past. The segment of life's poor circle through which I have gone has sprung again from its grave of memory, bringing with it each incident of pleasure and sorrow, each object of pursuing hope and lingering endearment. How mysterious is the spirit of memory—how painfully true to the objects of its trust—how quick and vital over the relics of joys that have fled, friendships that have ceased, errors that have been wept! How intensely it concentrates into a point, years of wisdom or weakness, pleasure or pain—pouring through the soul, in an unbroken current, the mingled sensations that have blessed or blighted its previous existence!

The ocean is its empire. I should not envy a guilty man his repose, who should here seek an escape from the deserts and the haunting remembrance of his crimes. Every wave in this vast solitude would speak to him as from eternity, and every dark cloud would bear in its folds a message of wildest thunder. If there be a cavern in hell, where anguish is without alleviation, it must be that where a guilty spirit suffers in solitude.

I am not a believer in supernatural intimations, yet the presentiment that I am never to retrace my steps, that I shall never see again the cherished beings that encircle the hearth of my home, clings to my heart with a dark and desperate pertinacity. You may smile at this, if you will, and expose its want of philosophy, but it is proof against all argument and ridicule. It is not the effect of fear, for this is not the first time that I have been at sea, and my confidence in the power and capacity of a ship to triumph over the conflicting elements, has increased with every day's experience. Nor is it from any apprehensions connected with those diseases which frequently scourge the places which we are to visit; for I have been in those putrid ports and cities, where one of the most familiar sights is the black hearse rumbling on its dismal errand. Nor is it to be traced to any fearful inferences from an extreme feebleness of constitution; for this very debility is frequently the best shield against malignant disease. The sturdy oak breaks before the tempest, but the pliant sapling yields, and when the storm has passed over erects itself. Nor is this gloomy presentiment ascribable to that melancholy mood of mind which darkly predicts ills that are never to be experienced, nor to that morbid sentimentality which affects sorrows that are never felt.

It is rather an undefined, involuntary, and inexplicable conviction which reason did not induce, and which reason cannot force away. Dr. Johnson believed in ghosts, and would not cross his threshold left foot first; and no arguments, however profound and ingenious, could have convinced that sagacious reasoner that he was unphilosophical or superstitious. The hare is not timid that trembles where the lion shakes.

Had any one told me a few years since that I was to become a sailor, that I should at this time be on board a Man-of-war, bound to the Mediterranean, I should have regarded the prediction with incredulous amazement. But

> "How little do we know, that which we are:
> How less, what we may be!"

Time and the force of circumstances work changes upon us of which we little dream. The very habits which fitted me for the contemplative quietude of the closet, by undermining my health, have driven me into an opposite extreme; for there is no situation where every element is more stirring and restless, than on board an armed ship. It would seem as if the principles of a perpetual motion had found a favorite lodgment in every particle of which this vast floating fabric is composed. There is not a spar, or plank, or rope, that does not appear to have caught this spirit of uneasiness; much more the jovial tar, whose home is on the mountain wave, who loves the quick breeze and the rapid sea, and who regards a life free from these excitements, as a state of listlessness and inactivity unbecoming a breathing man.

I am not quite a stranger to the peculiarities of my present condition. A former cruise in another quarter has familiarized me in some measure to the strange habitudes of nautical life. Alas! I can never think of that cruise without grief. We left there three of our dearest companions, who will return no more! They were in the spring-time of life, full of hope, enterprise, and lofty resolutions, but they have gone down to the silence and dreamless sleep of the grave. Their generous purposes and goodly promise have all perished in the bud. How often has the mother, in the depth of her anguish, doubted the melancholy tale; and how has the little sister, unacquainted with death, still expected her brother's return! Spring shall return with its buds of promise, summer with its purpling fruits, autumn with its golden harvest, but these come not again; there is no returning pathway through the grave.

The journal which I have now commenced, and which I intend to continue during the cruise, shall be confined mainly to my first and freshest impressions. I will cast into it the bright, the mournful, the deep or transient feelings, which the different incidents or objects encountered may awaken. There is only one subject upon which I shall reserve myself, and that is the government, the discipline of the ship. The moral and political mechanism of a floating community like this is too peculiar, too intricate and complicated for hasty opinion, and I shall therefore wait the results of the fullest experience.

Few situations involve a more perplexing responsibility or require a higher combination of rare talent, than that of a commander of a national ship. To be popular, and at the same time efficient, he must be able to enforce a most strict and rigid discipline, without giving to it that cast of unfeeling severity, to which the despotical nature of a ship's government is extremely liable. He must be open and undisguised, and express even his sentiments of disapprobation with a freedom and frankness, which may lead the subordinate officer to the instantaneous conviction that there are no suppressed feelings of bitterness, which may, in an unexpected hour, reveal their nourished and terrific strength. This plain and honest dealing is infinitely preferable to a heartless hypocrisy of manner; it relieves all around from those disquieting suspicions which duplicity never fails to excite; and where it is united with a generous disposition, a well-informed mind, and a dignified demeanor, cannot fail to secure affection and respect.

As my opinions may perchance, hereafter, be quoted as law on questions affecting the interests and etiquette of the service, there is another subject on which I must be for the present discreetly reserved. This involves the expediency and propriety of permitting us to take out our ladies on board our public ships. It will appear, as I am aware, ungallant to hesitate over an immediate and unqualified approbation of this license; but as my decision is to strike through all future usage in the service, and as its condemnatory features might be ascribed to the fact of my not having any one to take out, were the privilege granted, I shall withhold it till events may place it beyond the reach of such a cynical construction.

Yet, could any one disposed to arraign this measure, have seen the quantity of letters that went back by the return boat of the pilot, and above all, could he have glanced into the contents of those epistles, and marked the tears and passionate fervors that mingled there, like rain and lightning in a summer's cloud, he would have exclaimed, in relenting tenderness, let the cherished beings of their bosom go with them! Separate not, by a wide ocean, hearts so intensely united—beings so entirely formed for one hearth and home! Even Jack sent back the evidence of his truth: his scarcely legible scrawl may have given a fresh and bleeding life to affections, not the less deep on account of a simple, rude exterior. The vigor of the bow depends not on the beauty of its polish.

There is another subject upon which I must be a little reserved;—this touches the character of my immediate companions, the officers of the ward-room. We present, perhaps, in our assembled capacity, as great a variety of intellectual, moral, and social habit, as any group of the same size, ever yet convened on flood or field. There is no shape, which thought, feeling, or association ever assumed, that may not here find a ready, unbroken mold. We have every thing from the silent operations of a mind that expresses its action only in its priceless gifts, to the tumultuous agonies of an imagination that raises a tornado to rock a rose-bud, and rolls the globe over to crush a flea. We have the officer who walks the deck as if he were to be heard in whispers and obeyed in silence, and the one that gives his slightest order in a trumpet voice that might almost endanger the sleep of the dead. We have the ever cheerful and contented being, who would talk encouragingly on a famishing wreck, and the inveterate complainer, who would grumble amid the mellow profusions of a paradise. We have the man of method, who sleeps, dreams, and wakes by rule, and the unsystematized being who would lose, were it possible, his conscious identity; and who will probably be found at the great resurrection coming out of the grave of some other person.

We have a caterer who would purchase an ox for the sake of a sirloin, and a steward who would purchase an egg, were it possible, without the expense of the shell. We have a sailing-master who is seldom wrong when he conjectures, and as rarely right when he calculates; we have a commissary who would shoulder an Atlas of real responsibility, and protest against an ant-hill of petty inconvenience. We have a surgeon who would kneel in worship of the beauty, harmony, and matchless grace of the human form, and then dissect a Cytherean Venus to trace the path of an imaginary muscle. We have a marine officer full of professional pride and ability, but whose troops have never been paralleled since Jack Falstaff mustered his men. We have a Chaplain who vehemently urges us on like an invading army towards heaven, but stays behind himself, as he says, to pick up the stragglers; and we have over all a Commander who inspires the humblest with self-respect, but reinstates the absolute principles of the old school on the levelling doctrines of the new.

Our incongruities do not stop here. We have in our steerage light-hearted lads, unacquainted with a single rope in the ship, never perhaps from home, certainly never at sea before, and who are now giving orders to old weather-beaten mariners, who have ploughed every ocean known to the globe. I pen this not in disparagement of these inexperienced youth; for they have a quick play of intelligence and a freedom from vicious habit, that justly entitles them to esteem and affection. May they be able to preserve the "whiteness of the soul" untouched by the evils that await them, and revisit their sacred homes still worthy of a mother's fondness and a father's pride.

The tendency of early lessons of wisdom and piety, with the incipient habits of childhood, may at times be diverted and driven from their course, but they generally recover again their original channels. If there be any security in after years against a wide departure from virtue, it is found in the early instructions of an anxious, devoted mother. The course of the arrow is decided by the bow she holds in her hands.

Our ship is a frigate of the second class, of light, compact, and graceful architecture; she cuts her way through the water as smoothly and silently as the dolphin. Our crew are more youthful, more full of health and vigor, than are usually met with on the deck of a man-of-war. They are remarkably young, as years are reckoned on land, but the life of a sailor usually stops far short of that period commonly allotted to man. His occupation and habits shake his life-glass and hurry out its sands. I never see one of them die without those feelings we experience in seeing a noble being extinguished before his time.

He has points of character that penetrate to your deepest sensibilities. You see him dividing his last shilling with a pennyless stranger,—perilling his life for one who may perhaps never appreciate the self-sacrificing act,—living to-day in gay forgetfulness of the evils which the morrow must bring,—undergoing hardship, privation, and suffering with an unclouded cheerfulness,—and when death comes, resigning himself to its calamity with a composure that belongs more to philosophy and religion, than the characteristics of his rude life. If any being full of errors, generous impulses, and broken resolves, may hope for mercy in his last account, it must be the poor sailor,

—the man whom temptation and suffering have visited in every form, whose scanty enjoyments have been snatched from the severest lot, and whose wild profession has placed him essentially beyond the reach of those redeeming influences, to which every Christian community is indebted for its virtue and its hope of heaven.

I have been on deck at the close of every clear day to see the sun go down. This is a beautiful sight on shore, but more so at sea; for here the glowing orb appears divested of that excessive brightness, which on land frequently dazzles and pains the naked eye of the beholder. He seems to partake of that solemnity which is felt through nature at his disappearance. The clouds which attended him through the day in glittering attire, now assume a more sober aspect, and put on a dress of deeper richness; their full and flowing folds have a groundwork of purple and gold, and as they float together, they rear over this retiring Monarch of the sky a pavilion, compared with the magnificence of which, the splendors of the Oriental couch are but the tinsel which gilds the cradled sleep of the nursery.

When the last ray that lingered above the wave has vanished, and twilight is gone, the deep blue vault of heaven seems to sweep down to the level waters, and shut out all life, and breath, and motion, beyond its incumbent circle. It is then you feel alone—earth, with its ceaseless stir and countless voices, is shut out,—there is nothing around, beneath, above, but the silent sky and the sleeping Ocean. A man who can stand in such a breathless solitude as this, and not think with warm veneration of HIM, whose benevolent eye notices the fall of the lonely sparrow, must carry within him a heart as cold and insensible as the marbles of the dead.

This observation was made to one who stood near me, and whose fine susceptibilities were more deeply touched than my own. To her this twilight change, and desert ocean, seemed to call up memories in which the heart lingers with a bewildering fondness. She has exchanged the security of the shore, and the society of the most gentle and refined, for the perils and hard features of a man-of-war. Her feelings, as they break through her conversation, betray a freshness and elevation of tone that find their way to your affection and esteem. Cultivated and refined, without being supercilious,—cheerful and communicative, without being obtrusive or trifling,—with mental endowments to entertain the best informed, and a demeanor conciliating the most rude, she must be deservedly popular in her new condition, and cannot fail to enhance the estimation in which the fair of our country are held by foreigners.

> As soft as falls the silken shade,
>   Let every sorrow be
> Which grief, or care, or hope delayed,
>   May ever cast on thee.

And sweetly glide thine hours away
    As music from the string
Of woodland lyre, while o'er it stray
    The fragrant airs of spring.

And let each joy be pure and bright
    As dew on infant flowers,
Some tender theme of new delight
    To cheer thy pensive hours.

And as a soft melodious lay
    Dies on the still of even,
May thy rapt spirit pass away
    And mingle into heaven.

Death is a fearful thing, come in what form it may—fearful when the vital cords are so gradually relaxed, that life passes away softly as music from the slumbering harp-string—fearful when in his own quiet chamber, the departing one is summoned by those who sweetly follow him with their prayers, when the assiduities of friendship and affection can go no further, and who discourse of heaven and future blessedness, till the closing ear can no longer catch the tones of the long familiar voice, and who, lingering near, still feel for the hushed pulse, and then trace in the placid slumber, which pervades each feature, a quiet emblem of the spirit's serene repose.

What then must this dread event be to one, who meets it comparatively alone, far away from the hearth of his home, upon a troubled sea, between the narrow decks of a restless ship, and at that dread hour of night, when even the sympathies of the world seem suspended! Such has been the end of many who traverse the ocean, and such was the hurried end of him, whose remains we have just consigned to a watery grave.

He was a sailor, but beneath his rude exterior he carried a heart touched with refinement, pride, and greatness. There was something about him which spoke of better days and a higher destiny. By what errors or misfortunes he was reduced to his humble condition, was a secret which he would reveal to none. Silent, reserved, and thoughtful, he stood a stranger among his free companions, and never was his voice heard in the laughter or the jest. He has undoubtedly left behind many who will long look for his return, and bitterly weep when they are told they shall see his face no more.

As the remains of poor Prether were brought up on deck, wound in that hammock which through many a stormy night had swung to the wind, one could not but observe the big tear that stole unconsciously down the rough cheek of his hardy companions. When the funeral service was read to that most affecting passage—" we commit this body to the deep,"—and the plank was heaved, which precipitated to the momentary eddy of the wave the quickly disappearing form, a heaving sigh from those around told that the strong heart of the sailor can be touched with grief, and that a truly unaffected sorrow may accompany virtue, in its most unpretending form, to its ocean grave. Yet how soon is such a scene forgotten!

> "As from the wing the sky no scar retains,
> The parted wave no furrow from the keel,
> So dies in human hearts the thought of death."

There is something peculiarly melancholy and impressive in a burial at sea: there is here no coffin or hearse, procession or tolling bell,—nothing that gradually prepares us for the final separation. The body is wound in the drapery of its couch, much as if the deceased were only in a quiet and temporary sleep. In these habiliments of seeming slumber, it is dropped into the wave, the waters close over it, the vessel passes quickly on, and not a solitary trace is left to tell where sunk from light and life, one that loved to look at the sky and breathe this vital air. There is nothing that for one moment can point to the deep, unvisited resting-place of the departed,—it is a grave in the midst of the ocean—in the midst of a vast untrodden solitude. Affection cannot approach it with its tears, the dews of heaven cannot reach it, and there is around it no violet, or shrub, or murmuring stream.

It may be superstitious, but no advantages of wealth, or honor, or power, through life, would reconcile me at its close to such a burial. I would rather share the coarse and scanty provisions of the simplest cabin, and drop away unknown and unhonored by the world, so that my final resting-place be beneath some green tree, by the side of some living stream, or in some familiar spot, where the few that loved me in life might visit me in death. But whether our grave be in the fragrant shade, or in the fathomless ocean, among our kindred, or in the midst of strangers, the day is coming when we shall all appear at one universal bar, and receive from a righteous Judge the award of our deeds. He that is wisest, penetrates the future the deepest.

The day passed slowly and sadly away,—no sail broke the farthest verge of the horizon,—no passing cloud brought with it the incense of an unseen shore; but at night-fall a little bird was seen hovering in wide circles around our ship. It had been driven out to sea in a storm, or had wandered in its careless mirth too far from its native isle; it was unable to retrace its way, too timid to light, and too exhausted to keep much longer on the wing.

> Lonely wand'rer o'er the ocean,
>   Fainting for a place of rest,—
> Canst no longer keep in motion,
>   Durst not trust the billow's breast?—
>
> Feeling fast thy strength diminish,
>   Yet canst spy no friendly shore,
> And must sink, ere thou canst finish
>   One returning circle more?

Rest thee here—I'll softly pillow
    Thy too faint and feeble form,—
Bear thee safely o'er the billow,
    Through this night of cloud and storm.

I was once like thee a stranger,
    Searching for a place of rest,
But to peace and hope a stranger,
    Till I found the Saviour's breast.

CHAPTER II.

> In calms, he gazes at the sleeping sea,
>   Or seeks his lines, and sets himself to angling,
> Or takes to politics, and, being free
>   Of facts, and full of feeling, falls to wrangling:
> Then recollects a distant eye and lip,
> And rues the day on which he saw a ship.

FIRST SIGHT OF LAND—PEAK OF PICO—TERCEIRA—CITY OF ANGRA—VISIT TO THE SHORE—APPEARANCE OF THE INHABITANTS—CATHEDRAL—VESPERS—CONVENT—NUNS—GARDENS—SINGULAR MONUMENT—SHAVING THE HOG—A GALE AND WRECK.

There is one short exclamation in our language, which conveys to the heart of one at sea a more thrilling excitement, than the highest raptures of poetic inspiration. It has no meaning to a man who plods out his days on the uneventful earth, but to one who moves from zone to zone upon the "blue wave," and has many days since parted with the shore, it comes like a glad message from another world—"Land, ho!" I heard it this morning from mast-head just at the break of day, and sprang upon deck, with eye never so quickly cleared to catch a sight of what it conveyed; but I could see nothing except a heavy bank of clouds over our larboard bow.

"Don't you see," said the old cruiser who stood

near me, "that bit of a dark spot there, bobbing up like a buoy out of water—there, now it's gone, but keep it in your eye, and you'll see it again in a minute, just under the stern of that scudding cloud."

I fixed my eye on the cloud, which the fancy of the old seaman had converted into a well-rigged ship, which had just obtruded its dusky sides between us and that dark spot against the sky, but I was still uncertain at what precise point upon the hull to look, not being able to distinguish the stern from the stem in this aerial craft. "There, there, sir, it comes again," whispered the sharp-eyed tar. "At which end of the cloud?" I inquired, impatiently. "At her stern, sir, at her stern, close under her spanker boom," was the technical reply, which betrayed a much better knowledge of nautical phrases, than of an intelligible relationship between an obscuring cloud, and a sharp, elevated point of land.

This "dark spot" on the sky, of a towering sugar-loaf shape, and distinguishable in this respect only, from the thick and motionless mass of clouds which lay beneath it, proved to be the Peak of Pico, rising abruptly some seven thousand feet above the level of the sea, and which may be seen in clear weather at a distance of eighty miles. We were so near it, that two hours' sail brought into beautiful relief, upon the sides of its green acclivities, the white cottages of its inhabitants. I longed to leap upon its shore, and mount its steep cliffs, but we were sailing for Terceira. Adieu then to Pico, to its vine-clad hills, and its volcanic peak, beneath which the rainbow and thunder-cloud dwell in strange concord.

A fair and fresh breeze soon brought us in sight of the bold and lofty rocks which wall the circular shores of Terceira—furnishing its quiet inhabitants a defence, which may excuse in them their want of that chivalrous valor which exposure and danger inspire. Beneath the steep battlements which nature has reared along the breaker-beaten coast of this island, a thousand hostile fleets might exhaust their malice in vain; the iron storm of their batteries would make as little impression as the bubbles of a muttering wave. Upon the south side, this natural wall bends inward, affording a small harbor, of deep bottom and unsafe anchorage. At the foot of a mountain, which here freshly descends to the bright water, stands the neat city of Angra, the capital of the island.

We swung around into this inlet and let go our anchor, to the pleasurable surprise of many, who from their turrets and balconies were scanning our flag, and recognizing in it a long-absent friend. The blue and white banner, which floated from a small armed ship, and the two fortifications which defend the harbor, told us that Donna Maria was the infant queen of this romantic isle.

The necessities of an impatient dinner over, we hastened to the shore, where we met our quasi Consul, who politely offered us his attentions in any form that might be most agreeable. As we had but a few hours to stay, we declined the hospitalities of his hearth, preferring a ramble through the principal streets, and a hasty look at the strange aspect every thing wore. Under his guidance we passed from street to street, meeting everywhere new-fledged soldiers and little groups of citizens, who had been brought together by the sudden appearance of our ship.

The bells were chiming for vespers, and we turned into the Cathedral—a building of huge dimensions, in the Gothic style. We found about forty priests, or friars, and as many boys, who had the gift of music in them, sustaining the chant and occasionally breaking out with great animation in the chorus. When I inquired of our polite guide for the audience—the worshipping multitude that might here be accommodated—he pointed to one poor publican kneeling in the centre of the vast area, and observed, the people here do not attend vespers.

What a worship, I was about to exclaim, is this!—whether paid to God, or saint, or sinner. Why, the little brook, as it murmurs its vesper hymn in the ear of nature, has at least a lonely pilgrim or bird on its brink, to listen to its harmony, and catch the spirit of its homage. But here is a magnificent temple with its sweeping aisles, perfumed altars, white-robed priests, and melodious choir, all consecrated to the worship of the Most High and the sacred edification of man—and only one poor penitent, of the thousands whose sins or gratitude should bring them here, is seen to come and kneel. Surely there must be "rottenness in Denmark."

Breaking from this partial reverie, I joined our company at the extreme end of the aisle, where our guide was leading the way to some recess, or shrine, with an air of peculiar awe—it was the sanctum sanctorum of the place, and we paused upon its hallowed threshold. Three large wax candles were burning within, and before these a venerable priest was walking, as one that meditates alone. The solitary prelate instantly invited us in, and seemed to excuse our not crossing ourselves to the sacred pictures which hung upon the walls. This consecrated cloister was distinguished for the sober richness of its furniture, its silent solemnity, and the multiplicity of images, which cast upon us from every quarter their looks of penitence and celestial hope.

Around the embroidered curtain, which inclosed the Host, bloomed several vases of fresh flowers. The priest from one of them, as we retired, plucked a rich carnation and gave it to Mrs. Read with the most graceful inclination that I ever saw in a man of his years. There was something in the manner of his presenting this beautiful flower, which made one for the moment forget that we can ever grow old. The rose was a delicate compliment, and will be cherished by her to whom it was given, long after the perfume has passed from its withered leaf, and long after the thin pale hand which tendered it shall have forgotten its kindly office.

From the Cathedral we wandered into a street, leading past a favorite convent, beneath the high walls of which, scarcely a blade of grass was seen to shoot. On inquiring the cause of the sterile and trodden aspect of the ground, we were informed that the young men of the city were in the habit of frequenting that place, hoping to catch an answering glance, or word, from the truant nuns within. The windows had balconies, in which were placed various pots of flowers, the care of which afforded the veiled inmates a pretext for visiting the light; but while hovering over their cherished plants, their eyes it seems are wont to meet those of some romantic Romeo below,—and then a devoted word goes up, and another, with some sweet flower, comes down; and now and then, the gentle Juliet comes down herself—not to descend into a tomb, but to make a heart happy, that has turned away from the gay saloon to the pensive convent.

I like these romantic touches in human life; they are green spots in a desert. I know not what His Holiness the Pope or the Lady Abbess might say to such a charmed elopement of one of their nuns, but sure I am that if I am ever concerned in what is coarsely termed a run-away match, the object of my pious plunder shall be some brilliant being, suffering an involuntary confinement in one of these living graves. Nor am I without an encouraging example: a captain in the British navy recently ran away with one from a convent in Teneriffe, and found in her all

"Which Eve has left her daughters since her fall."

The next object that arrested our steps was an extensive and neatly arranged garden, connected with an herb-growing monastery, and which, as our conductor informed us, was rather a flattering specimen of the horticulture of the island. In the midst of plats, upon whose varied bosom the rose and geranium were intertwined, appeared most of the tropical fruits and plants in vigorous growth. To one who has been many days at sea, living on hard bread and salt meat, the slightest vegetable, even a head of lettuce, appears a tempting luxury; but an inaccessible orange or banana is like the stream which mocked the parched lips of poor Tantalus. But we left this ample garden, so full of vegetable life, with all its budding sweets untouched and untasted; not a flower was plucked, or a leaf disturbed in its green quietude. Though sorely tempted, we kept this once the eighth commandment.

After strolling through several more of the streets, we found ourselves in a public square, upon rather a confined scale, in the centre of which stood a somewhat singular monument. It was constructed of a species of calcareous stone, of dark hue and compact texture, and consisted of an elevated quadrangular pedestal, upon which rose a cylindrical column, bearing a capital with a device, which no one could trace to any definite order of architecture, or particular school of sculpture. The whole betrayed the wasting effects of time, though the outline had been preserved quite entire.

One of our company, having a great fondness for antiquities, immediately commenced transcribing a half obliterated inscription upon its base; others descanted on the beauty and harmony of its proportions; the rest of us wandered back in thought, through the depth of centuries, to the virtues of those whose achievements were here rendered immortal. Our conductor, who had been detained by some company we had met on the way, now joined us; and observing the rapt air in which each stood, and the antiquary with his busy pencil, remarked that the time-worn object of our contemplative wonder was a *pillory!*

Romance, a love of the marvelous, self-complacency, all died within us, as we blushingly turned away from this only monument which we met with in Angra. Our mortified vanity, however, was soon exhilaratingly revived, by a glass of native wine, and a cup of excellent coffee, at the house of our Consul.

The streets of Angra, though narrow, are uncommonly clean for a Portuguese city. The houses are generally of two stories, and have many of them balconies, screened by vines and trellis-work, which, without excluding the air, afford a green protection to the black-eyed beauty as she catches a glimpse of the moving crowd below. The apparel of the poorer classes is clean, but it is obvious that the needle has in many cases been put in extensive requisition to repair the rents of time. The costume of the better-conditioned circles, though not glaringly gaudy, is rather showy than rich.

There is very little about the place indicative of wealth or earnest enterprise. It must have paused for many years in the march of improvement. This is owing to the unsettled state of its political relations, its frequent revolutions, the rapacity and poverty of its successive masters. Even the bells of some of the churches have been taken down and coined. There are men, who, if they could get there, would pick out and peddle the gems which glow in the pavements of heaven.

The wines of this island are inferior to those of the Canaries, and the birds less musical; but the lands are abundantly productive of grain, pasturage, and fruits. Little attention, however, is paid to flocks and herds, unless the treatment which the hog receives be considered an exception. This coarse animal, which of late has become among us little more than a strong political metaphor, is here remarkable for his anti-

Jew characteristics; he is not only obnoxious to this class of people, from his very nature, but this antipathy is enhanced by the instrumentality of the razor, applied, it is true, not to his face—only his back. This is done, not out of disrespect to those who have repudiated this humble quadruped, but for the sake of giving him a greater breadth of beam. Whether this is really the effect, or a mere conceit, I did not particularly inquire. I ask pardon for introducing here this unseemly emblem of the spirit of our party devotedness; though Byron, in his masterly letter to Bowles, contends, that if pure, unsophisticated nature be the highest theme of the muse, then the most poetical object in the world must be—" a hog in a high wind."

At a little before sunset, we returned on board, for the sky had already begun to assume an ominous change, when orders were immediately given to get underway. We had no sooner weighed anchor—leaving our fluke among the ragged rocks of its bed—and made sail, than night set in with an aspect of terrific gloom. The wind, which had been blowing fresh during the afternoon, now came with the violence of a gale;—the clouds which had hung around us at twilight, in huge black masses, suddenly heaved their distended forms over the heavens and increased in density and darkness, till they shut out its last struggling ray. Of the sea, which began to speak to us in the shock and terror of its resistless motion, nothing was seen but the fitful light, which occasionally flashed from the crest of a plunging wave.

In this world of wild convulsion and impenetrable night, through which the sheeted dead and a shaking earthquake might have passed unperceived, our ship sustained herself with singular steadiness and resolution. With her magnificent wings furled, and her loftier spars taken down, she resembled the battling hero, remaining firm, with his plume and helmet swept away, and his sword broken at the hilt. At midnight the gale began to subside, and at break of day there was little evidence left of its fearful energy, except the heavy sea it had raised, and the dismantled condition of our noble ship.

In the course of the day, a sad memorial of its violence drove past us in the shape of a wreck. It was pursued by huge waves, that broke over it with an exulting fierceness and savage glee. Her masts had been swept by the board,—her helm carried away,—her gunwale broken down,—not a living being remained, or even a breathless corse, to tell who there wept, prayed, and despaired! This is only a type of that universal wreck that is coming on: for

> This mighty globe, with all its stretching sail
> And streamers set, is speeding wildly fast
> To that dim coast, where thunder, cloud, and gale
> Will rend the shrouds, lay low the lofty mast,
> And bear her down, 'mid night and howling wave,
> With wail and shriek, to her engulfing grave.

No Pharos then will cast its cheering ray
    To show the mariner the welcome shore;
No friendly star come forth, as dying day
    Darkens above the breakers' ceaseless roar;
No minute-gun through calcined cliff or steep,
Startle the wrecker from his savage sleep.

Monarchs will seize the helm to stay its roll,
    Then fall upon their trembling knees in prayer,
Hoar voyagers scan again the chart's dim scroll,
    And drop its idle page in mute despair;
While pallid myriads, on the plunging deck,
Grapple with death, in that tremendous wreck.

And down 'twill sink amid the tide of time,
    And leave no relics on the closing wave,
Except the records of its grief and crime:
    The gentle heaven will weep above its grave,
And universal nature softly rear
A dewy urn to this departed sphere.

CHAPTER III.

> It is a sweet and sunny isle, just swelling
> From out the ocean of a rosy dream—
> Crowned with ambrosial bowers, where love is telling,
> In modest violets, its tender theme,—
> A theme too delicately sensitive for words,
> But may be conned in flowers, and sung by birds.

MADEIRA—FIRST APPEARANCE—GLORIES OF SUNSET—RIDE INTO THE INTERIOR—PONIES AND BURROQUEROS—DEEP RAVINES—PEASANTRY—A MADEIRAN BEAUTY—AN ENGLISH LADY—DINNER AND DANCING.

As the white clouds, which hung this morning like a widely distended veil over our weather-bow, were occasionally ruffled by the breeze, we caught momentary glimpses of the lofty and varied outline of the heights of Madeira. Here a steep cliff presented its wild features, there the green side of some hill smiled forth, while upon gentler elevations appeared the white dwellings of the inhabitants, in beautiful contrast with the deep verdure in which they were embowered. Upon the beach foamed the successive wave, or cast its white crest high up the jutting rock. The whole appeared the work of enchantment—a mere illusion sent to please and mock the senses; and this impression was almost confirmed, as the spreading folds of the floating clouds again snatched every vestige of the entire scene from our fixed eyes.

Had death come upon me at that moment, I should have departed with a full belief in the mystery and power, which fancy or superstition has ascribed to those fairy agents, who dwell in subtle essence, and work their marvels upon the palpitating experience of man. But a springing breeze unveiled again the hidden object of our curiosity, and brought us at length so near it, that it appeared before us in all its unrivalled wildness and beauty. Could I see but one island, in its progressive development from the obscurity of cloud, and sky, and wave—it should be Madeira. There is no isle, even under the glittering skies of the West Indies, that has such an enchanting effect as this; none that seems so completely a thing of light, laughter, and beauty.

As we floated into its open roadstead, we passed an English frigate lying at anchor, which saluted us with a "Hail Columbia;" a compliment which our band returned with a badly played "God save the King." Our anchor was now let go, our sails clewed down, and a boat lowered for the shore. I remained on board, to witness the effect of the setting sun upon the scene before us. Twilight here is of short duration, but atones for its brevity by its richness.

The city of Funchal, before which we were riding at anchor, stands against a green amphitheatre of hills, which rapidly ascend to an elevation of three thousand feet. These steeps are crowned with pinnacles, which shoot up wild and high, and which are burning with living splendor, after the advancing twilight has cast its purple shadows over the hushed dwellings beneath. The contrast of these flaming turrets, with the dim and dark aspect of that which slumbers in sunless depths below, produces an effect which can never be described, and which would only be feebly mimicked, by setting the towering bastions of some hugely-walled city in flames, while silence and night reigned through its untrodden streets. How triumphant is nature, both in her magnificent and minor forms, over the proud pretensions of man! The cliff which sunset kindles, and the violet which the dew-drop gilds, alike baffle his art and mock his vanity.

In the morning we took a boat for the shore, for the purpose of riding into the interior of the island. We were met at the landing by Mr. Perrigal, our Vice-Consul, who had politely provided Mrs. Read with a palankeen, in which she was carried by two broad-shouldered men to the Consular mansion. As for the rest of us, the question was not, how we should obtain the means of conveyance, but how we should manage to mount one saddle, instead of two or three; for we were surrounded by thirty or forty Burroqueros, leading their donkies into our very faces, and vociferating "This one, this one, this one!" with an earnestness and impatience which rendered all choice impossible. Indeed we were glad to jump upon any thing to escape from such a snarl of animals, and importunate drivers.

In a moment we were mounted, and rushing through the city, with a Burroquero holding on with one hand to the tail of his pony, and with the other belaboring his limbs with a long stiff wand. We brought up at the door of the Consul, where we halted for a few minutes, till Mrs. Read could mount her pony, and then started off, full gallop, for the interior. The clatter of hoofs which we left behind, brought to the window many an eye, whose look came too late. Echo and wonder only remained, with dust, distance, and laughter. John Gilpin's race with all its involuntary speed was gravity, compared with our ludicrous appearance: it was enough to shake the powder from the wig of a Chief-Justice.

I found myself bestriding a pony about as large as one of farmer Darby's black sheep, but as sure of foot as any fox that ever jumped; yet in the gallop, his fore and hind quarters went up in such quick alternations, that the most rapid vibrations of the body were necessary to preserve the even balance, and keep one from falling over the stem or stern of this tossing craft. I thought, after all, the animal was more to be pitied than his rider; and when we had been on the tilt about two hours, and were come to the foot of another long and steep ascent, I dismounted, to the no small amusement of the driver, who, it would seem, much better understood the ability of the little hardy fellow, than myself.

At the top of this arduous ascent, we found ourselves suddenly recoiling from the crumbling verge of a ravine, that dropped down in nearly a perpendicular descent two thousand feet. As we discovered no road leading away from this perilous position, except that by which we had come, we concluded, of course, that this was the *ne plus ultra* of our ride. But crack went the huge sticks of the drivers against our donkeys, and away they sprang up an extremely narrow ledge of rocks, that beetled out over this frightful abyss.

There was no stopping them, for a concussion of the animals against each other would have precipitated the whole of us to the bottom. Go on we must, but whether for good or ill, for gratification or broken bones, we could not tell. Nothing but the instinct of our steeds saved us; they balanced along with well-poised frame, when their riders would have lost their footing, and with a spinning brain would have reeled toppling down.

Another hour of this hair-breadth riding brought us to the Curral—the main object of our adventure. This is a little fertile valley sunk into the heart of the island, surrounded by a wall of natural rock rising to a height of twenty-five hundred feet. Upon the verge of this wall we now stood; but every object below was buried beneath masses of cloud: nothing could be seen; nothing heard, except the tones of a church-bell, as they struggled up through this heavy sea of vapor. The wild cliffs and pinnacles, which

FUNCHAL MADEIRA.

still towered far above us, shone conspicuously in the light, and their sunny aspect served to deepen the gloom which rested upon the unpierced depths below. There was light, and beauty, and resplendent grandeur above; but below, brooded a night, upon which the quick rays of the sun fell at once quenched and powerless.

After partaking of a very welcome lunch, and some excellent wine, which Mr. Perrigal had hospitably provided for the occasion, we started on our return, fully determined, if we should get back without any serious accident, to make another excursion to this inland wonder. I never left a place with greater reluctance, or a deeper conviction of the power of man's curiosity.

On our return, we frequently overtook, as we had encountered in coming out, many of the peasantry, bearing their burdens of fuel to market. This essential article consists here, principally of the fern, and the roots of the broom. It is borne from the interior upon the head; we met women with large bundles of it in this position. This indeed is the only mode in which it can be transported. The paths in many places are notched into the steep face of a mountain, and are so extremely narrow, as to afford a passage for little more than the person of the individual. The burden is therefore done up like a sheaf, and placed on the head in a line with the path. With one hand, the patient bearer steadies her load, and with the other, by the help of a pointed cane, she steadies herself. When two encounter each other with their loads, one of the parties looks out for a jutting cliff, or a deeper nitch, where she stands till the other has passed. It was only in this mode that we were able to get along with our ponies. In this form the city of Funchal is mainly supplied with fuel. Fortunately the climate is habitually so very mild, that little is required, except for culinary purposes.

I never had such a feeling of sinking sadness, as when I saw these females with these enormous bundles on their heads. There was something in their condition so strangely at variance with the delicacy and tenderness which are usually the pride and privilege of their sex: when I observed, too, the unmurmuring patience and cheerful resolution with which they perform the incredible task, I could have stopped and wept. Had I possessed a key to the mines of Peru, I could have cast it at their feet. They carry these wearisome loads, from many miles in the interior, through the most rough and perilous passes, to the city, where they are obliged to part with them for a few farthings, and then start at night-fall, faint, and perhaps unattended, for their cabin in the mountains.

The self-adapting disposition of woman, the uncomplaining trust with which she submits to reverses of fortune, and the hope and cheerfulness with which she strives to inspire others, while her own heart may be desolate, are high and affecting attributes which belong only to her. She is essentially the same in the cottage and palace, at the couch of pain and the hall of festivity, in all that constitutes her highest excellence and man's chief happiness.

But I am wandering from the thread—not of my discourse, but of our return from the Curral. We arrived at the Consul's quite late in the afternoon, and sat down to a sumptuously furnished table, where we met several agreeable ladies and gentlemen of the island. The dinner passed off with many good feelings, and amiable sentiments lit up with many kindling recollections of home. I saw, neither on this occasion, nor on any other while in the island, excessive drinking, even of the pure and harmless juice of the grape. There was no ardent spirits of any kind upon the table, nor any lurking upon the sideboard, to tempt the lips of the unwary guest.

When the table broke up, we found in the ample mansion every facility for disposing of ourselves, as our different tastes and dispositions suggested. Some took the cigar, and talked of politics; some amused themselves in the garden, among its fruits and flowers; and others, like myself, took a siesta—that dreamy quietude in which weariness forgets its exhaustion, and the spirits rally for fresh action. I always had a great respect for sleep, and a deep love of dreams. The first is the most innocent occupation in which we engage; the last, the most sweet and beautiful.

The evening presented us with a brilliant circle of ladies. The most striking feature in a Madeiran beauty is her eyes: these are usually full, black, and floating; and shaded with a long, silken lash, from beneath which the kindling ray flies with an electrical effect. You would hardly think that an eye, which verges so close upon the melancholy in its general expression, and around which a living languor seems to sleep, could contain such vivifying power. The outline of her face, perhaps, approaches the circle too closely for depth of sentiment, but for an exhibition of cheerfulness, it could hardly be improved.

The contour of her person has also too much fulness to appear in perfect consonance with the most pliant and airy motion; but this is gently relieved by a foot that needs no compression to give her carriage a light and airy cast. Her complexion is a shade darker than the brunettes of our clime, yet equally transparent: her locks are long, and black as the raven's wing; and when she speaks, it is not simply with her lips,—her whole countenance is lighted up and eloquent.

Among the English ladies, there was a Miss E———s, whose winning sweetness of conversation and demeanor came upon one like a soft, mysterious charm. It was merely nature speaking and acting without affectation and without disguise. There was no effort, no ambition, and not the slightest indication that she was even aware of the interest she inspired. Indeed, there was a delicacy and half-retiring diffidence about her, that would have shrunk from an idea of the attraction which encircled her. The pretensions of dress and the show of studied airs utterly faded under her manner. Her thoughts and language seemed to come forth unwrought and spontaneous from their pure fount, yet they beamed with beauty and native intelligence. I never met with but one lady before, in whom nature appeared so unmingled and sweetly triumphant. That lady was Mrs. G., of W———, whom I shall never cease to remember, till all that is amiable and excellent in woman has ceased to affect me.

The evening passed off in music, scattered conversation, and dancing. As for the first, I was a delighted listener; the more so, because there was one voice breathing most melodiously there, that had come with us over the wide water; and as for the last—I was a mere looker on, though in no surly, censorious mind. I never could see much sense or pleasure in grown people bowing, wriggling, and skipping about the floor to the sound of a fiddle-string. It may perhaps become that age, when we are justly "pleased with a rattle, tickled with a straw." But leave it, I pray, to the dear little girls and boys, on the Green, such as I made a ballad for in my young days.

While ambling round a cottage green,
    I met a little child,
The merriest object in the scene—
    Where she was playing wild.

No bonnet screened her from the sun,
    Her neck was white and bare—
Except around it loosely hung
    The ringlets of her hair.

There was a gladness in her air,
    A laughter in her eye;
Her little hands went here and there—
    As she was racing by.

Whither so fast, my little one?
    She made me no reply—
But chattering to herself—ran on
    To catch the butterfly.

The fluttering beauty soon she caught,
    But then it was so bland,
So fine and delicately wrought,
    It perished in her hand.

So giddy youth for pleasures run,
    And think they shall be blest,
But find them, after all is done,
    To perish when possessed.

CHAPTER IV.

But now methinks 'tis time to change this theme,
  To say a word of matters and of men,
For neither of them are just what they seem,
  And never were what they will be again;
But both are changing in the wax or wane,
Like floating fire along a field of grain.

MADEIRA CONTINUED—EXCURSION—VILLA OF AN ENGLISH BACHELOR—TRAGICAL DEATH OF GEORGE CANNING—WILD RAVINE—SINGULAR WATERFALL—LADY OF THE MOUNT—SUPERSTITION—THE DYING MOTHER'S REQUEST—STAR OF BETHLEHEM—VISIT TO THE CONVENT OF SANTA CLARA—INTRODUCTION TO A BEAUTIFUL NUN—HER INVOLUNTARY CONFINEMENT—PERSONAL ATTRACTIONS—MENTAL ACCOMPLISHMENTS—PROPOSED SCHEME OF ESCAPE.

The cloudless heights of Madeira promising this morning a fine day to those who might be disposed to make an excursion among their wild scenes, we started, full of glee, at a very early hour. The ponies which we had taken from the multitude that were clamorously urged upon us, were in high spirits, and we started at a speed that would have left the quickest footman in our country panting and puffing in the distance. Not so with the mountain boy of this isle; for quick or slow, he is ever singing, whistling, and cracking his whip, close at the heel of his animal.

The first place at which we alighted, and to which

we had been politely favored with an unceremonious invitation, was the Til Villa. This is the residence of an English gentleman, situated at a small distance from the city, upon the sunny side of one of those hills which slope up so gradually as to be capable of cultivation, especially when thrown off into parapets, as in the present instance. This villa is quite in the Italian style; the grounds are laid off with a strict regard to beauty and effect; and though the rigid utilitarian would find but little here to applaud, yet the lover of flowers, of the green shade, and the sparkling stir of waters, might easily be in a rapture. In the centre of the garden towers a majestic Til, one of the indigenous evergreen forest-trees of the island, *ingens arbos, faciemque similima lauro.* This tree has given name to the place, though its right so to do might well be questioned by a venerable chestnut standing near, and measuring, with its neighbor, over thirty feet in circumference.

This villa derives a melancholy interest as having been the scene of the tragical death of George Canning, a captain in the British Navy, and eldest son of the late distinguished Premier of that name. He had come to this villa with a party of gentlemen to dine,—had been playing at racket, and being somewhat exhausted, had thrown himself, for a moment's repose, upon the sofa, on which I am now sitting to sketch this note. But being heated, he soon left the apartment, and went, unperceived by any one, to the pool, a place convenient in many respects for bathing.

When the table was announced, the host looked around for the guest, in honor of whom the entertainment was intended, but he was not in his place. Inquiry was raised, a search commenced, when, coming to the pool, they discovered the pale form—but the noble spirit—of Canning had fled forever! Tears and lamentations, and the kindly efforts of affectionate grief, were unavailing. The hall of festivity was wrapt in sorrow, and many a heart that came there gay, retired to weep. As died the lamented father, so perished here, still more suddenly, the beloved son. Their remains may molder in the untimely grave, but their virtues are stamped with immortality.

The Til Villa begins to wear the aspect of neglect and decay. Its proprietor is one of those men who tread life's circle *alone*. This may do perhaps through half the round, while the heart can look abroad, but then the other half becomes a listless solitude. The very objects in which the solitary once delighted, and in which, through his more salient years, he placed his pride and trust, will in age lose their attraction, and disgust him with their frivolous memories. There is but one object that can perpetually interest and charm the heart,—but one that can fill the native void in its affections,—but one that can render nature truly beautiful and lovely; for Eden itself was but

> ———"a wild,
> And man, the hermit, sighed, till woman smiled."

All this is, perhaps, as much as I can consistently say, committing myself the mistake which I deprecate in others. But I cannot pen here a deeper truth, than that an individual vitally consults his happiness, honor, and wealth, by an early union with one, who may perhaps bring to him no dower, except her gentle virtues and affections.

But I forget our ponies, and the distant waterfall, to which we were bound. From the Til we wound up the steep hills, which tower in quick and long succession above each other; but before we had reached the object of our curiosity, a part of our company were so well satisfied with a scene we had met, that like a wise man looking out for a wife, they would go no further.

The object which arrested them was a section of the ravine, which, in its progress to the ocean, intersects the eastern end of Funchal; and which, from the projecting height where they were standing, appeared to divide the very foundation of the island. In its lowest depths sparkled a current, which any miser would have taken for a stream of silver. The imagination of a believer in a central sphere might have taken this mysterious chasm as the authorized medium of communication with his inner world; and his fancy would have converted the streamlet, which wanders through it, into the narrow and glittering outline of its concealed ocean.

Leaving our charmed companions to wonder and speculate at will, Lieut. L. and myself proceeded for the Waterfall. After ascending several difficult elevations, we arrived at the foot of one, from the top of which, our native guide informed us, the Fall might be seen. But how to get there, was now the question; for the ascent was entirely too steep for our ponies, and seemed likely to prove too much for our strength. But the force of curiosity and the pride of conquest urging us on, we dismounted, and when an upright posture became impracticable, resorted to our hands and knees; and by catching to this stone and that shrub, we at last drew ourselves up to the top. The cascade instantly burst on our view,—a magnificent sight—being a large sheet of water, falling unbroken three hundred and fifty feet.

From the position which we occupied, it appeared to burst from the solid side of the mountain; there was no warning of its coming—no "note of preparation"—nothing that led you to expect the splendid exhibition. It rushed upon you at once, unnoticed and unprepared; and when you saw it plunge down its terrific way, to the then concealed gulf, it was as if that were the all of its magnificent existence.

It appeared a miracle in nature—a river without a source—a fall without an admonitory rapid. The rushing wave of Niagara prepares you for the plunging thunder of its might. It speaks to shore and cliff, and echoes the footsteps of its coming in the caverned rock. You expect its wild leap, and wait with awe the crushing force of its gigantic strength; but this mysterious wonder in the fall of waters dashes down, without having awakened an idea of its existence. It deigns to exhibit only its splendid flight, —its wings are spread and furled unseen.

Before our return we renewed one of the recreations of boyhood, but upon rather an enlarged scale. We disengaged, successively a number of rocks, weighing several tons, and saw them sweep their resistless course to the bottom of the ravine. When they reached their shaking bourne, they sent up a crash of echoing thunder, that lingered long in sullen reverberation among the hills. We hove off the very mass upon which we had been incautiously standing: —it was dashed into a thousand fragments upon a projecting ledge, while each went indiscoverably beneath, in muttering wrath. I thought of the erring spirits, smitten from heaven's verge to Tartarean night. Bidding the waterfall adieu, we returned to our companions, whom we found lingering around the very spot where we had left them. Nature never tires; in the magnificent or the minute, the severe or subdued, she is an exhaustless source of interest.

Our descent, which we commenced after partaking of an excellent lunch, and a short repose, brought us into the neighborhood of the Mount Church, to which we paid at least the respect of curiosity. This edifice is one of the first objects which attract the eye in approaching the harbor. It is situated half-way up the mountain which ascends in the rear of the city, and commands an elevation of two thousand feet. It is surrounded by a fresh chestnut grove, in which you mount to it by sixty granite steps. The style of the building is modern, and not destitute of architectural pretension.

As we approached the altar, the priest, who was directing our attention to the points of strongest interest, and who had hitherto evinced an air of utmost ease and playfulness, seemed suddenly impressed with a strange reverence. I shall never forget the incommunicable solemnity which pervaded his countenance, as he slowly drew aside the rich curtain that hung over the altar-piece, and breathed, in a whisper —Nossa Senhora do Monte.

The object of his deep devotion was a little image of Our Lady; which resembled in every respect a child's doll, only its ornaments and attire were more expensive than are ordinarily thrown away upon a toy. A string of beads, in imitation of jewels, went round its filleted head, and a number of tinsel stars bespangled its little petticoat. I could hardly preserve my gravity of countenance, while looking at this Nossa Senhora do Monte. Yet it seems she is an object of peculiar veneration and homage here; on her festival day, half the population of the island go in solemn procession to kneel at her feet. Those who would be classed among the most devout, or who may have committed some sin of deeper dye, in their earnestness to secure her compassionate grace, mount the sixty stone steps, which lead to her sanctuary, upon their naked knees.

The following circumstance, which came to me from a source too credible to admit of doubt, strikingly exhibits the spirit in which this our sainted Lady of the mount is regarded. A mother, being about to depart this life, summoned her daughter to her bedside, and told her that in her younger years she had committed one unconfessed and unatoned-for offence, and that she could not leave the world in peace and with a consolatory hope of heaven, till she had given her a solemn promise that in expiation of this sin, she would on the birth-day of her eighteenth year, at twelve o'clock at night, climb the steps of this church upon the bare knee. The pledge was given, and in a few months from this time will be redeemed with the most religious punctuality. I subsequently met the young lady who is to perform this painful penance, and might perhaps have quoted to her the first Commandment, had there been any probability of her justly appreciating its awful sanctions.

Far be it from me, however, wantonly to disturb the performance of a vow, given even in a spirit of religious delusion—or to trifle with a pledge, which may have served to console the dying. When that fearful hour shall become a reality with me, God only knows the anxieties it may awaken, or what infinite need this trembling spirit may be in of the smallest ray, to relieve its gathering doubts and sorrows. Yet I would not descend to the grave under the light of a false trust—under the guidance of a star that is to vanish away in perpetual night. But there is one star, that will never disappoint the hope which it awakens; its ray is never dimmed, and it knows no going down; its cheering light streams on through ages of change and tempest. The earth may be darkened, the foundations of nature broken up, and the planets shaken from their spheres, but this sweet star will still smile from its high and holy dwelling. No wonder the Poet of truth and piety determined to celebrate

> First in night's diadem,
> The Star, the Star of Bethlehem.

I must now introduce the reader to an individual who has been for several years an object of deep admiration and sympathy among visitors at Madeira. This person is Donna Maria Clementina,—a nun in the Convent of Santa Clara. She was immured in this prison at the early age of ten, by the wicked cruelty of a step-mother;—her tears and prayers were of no avail. Thirteen long years have now passed away, and she still gazes on the dull wall of the convent, and sighs for the light and free air of heaven. Her situation has been partially relieved by the interest which her youth and beauty have awakened. The companions of her early years have never forgotten her, and now, when inquired of for the most beautiful lady of the island, they will take you to this convent, and call to its impassable grate the blushing Maria.

Another circumstance has cast a momentary smile into the solitude of this sweet creature. When the constitutional government was established in Portugal, an order was issued by the Cortes that the doors of all religious houses should be unbarred. The consequence was, that Santa Clara was freely visited by those who had affection or curiosity to be gratified in that form. Among others who availed themselves of this privilege, was a young and accomplished officer in the Portuguese navy. He saw Maria, and felt at once, as every one must, the charm of her beauty. She returned his affection, with a gentleness and sincerity, which showed the delicacy and truth of her heart. She was now free from the authority of a cruel parent, and of the coerced obligations of the veil; and she engaged to receive the hand of the gallant officer, whose heart she had so unintentionally won.

The wedding day was appointed, and she left the convent to mingle with her friends a short time, before her happy union. But during this interval she was taken seriously ill,—the excitement of society came with a too sudden power upon one of her sus ceptible nature,—the wedding day was deferred—fatally deferred!—for, before its arrival, the Constitutional Parliament was forcibly dissolved, the liberating act of the Cortes revoked, and Maria remanded back, in tears and despair, to her solitary cell.

He in whom she had wound up her gentle affections, and who had fondly identified her with the hopes and happiness of his coming years, was now debarred all access to her presence. Yet would he ascend a rock which towered near the convent, and wave his white handkerchief, and joyfully catch the answering token of hers, as it gleamed from the grate of her high window; and in the still night, he might often be seen on that cliff making the expressive signal, and by the light of the full clear moon, exultingly discovering, at the shadowy grate, the replying evidence of an affection that could outwatch the morning star.

He was soon ordered by his government upon a foreign station, where he fell an early victim to the diseases of the climate; and there is now no evidence of his having been here, except what lives in the melancholy remembrance of poor Maria; and there seems to be nothing in sympathy with her, in her disappointment and grief, but the moaning of the wave, as it dies on the broken shore.

Such is an outline of her history, to whom Mrs. R., Dr. M., and myself were introduced this morning, by the amiable Miss S. E., of Madeira. Upon ringing the outer bell of the convent, we were conducted to a well-furnished parlor in the second loft, communicating with the more secluded interior, by a double grate. The lady Abbess was called, permission to speak with Maria solicited, and the name of Miss E. sent in, as an attraction that never fails to bring her forth.

Maria had no toilet to make, no curls to arrange, and she was soon seen approaching the grate, with that easy and subdued air, which refinement and grief only can mold. Her eye kindled instantly as it met that of her friend, and though our unexpected presence seemed at first slightly to disconcert her, yet it was only a momentary embarrassment, which bespake the retiring delicacy of her nature. We were all immediately at ease, and she was speaking to each, in a tone so cheerful and animated, that we quite forgot the sorrows which had so early overshadowed her life.

I stepped silently to a position where I could study, with less exposure, the sweet being before us. Her veil was drawn aside, and she was telling Mrs. R. of the glimmering hope which still lingered in her solitude. I have met before with many a face justly regarded as lovely, but never with one of such serene expressive beauty. This indescribable charm was confined to no particular feature,—it dwelt like a sweet dream upon the whole countenance,—each turn, and shade, and swelling line contributed to its perfection. Yet there was no want of distinct expression,—her full blue eye alone contained the breaking mystery of a world,—all the voiceless thoughts, feelings, hopes, and desires of the spirit within, seemed to float there in melancholy life.

The sentiments of the spectator followed in quick sympathy each token of this mute oracle of her heart. If its glance fell to the earth, he thought of broken hopes and blighted expectations; if it turned to heaven, he felt the aspirations of a confidence which no sorrows can wholly quench; if it dwelt for a moment on him, he would find himself in smiles or tears, just as its look and tone might be.

Around her dewy lips dwelt a wonted smile, which appeared as if it had been checked and shaded in its sunny flow, by some counter sentiment of grief; and yet her lips did not suffer, in the breathing sweetness of their expression, by these mingling emotions. You felt no intense desire to approach those lips too nearly, and yet you could not turn away without looking again to the pensive, half-formed smile which slumbered there.

The oval outline of her cheek had been very slightly invaded by her sorrows, though it still retained its delicate transparency, and was ever and anon mantling with exquisite life and loveliness. The exulting thought, that she might one day be free, would now and then rush to her glowing cheek, and gleam among its paler hues, like that deceptive flush, with which the hectic sometimes beautifies the dying; and then the chilling suggestions of doubt and despair would blanch it again to its marble whiteness.

Her forehead, from which her raven hair was rolled back, rose in a fulness and serenity of aspect, that imparted a feminine dignity to the more tender and playful features of her face. It was a brow that bespake intellect, without any of its sternness, and a serene enthusiasm, without any of its impatient passion. She seemed as one formed to please, and sensible to the gentlest impulse, yet capable, in an hour of trial, of leaning upon her own energies, and of sustaining herself upon the strength of a spirit which no misfortune can wholly subdue. Still she appeared as susceptible, sweet, and childlike, in her being, as if she had been wholly ignorant of this undying resource in herself.

Her form was in keeping with the delicacy and richness of her mind and countenance. The proportions were molded into that flowing curve, which fills the eye, without going beyond the decision of its chastened taste. Her whole person, in its more slender and full expressions, was a rare and happy triumph of nature; no art could improve it, and no heart be insensible to the exquisite perfection of its symmetry and beauty.

Such is only a faint outline of the animated being, near whom I now stood as one enchanted in some dream of immortal loveliness and grief. If the power had then been lent me, the grate of that convent had fallen in twisted fragments; and I half accuse myself now, for not having tried the wrenching force of my arms upon it, although the most entire success would have been regarded by many, merely as an act of romantic folly. But cold must the heart be, that could turn away from that grate without being kindled, and filled with indignant regret. I never yet could see woman in tears, without being deeply moved. Man in his prison, may busy himself in the projected and daring intentions of an escape, but these bold and hardy adventurers are above the cope and bearing of the timid and retiring female: she might, perhaps, nourish them silently in her heart, yet when she came to their execution, her diffident hand would fail in its perilous office.

Her voice possessed a singular sweetness, and liquid fulness of tone; its modulations came warbling on the ear like the musical flow of a rich harp-string; it was a breathing harmony, living a moment, and then melting away in the soft atmosphere, which her presence created. It appeared to possess a mellowing and pervading influence, bathing her lighted countenance, and steeping in music each eloquent feature. It resembled, in this spreading sweetness, the flowing of the dew-drop over the delicate veins of the violet.

Yet Maria listened eagerly to the ingenious suggestions of Mrs. R. respecting an escape, and deemed it, in the shape contemplated, as practicable. But what could she do, provided this escape was effected; there was no concealment in Madeira, that could long secure her from the searching pursuit of her oppressors, and she could not fly away unprotected into a land of strangers. Mrs. R. was ready to offer her the protection and patronage of a sister, but her connection with a public ship, and with the commander of that ship, forbade, for the present, this generous expression of sympathy; besides, Maria had too much delicacy to allow her liberation to involve her friend in any embarrassment. I regretted, for once, that it was not in my power to absolve myself from the obligations and responsibilities of a commission in the navy. I know not that the beautiful creature would have taken the adventurous flight with me, but sure I am that I would not have parted with such a prize for all the pearls of Omer and the gems of Golconda.

These sentiments of admiration were by no means confined to myself. Dr. M., in this animated interchange of thoughts with the lovely captive, had unconsciously caught the pleasing infection; indeed, it could not be otherwise with a man of his discriminating taste and fine susceptibilities. And then the object of our sympathy and affection was before us, so lovely, helpless, and surpassingly beautiful: a heart that never moved before would have melted then.

I wish I could trace the various turns which her conversation took, and the refined mental accomplishments which it betrayed. The varied topics upon which her brilliant imagination lighted, she instantly animated with the very life of her feelings. Silence and solitude, with the contemplative habits which they bring, seemed to have attuned her mind into harmony with the most pure and ethereal sphere of thought. Her spirit had a home there, far above the tumult, and strife, and sorrows of earth.

But our parting moment had now come, yet we did not go without a token of Maria's affectionate regard. She put into the hand of each a cluster of fresh flowers. Among those which she presented to Mrs. R. were several of her own fabrication, but so delicately pencilled, you could not have told them from the living blossoms, with which they were intertwined. Mrs. R. tendered her in return an elegant ring, on which were appropriately represented two clasped hands in cameo. As for myself, I had nothing about my person indicative of my feelings, except two hearts cut in carnelion, and so peculiarly united, that a destruction of one must be the ruin of the other. These little offerings Maria accepted with a look of gratified sadness; and now, as we breathed our adieu, and turned to go, her small white hand came quickly through the grate to Mrs. R., and before it was withdrawn, we each pressed it to our lips, and then wound off

"With lingering step, and slow."

CHAPTER V.

> How freshly on our slumbers broke the morn,
> How sweet the music of the mountain stream,
> How all things seemed of bliss and beauty born,
> And bounding into life, with day's young beam!—
> Alas, the sin that could such joys forego,
> And fill an infant world with guilt and woe!

A SINGULAR MARRIAGE—CATHEDRAL—CLERGY—WEIGHING A PROTESTANT—THE PROSCRIBED FIDALGO—CAMANCHA VILLA—ITS LADY—THE RIBEIRO—A SLEEPING SENTINEL—FORCE OF HUMAN SYMPATHY—MYSTERY OF SLEEP—JOY OF MORNING—MATINS OF MARIA—RIDE TO THE CURRAL—STUPENDOUS SCENERY—QUIET HAMLET—FORCE OF HABIT—SAINT'S DAY—HOMAGE OF GUNPOWDER—RECOLLECTIONS OF HOME—TWILIGHT—THE VESPER-BELL.

A SMALL party of us left the ship to-day to dine with Mr. B., at his Camancha Villa. On reaching the shore we were met by a little girl, who came running up to us, with an eye full of laughter. I could not at first account for her delight, but it seemed that she sought in smiles, what many seek in tears. When the little boon which she asked, simply *por sua saude*—for the sake of your salvation—reached her hand, off with it she ran to a matronly looking person, in the most simple attire, who received it with a grateful countenance.

It appears this lady is the mother of the girl, and in her more youthful and romantic years, gave the very highest evidence of the bewildering power of the " capricious passion," for though of a respectable family, she gave her heart and hand to a blind beggar—

"The current of true love never did run smooth,"—

and lived with him in a small cave, till his death, an event which occurred a few years after their marriage. This playful child was theirs, and now supports her forsaken mother by smiling you into a benevolent humor, and then taking your cheerful offering to one, whom all should regard with charity, who believe in the resistless force of love.

We now entered the Cathedral, and found the priests extremely polite and attentive; indeed, they could not with a good grace be otherwise, for they had been telling the lower orders of the population—who regard them as little less than oracles—that we had been sent of heaven, to break up the alarming blockade of Don Pedro, and afford an access to provisions, which had begun to grow scarce in the island. We had, indeed, broken up the blockade, but I seriously question whether our commission emanated from a higher source than the president of the United States; much less could it be regarded as an expression of divine pleasure towards the ambitious designs of the ex-emperor of Brazil, or of fostering favor towards the riveted despotism of his brother Don Miguel, or of holy sanction towards the political influence of a priesthood whose power is here based on the most humiliating ignorance and superstition.

The cathedral is a large structure of no exterior pretension, in the modern style, and lined with many pictures of the dying and the dead. Among these paintings, one, from its more conspicuous position and characteristic design, instantly caught my attention. It held forth, in strong relief, the most unevenly balanced scales ever known since the weighing of man's prospects of heaven. In one lay a good favored Catholic, plump down to the counter, solid and sure; in the other, an unlucky Protestant, keeled up in hopeless despair. He had been laid in the jesuitical balance, and found wanting. We might smile at this symbol of bigotry, were it not that it whimsically forestalls the decisions of the Judgment-day.

We now mounted ponies for Camancha, distant six or seven miles. The road which we took led past the magnificent villa of Seignor Joas de Carvalhal, the richest Fidalgo of the island. Having in our company a gentleman quite at home there, we halted, and, dismounting, entered a heavy iron gate whose rusty bolts spoke of change and misfortune. The winding vistas of the orange, lemon, myrtle, and banana, with the reeling vine and fragrant flower, opened before us in tropical luxuriance. To the eye of one just from a frost-bitten clime, it was as the first blush of Eden to the eye of Adam.

Through the green depths rippled a stream that

had been induced from the distant mountain. Here it fell in a glittering cascade; there it supplied a calm lake, upon which floated a swan joyously, as if ignorant of the exiled and unhappy condition of its lord. Alas, for him! a man of noble qualities, whose munificent hospitality was in keeping with his wealth; but he was suspected of entertaining principles that breathed too warmly of freedom, and was forced to fly, leaving his immense estates to confiscation and plunder. I saw, but a few days since, a number of the hundred pipes of wine found in his cellar, and which had been seized by the government, exposed to sale. But no purchasers appeared; they would have nothing to do with "Naboth's vineyard." Ahab might revel in its sweets, and share alone the fruits of his crime. After a saddened walk of two hours through the neglected park, the deserted mansion, the silent chapel, and forsaken summer-house, we whispered a deep denunciation to tyranny, and departed.

We were soon at the Camancha Villa, which is nestled in a small verdant valley, and sheltered from the drifting winds by a circling range of densely wooded steps. It is just such a spot as one would choose, who wishes to retire from the dusty jar of the world and drink in the fresh spirit of nature. It is in perfect consonance with the tranquil cast of her taste who fixed on this spot, not so much from a settled disaffection to the more stirring scenes of life, as the desire of an occasional refuge, where she might indulge her classical and contemplative habits. I have seen this accomplished lady in the circles of the gay, and though she would there enchain the capricious waywardness of youth in a sparkling flow of thought, yet it is in this hushed place that she seems to fill the full measure of her sphere. She is here as the Queen of night moving through the silent heaven.

We had taken our walk through the garden which, like that of Tasso's muse,

> " Apriche collinette, ambrose valle,
> Silve e spelonche in vista offerse,"

where the plants of India, Africa, and Mexico, breathe their mingling perfume. We had seen the little boat that on its crystal element trims its own sail to the breeze, and the gold-fish sporting in the ripple of its wake; we had traced the streamlet ever murmuring its music to the spirit of the place, and living on in freshness and harmony when decay has stricken the blossoming year; the festivities of the day were over, our sentiments of friendship plighted, and now the purpling twilight bade us depart. Adieu to thee, Camancha,—adieu to thee, fair lady,—many be thy years, and happy as he is blest, who won and retains thy affections.

On our return we crossed the *ribeiro*, which intersects the eastern end of the city; it now shows itself only as a little babbling brook, but some twenty years past, I am told, it was so swollen by the bursting of a cloud in the mountains, that it carried off in its torrent sweep a hundred dwellings with their unwarned inhabitants. It occurred in the dead of the night, and before the sleeper could wake to his peril, he was whelmed in the rushing mass of ruin:

> ———— " lapides adesos,
> Stirpesque raptas, et pecus, et domos
> Volventes unâ."————

Tne gigantic remains of a church are still shown as the sad evidence of this terrible catastrophe, which indeed seems to have anchored itself so frightfully in the recollections of the people, that they speak of events which took place before the flood, and leave you in danger of confounding the miracles of this little streamlet with the destructions of the general deluge.

On reaching the gate which communicates with the shore, we found it bolted, and a sentry sleeping beside it, with as much composure as if the days of hanging and shooting for this defection from duty were over. His gun lay beside him, wet with the dew; and even his dog, whom it would seem he had appointed a sort of deputy watch, did not feel sufficiently the responsibilities of his trust to keep wholly awake.

All this was well for us, not that it enabled us to pass the gate, but the poor soldier on awaking was so happy in ascertaining that it was not the patrol who had caught him asleep, that he unceremoniously turned the key, and saved us the trouble of going to the guard-house for a pass. Poor fellow!—let him sleep and take his rest; for what is life to him—what its thousand sources of wakefulness and interest? His days molder through a narrow round of unmeaning duties. In peace there is nothing to quicken a solitary pulse; and if war come, it is only that he may be hacked to pieces for the ambition of another, and then cast into a hospital to be forgotten and die!

My feelings, while looking at the condition of this poor soldier, would alone convince me of the force and sacredness of human sympathy. We are so mysteriously made that suffering and virtue, in whatever form presented, never fail to excite our pity and veneration. Even where this affecting trait is an exception to all the other characteristics of the individual, still we admire and weep. The tender affection of Conrad for Medora half reconciles us to the wild life of the Corsair; and we tremble to each doubt and hope, as he springs from shore to cliff to greet once more—alas! that changed and changeless countenance.

We yearn to let Othello know that the object of his love and fatal jealousy is innocent, and that Iago is the wretch on whom the lightning of his indignation should fall. We rejoice to see the "Birnam-wood move towards Dunsinane," convincing us no less than Macbeth, that he may be put to death by "man of woman born." When Romeo with his mattock thunders on the portal of the tomb in which Juliet sleeps, we hear the marble break, and would give a world could Juliet hear it also. When Gloucester loses his eyes, and with them, his desire of life, and hires a poor peasant, as he supposes, to lead him to the verge of the precipice that beetles over the sea, and bidding an eternal farewell to the world, makes the desperate leap, it is quite as difficult to persuade us as it was him, that he has not actually fallen many a fearful fathom down.

This sympathy extends beyond our own species. Cowper is not the only being who has wept over the untimely end of some favorite prisoner of the cage. I should not envy a man his sensibility who could be at ease, and hear the bleatings of a lamb that had fallen into the clutches of a wolf. Nor is this sympathy confined to animal existence. The mariner has a strange affection for the plank that has saved him from a watery grave. The octogenarian looks upon his old familiar cane rather as a companion than a support. Even the dog will bark at the stone that has rolled too carelessly over his foot. Thus are we strangely linked in our perceptions and sympathies with all the animate and material objects of the world; and the slightest of them may often strike this electric chain with vivifying force.

Enough of this philosophizing humor. The night

wears late—the lamp that lights this vagrant page burns dimly: I must rest—must sleep. Strange state of being—to live, yet be unconscious—to breathe, yet feel not the pulses thrill—to sigh, love, smile, and weep, yet be insensible to the quick presence of all outward things! Would that one could penetrate this state—reveal its mysteries—its deep, tongueless secrets:—does it resemble the slumber of the shroud? or do we there dive still deeper from the realities of life? how shall *that* sleep be broken up?

<blockquote>"When will it be morn in the grave?"</blockquote>

Nature here awakes from her night's repose with a freshness and vigor which fill one with the most vivifying sensations. Each mount and vale and wood and waterfall break upon you with an exulting life, that calls up within you the joyous and irrepressible feelings of your earliest years. Your first impulse is to bury yourself in some more favored recess, or ascend some height, around which the fragrant earth sends up the incense of its thousand altars. To gratify these feelings in their widest scope, we started this morning, with the freshening light, for the Curral—that great marvel of Madeiran scenery.

We were well mounted, and soon moving through the high-walled street which leads past the convent of Santa Clara. It was the hour of Matins, and the early prayer of the beautiful Maria was ascending, in unison with the pure homage of nature, to the great Source of all light and blessedness. I could have stopped and listened to the solemn chant that stole through the grate of the chapel window, but sterner hearts were near me, and I must move on, with only time to whisper an earnest blessing to the unseen worshipper within. Who could endure to be cut off, like this lovely being, in the first flowing of the heart's affections, from all the congenial objects of its fervid desire—never to mingle in the delights of social endearment—never to feel the sweet influences of the varied year—never to see the return of purpling eve, or

> "Morn, in russet mantle clad,
> Walk o'er the dew of yon high eastern hill!"

From the convent we passed the humble church of St. Antonio, and thence onward and upward through a continuous series of vineyards, all sheltered from the chilling effects of the north winds by the heights to which we were tending. The orange-tree was bending under its golden burden; the banana revealing between the bright expanse of its broad leaves its delicious treasures; and the low winds, which had slept amid the flowers through the night, were abroad, scattering the perfume of their gathered sweets. A mile or two further of these gradual ascents, and cultivation ceased; the vine, save here and there, could not find soil in which to strike its roots; and even where it could effect this foothold, was chilled into sterility. We continued on, now in a zigzag motion, up the steep height, and then on a path of frightful narrowness and elevation around its sharp pinnacle, till our steps were at length suspended on the verge of the Curral.

This island wonder is a valley of a wild ravine character, lying at a depth of three thousand feet beneath the cliff on which we stood, and surrounded on all sides by an equal, and at many points, by a still loftier range of rocks. Far down in its green bosom, a cluster of white cottages may be seen, in the midst of which stands the delicate church of Nossa Senhora do Livramento, and near by, the humble mansion of the goodly padre. These habitations, from our elevated position, appeared not larger than what might well accommodate the prattlers of the nursery; and the hawk, which wheeled midway, dwindled to the form of a bird that might rock itself to slumber in a rose-bud.

The quiet aspect of this little village contrasted strangely with the mountain barrier which towered in wildness and grandeur around it. In many places these precipices dropped to the bottom with an almost perpendicular front; in others they were broken, and there the Til and Vinhatico cast below the deep umbrage of their forest gloom; while over the wave-worn steep rushed some stream on its exulting course to the torrent that called to it from beneath. It was a place where the thunder-cloud would seem most at home; yet, as the calm bow will sometimes attend this minister of sublime terror, so this sweet hamlet smiled out from its terrific dwelling-place.

We now commenced our descent to the valley, which we reached by an extremely narrow path, cut along the steep face of the rocks, and requiring in us a philosopher's steadiness of brain, and a rope-dancer's dexterity of balance. The ingenuity displayed by our Burroqueros in getting down our ponies, was quite original, and but for the perils attending it, would have been burstingly ludicrous. When a smooth precipitous descent of several feet occurred, where the animal could obtain no foothold, they would let him down upon his patient haunches, by the flowing length of his tail, with many appliances of a steadying character, nicely adjusted to the emergency of the occasion. This will appear about as credible as the story of the flying-horse; but if there never be a greater deviation from truth, exaggeration and falsehood will cease among travellers.

On reaching the small church of the hamlet, we found a tiny flag flying from something like a liberty-pole, in its court, and a little cannon sending out its noisy breath. On inquiring for the occasion of this military display, we were informed that it was in honor of the sainted lady, whose image we now discovered on the flapping banner. I had heard of prayers being offered to saints, but the homage of gunpowder was a novelty. It is a little singular that the same element which the assassin employs for the destruction of his victim, the suppliant should use in worship of his saint. But enough of this heterodox deviation.

Standing in the centre of this deep valley, though the indications of human life and industry are around one in a variety of forms, yet there is very little that forcibly reminds him of man. This domestic sentiment is overwhelmed in the mightier impressions of nature. From the bottom of a profound abyss, he is looking up to mountains which steeply inclose him on all sides, and tower to the very heavens in the wildest magnificence. From the broken summits, around which the cloud rallies in darkness, down to the torrent that rolls at his feet, every thing awes and subdues him. Wherever he turns, the threatening mass of some lofty cliff, or the shadowy mysteries of some unpierced chasm, or the hollow voice of some unseen waterfall, or the perpetual gloom of the forest-tree, impresses him with sublime terror. He feels as one shut out from the gayer scenes of earth—confined within an insurmountable barrier of precipitous rock, and doomed forever, in his helplessness and desertion, to tremble under a sense of height and depth, solitude, solemnity, and danger.

Yet the unpretending tenants of this secluded spot pursue their quiet vocations as free of alarm as they are of molestation. They cultivate their vines in the very crater, whose bursting energies threw up this island from the bed of the ocean. Every thing around them has upon it the marks of volcanic violence, and seems still to be pillared upon a slumbering earthquake; but these ominous appearances and recollections do not disturb their calm and ever-cheerful contentment.

This results from the force of habit. It is this mysterious principle in our nature that enables the mariner to sing under the dark frown of the coming storm; that makes the peasant sleep soundly at the shaking foot of Etna; and the chamois hunter pursue his game, in lightness and glee, along the glittering verge of the avalanche. Can any thing within the range of our conceptions more thoroughly adapt man to his condition, than nature? This she effects so silently and unperceived by the individual himself, that before he is aware of it, he is singing under the cloud that mantles the tempest—looking with exulting sensations into the eye of the volcano—or holding a carnival over the ashes and bones of an entombed city. Let those who treat with lightness the untutored influences of nature, find in reason, if they can, a more effective and pervading power.

I return to the Curral. This is a part of the domain of the Santa Clara Convent; and is contemplated as a refuge for the nuns, in case a hostile invasion should render it necessary. I should be tempted myself to join an expedition to storm the nunnery, if it would be the means of planting in this retreat the imprisoned Maria. Her romantic heart would here find objects fitted to its high and enthusiastic nature.

She is now like a bird of adventurous wing and gifted song, caged to the lattice of one that is steeled to the injury inflicted, and incapable of grief for the melody lost. I must unwire that cage and liberate the captive: there will then be music sweeter than that breathed through the star-lit bowers of Eden by

——— "The wakeful nightingale,
Who all night long her amorous descant sung."

The spot on which we had fixed for a half-hour's repose, was a large rock, rising boldly out of the rushing stream, and commanding the most comprehensive view of the stupendous scenes around. We here spread out the welcome collation, which the provident forethought of Mrs. R. had munificently provided. The severe exercise which we had undergone gave a keen relish to the occasion. There is no appetite so unfastidious in its demands, and so happy in its gratification, as that produced by mild fatigue, especially when the effort has been sprinkled with adventure, and enlivened by agreeable company. We suspended a bottle or two of the purest Madeira in the stream—which was indisputably an excellent cooler—and then, in the flowing cup, remembered those far away, and some of whom, perhaps, we never more might see.

With what yearning fondness the affections of one in a strange land will turn to his native shore, though oceans roll between! I am not astonished that the exiled Swiss thinks of his wild hills with mournful regret; much less do I wonder that the Hebrew captive hung his harp on the willow, and wept by Babel's stream, when he remembered Zion. Home never appears so sweet to us as when deprived of its endearments; all that may have been coarse or repulsive about it, is then forgotten, and every attraction is invested with an additional charm.

Our repast over, Capt. Read proposed that we should climb the side of the Curral, opposite to that which we had descended. The task was one of extreme difficulty, for the face of the mountain, though broken into chasms, cliffs, and crags, was very precipitous, and presented an elevation of four thousand feet. But by winding along its front, and improving every slope of less boldness, we at last gained the top. Thanks to the roots of those shrubs for the pertinacity with which they clung to the rocks: it was often our only hope and safety.

I thought we had taken a final farewell of our ponies, but their attendants forced them up. The dexterity of both is incredible; they seem to be strangers to fatigue, and superior to any obstacles which nature, in her fiercest fit of defiance, may cast in their way. We now picked our way along the sharp ridge, with the Curral on our left, when the

Serra d'Agoa, a ravine of equal depth, and perhaps of more rugged magnificence, opened beneath us on the right. A current of white clouds was pouring down its opposite side, and so closely resembling a foaming cataract, that the illusion for a few minutes was entire. The lingering splendors of the setting sun, the silence of the approaching twilight, and the long shadows which began to cast their dark forms below, imparted a fearful interest and solemnity to the scene.

I have stood by the plunging tide of Niagara, and seen its mighty wave roll down into its abyss of agony and thunder; but there is not in all its fierceness and crushing strength, that which fills the mind with such a deep and mysterious awe as these hushed and fathomless ravines. We could have lingered here for hours, but the fading light warned us to go. Woe to the luckless wight who sings his Ave Maria on that height; it will be his last vesper; the dryads of the untrodden chasm only will know the place of his grave.

We descended without any serious accident, and were happy in finding ourselves once more on a road where we could mount our ponies. Our return, in consequence of having crossed the Curral, was much more circuitous than our route in the morning; but the picturesque novelty of the varying scenery, as it opened upon us in the depths of the twilight hour, more than reconciled us to the length of our way.

The light that is shed here from an evening sky, lies on the landscape in a rich mellow slumber. There is a softness and liquid fulness about it, that makes you think you can drink it as you would nectar. Were I to turn idolater here, the objects of my worship would be the genius that reigns in the awful Curral, the spirit that breathes through the star-lit night, and the beautiful being who dwells in sweetness and grief within the veil of Santa Clara.

  Hark to the bell in Clara's turret ringing,
   Bidding the vestals for their rites prepare;
  When low before the white-robed altar kneeling,
   Maria meekly breathes her vesper prayer;
  A prayer so full of holy, fervid feeling,
   She seems a sainted spirit, lighted there
  To pray,—giving to this one spot of earth
  The heavenly charm that hovered round its birth.

CHAPTER VI.

> OH, there is something in this stirring hour,
> Just as the sun is circling from the sea,
> Which has, if any thing can have, the power
> To make men feel that it were good to be
> Like HIM whose smiles, descending in a shower,
> Now wake the living world to ecstasy!
> Yet many rise, as they lie down at even—
> Without one thought of either God or Heaven.

SKETCHES OF MADEIRA—PHYSICAL FEATURES—WINES—CLIMATE—CITY OF FUNCHAL — PRIESTS—SOCIETY—MORALS—PEASANTRY—MERCHANTS — POLITICAL OPINIONS—HABITS OF THE LADIES—COURTSHIPS—OUR PARTING AND FAREWELL.

THE island of Madeira is full of marvel and romance. It was thrown up into this breathing world by some volcanic convulsion; it was discovered by a wandering love-adventure; its every aspect is one of wildness and beauty; and its wines prompt the most rich and unearthly dreams. There is nothing about it that has the smallest cast of sameness, except its climate; and that could hardly be improved by any changes wider than the slight vibrations through which it passes, and which are full of softness and vitality. It is indeed a fairy land,—the paradise of the Atlantic,—the gem of the ocean. But I will look at some of the more marked and discriminating features of this singular island.

Its southern coast descends in easy and green declivities to the sea. These warm slopes are covered with the choicest vineyards; the vine seems to reel under its purple burden. Where the ascent is so steep as to render it necessary, it is thrown off into parapets, which may be seen rising above each other in a lengthened series. So precious is this southern exposure, that where there is no native soil, the rock is covered with earth brought from a distance with great labor and expense. The wines of these vine yards, for richness of body, deliciousness of flavor, and immunity from injury by time and indifferent treatment, are not equalled in the world. Who has not seen the hospitable host half in a rapture, as he bade his delighted guests fill their glasses from a little of the "old south side" left him by some worthy ancestor? But "who hath redness of eyes?—they that tarry long at the wine."

The northern shore of the island rises from the wave in a bold, elevated range of rock; but what it gains in majesty it loses in other respects. The vine is inferior to its sister of the south; and, as if to punish it for its want of sweetness, instead of being supported by fine trellis-work of cane, it is left to climb up some bramble or reluctant tree, as it can; and then, after all its best efforts, is still more deeply punished by being worked up into brandy. Sometimes, indeed, it has the good fortune to be removed in its infancy to the south side; and then it never fails to secure affection and esteem.

The centre of the island has the Curral and the magnificent heights which surround it, and which are filled with gushing fountains that send their laughing waters in every direction to the shore. Every cliff, and chasm, and cascade, has around it the deep shadows of some indigenous wood,—the mystery of some romantic legend,—the despair of a lover's leap, —or the yielding affections of beauty, flying from the stern mandates of parental authority.

The climate is one of unvarying mildness and salubrity: it is a continual spring with its fruits, and flowers, and fragrant breath. This uniformity of temperature is one of its most charming features: you are never oppressed with heat; never pinched up with cold. The thermometer usually ranges from sixty to seventy-five degrees; and in the greatest extremes, rarely rises or sinks more than five degrees above or below that agreeable medium. This place is a favorite resort for invalids, especially those afflicted with pulmonary complaints. You meet with them from the most distant climes. The atmosphere has a peculiar elasticity and softness; it flows through the delicate lungs with a soothing, healing influence.

The patient fears no attack from any diseases foreign to his own malady; for a malignant fever or fatal epidemic is not known here. And so entirely has nature intended the place as one of harmlessness as well as health, that she has excluded from it every description of venomous reptiles and insects; even the musqueto has never been able to obtain a citizenship. Whether it be owing to natural causes or not, I cannot say; but during the time that I have been at this island, I have never once heard a child cry. The little nestler appears to be so well satisfied with the new world in which he has arrived, that he troubles no one with the fretful calls of any ungratified want. Who would not venture to get married at Madeira?

Funchal is the principal town of the island; it is delightfully situated on the south side, and contains a population of about twenty thousand. The streets are very narrow, and ascending as they lead from the shore; but they are remarkably clean; and a refreshing air is given to them by a little runnel of water that courses down the centre. The buildings are generally of two stories; many of them have iron balconies at the windows, and a belvedere or turret, which is a favorite resort in the evening.

Some of the wealthier class, especially the English merchants, have Quintas—beautiful summer residences—in the vicinity of the town. Around these fresh retreats the vine, shrubbery, and flora of the island, appear to the highest advantage. The grape, with its creeping tendrils and exuberant foliage, shadows the cool corridor; the geranium and fussia rise in a firm aromatic wall; while a vast variety of flowers bloom in their tasteful arrangements: many of them are sweet exotics, but they seem here not to pine for their native skies.

Among the natives there is very little of that free, social intercourse, which constitutes so prominent and pleasing a feature of society with us. This reserve is owing in part to a wider distinction of classes, but more to a useless jealousy. The husband has little confidence in the fidelity of his soft companion, and the good lady has just as little in the virtuous education of her daughters, and the Argus-eyed vigilance of both is frequently eluded. In the annual returns of births in the parish of the cathedral, the number of children *espostos, que não se sabe quem são seus pays*, generally equals that of those born *de legitimo matrimonio*.

This laxness of morals will always be found where a blind indiscriminate jealousy is substituted for the restraints of an enlightened conscience and a high tone of public sentiment. If a parent wishes to keep himself and the members of his household in the paths of virtuous peace and happiness, he should introduce among them the Bible, and bind upon the heart the spirit of its sanctions: this will do a thousand times more to aid his better purposes, than all the bolts, and bars, and sleepless suspicions that ever yet embarrassed the wandering or punished the guilty.

Yet it is astonishing what a degree of composure the domestic relations maintain here, notwithstanding this frequent profanation of their shrine. It can be explained only on the supposition of a want of innocence to cast the first stone. Nothing so disarms the injured and incensed, as a consciousness that he is guilty himself of the very crime which he would expose and punish in others.

The man who requires fidelity and purity at home, must not carry treason and contamination abroad. If he breaks within the sanctuary of his neighbor, it is but a just retribution that his own hearth should be profaned. If he wanders in search of forbidden pleasures, he must not expect even his own children to escape the contagion of his example. The censor should be immaculate of the crime which he condemns in the culprit.

The more influential and better-informed portion of the population of Madeira, are in favor of a government based on liberal principles. They utterly loathe the miserable despotism to which they are now forced to submit. They do not speak out, but there is deep thunder ready to rend the cloud. That the present state of things must soon change, no one who has any knowledge on the subject, can doubt. It is not in human nature long to endure such wrongs unredressed. Whether the condition of the people will be improved by the success of those who have espoused the cause of Anna Maria remains to be shown; but one thing is very clear, it can hardly be rendered more deplorable.

A revolution would have taken place before this, but for the unaccountable influence of the clergy over the lower orders. These men of sables, I regret to say, appear to have forgotten their high and holy calling; for, instead of being interested in multiplying the sources of intelligence and sacred influences, they seem to be engaged in suppressing inquiry, and stifling the breaking light of the age. They sympathize with every movement that casts a new weight upon the drooping energies of human nature. There was a great exultation among them when it was announced here, a few days since, that the administration of Earl Grey had been overthrown, and that the Wellington party, with its high-toned aristocratic sentiments, had been installed upon its ruins. The aged bishop, in the plenitude of his thankfulness, crept up the stone steps of the cathedral three times, at the dead of night, upon the naked knee. But his hopes were blasted in the bud; Grey was soon recalled, and the Reform Bill passed in triumph. So perish the hopes of all who seek to trammel the public mind.

The condition of the peasantry is not one of such unrelieved wretchedness as its external form would intimate. Who would suppose that the comfort, inseparable from the smallest portion of happiness, could be found in a cabin without a floor, or window, or chimney, and where the only edibles seen are the yam, the pumpkin, the batata, and a fish over which even the gull might hesitate? Yet I found in these very cabins, a kindness, contentment, and cheerfulness, to which the abodes of refinement and luxury are often strangers. Yet this smiling contentment was not of that animal sort which consists in an insensibility to its condition; through all the shades of its deprivations there was a quick intelligence, and a hope of better days, as irrepressible as the mountain wind.

The peasants are a healthy, muscular, and active class of people. The dress with the men consists of a conical cap thrown on the top of the head, a coarse linen shirt with an extremely narrow collar and flowing sleeve, and which is confined, just above the hip, by the band of a pair of loose kilts of the same material, which in their turn descend to the knee, and are there gathered and confined, while a short boot, leaving a part of the leg bare, completes the costume. The women wear a similar cap, with short petticoats, and a pelerine which protects the ample chest and firm-set shoulders, and is fastened behind. Such a dress has one thing to recommend it at least, it leaves nature free in the discharge of her noble functions; there is no narrowing, pinching, torturing whalebone, or constricting cordage about it—inventions which death has introduced to flatter the fancy and fill the grave.

The English ladies at Madeira form a small, but intelligent and attractive circle. The mild climate appears to soften down those more sanguine traits of character, to which the daughters of Albion are a little prone, and which are slightly at variance with a perfect delicacy and sweetness of disposition. I observed similar effects of climate, upon the same polished class, in the island of Santa Cruz. The climate of England wants that softness which breathes such a mellowed harmony through the spirit of the fair Madeiran. It is this melody of soul which imparts such a tranquil and exquisite beauty to the countenance of the gentle inmate of Santa Clara. As I saw this peerless one conversing with the sister of her heart, in her early visit, it appeared like the meeting of two light clouds, without an element to disturb the amalgamating flow.

A Madeiran lady seldom walks, and very rarely rides except in her palankeen. This is a sort of swinging cradle, suspended from a slight pole, and borne upon the shoulders of two men, and is so closely inclosed by curtains, as entirely to secure the fair occupant from observation, save now and then when her small hand feigns to adjust the drapery, or her flashing eye finds some intended aperture, through which it can exchange the exulting glance. In this mode she goes to mass, and makes morning calls, and sometimes steals a look at one whom she may not yet openly encounter.

But the matrimonial preliminaries are generally conducted in a quite different form. The gentleman passes in front of the lady's house, with a frequency which cannot escape her notice: if she is pleased with her out-door visitor, she manifests her interest by appearing at the window of the upper story. As his attentions are continued, and her complacency increased, she gradually descends from one loft to another, until she reaches the window of her parlor; from this she casts him some flowers, significant of her pleasure. At length she permits him to pay her the passing compliment of the morning, while she returns him some word or broken sentence of mystical and magical import; but she never permits him to come in, until he has obtained the consent of her parents—and then not to address her a few months and run away—but to marry her; and his request and their consent are regarded as a bona fide contract, which neither party can violate without dishonor.

There is something in this mode of approximation and union that I like. It has none of that long, feeling, sounding, experimental process about it, which obtains in our country, and which too frequently ends only in the disappointment and mortification of one of the parties,—unless, as is sometimes the case, the farce has a still more tragical close, in a blighted name, or a broken heart. Ladies, who have usually the most to apprehend from these unmeaning pastimes, should be careful how they set the example of a trifling disingenuousness, for if they are honest and sincere, the men will not dare to play the hypocrite. Nothing is more calculated to make a gentleman honest, than the presence of an honest lady.

I leave Madeira with regret. I could never be wearied with its climate, its scenery, and society. The pleasures of our visit here have been much enhanced by the polite attentions of our vice-consul, Mr. Perrigal. Though under no obligations to be peculiarly civil, yet his time, his well-furnished table, and ample mansion were proffered to us in that cordial, unceremonious manner, which makes acceptance easy, and leaves one at liberty to come and go at pleasure. It was a true specimen of the politeness and hospitality which adorned the olden times, and which may be met with occasionally in these later days. No one can enjoy such favors, especially in a strange land, without cherishing, what I know we do on the present occasion, the liveliest sentiments of gratitude and esteem. We shall look back to the hospitality of this shore, as the pilgrim to the sparkling waters of the desert spring.

But our anchor is up—our sails are unfurled—the springing breeze comes fast—and we must bid adieu to Madeira and Maria. Farewell, thou wild and beautiful isle!—nothing lovelier than thee ever rose from the ocean, or possessed a more captivating claim to the first smile of the morning star. Farewell, Maria!—the veil never shadowed a sweeter countenance, nor hath convent-wall imprisoned a purer heart than thine! May thy footsteps soon be unconfined as thy spirit; but whether free and bright, or chained and mournful, be the lot of thy coming years, thou wilt long be remembered by those who never met thee but with increased fondness, and now leave thee with lingering affection and grief!

> Farewell!—and should we meet no more,
>   Except in memory's dream;
> Yet sweet the visions that restore
>   The semblance thou dost seem.
>
> Adieu!—the last that thou wilt hear
>   From him that knows thy worth too well—
> To stifle one relenting tear,
>   That mingles in this last—farewell!

CHAPTER VII.

In Portugal, Don Miguel holds the throne,
  In spite of Pedro and his lovely daughter;
John Bull affects to think the girl hath shown
  The clearer title, and will whelm in slaughter
Her Uncle's forces, if the Miss, when crowned,
Will pay for every sailor shot and drowned.

PASSAGE FROM MADEIRA TO LISBON—SEA-SICKNESS AS A PURGATORIAL STATE—SITUATION OF A MEMBER OF CONGRESS AND OFFICER OF THE NAVY COMPARED — ROCK OF LISBON — PILOT — TAGUS — CHEERING — ROCKETS—DON MIGUEL—CITY OF LISBON—CABRIOLETS—POSTILLION—MADAM JULIA'S HOTEL—A PARTISAN MERCHANT—ALCANTRA AQUEDUCT — CHURCH OF ST. ROQUE — MOSAICS — QUEEN MARIA FIRST — CHURCH OF ST. DOMINGO — STATUE OF KING JOSEPH — THE EARTHQUAKE—INQUISITION.

I HOPED, when we had reached Madeira, and quite crossed the Atlantic, that the horrors of sea-sickness were over, at least, for this cruise; but this persecuting plague of the ocean has come again, foul and ghastly as Milton's personification of sin at the portals of the lower world. A heavy head-sea is heaving against our bows the mass of its violent strength; while our ship shakes through her sides, like a whale in the convulsions of death.

This frightful paroxysm, were it all, might be endured; but then to be yourself sickened beyond all the powers of the most nauseating drugs—to heave up, in wrenching throes, your very vitals, from their bleeding roots—to be battled, and bruised, and tumbled about, as a loathsome thing, which even the sea would spurn from its presence, and almost deny a grave—this is enough to torture and disgust one out of life. I wonder not that the sea-sick, sometimes, while the power of motion remains, roll overboard, and bury themselves before their time; for if suicide be ever without guilt, it is where the poor wretch has every thing of death but its insensibility.

It is astonishing to me that the ancients, whose imaginations were so prolific of woe, never introduced, among their Tartarean torments, the horrors of sea-sickness. For what is the plight of a wandering ghost, or the thirst of a Tantalus, or the recoiling task of Sisyphus, or even the inexorable wheel of Ixion, compared with the condition of one who is forever straining and retching to heave up from his inmost being, a rankling, broiling, clinging nest of torture—and in his agony, and faintness, and swimming delirium, calling in vain on death for relief! If I ever construct the machinery of a purgatorial state, I will place, in the very centre of its horrors, a rolling deck, strewn with the ghastly victims of sea-sickness; for the man must be lost to reason who could think of long enduring such a retribution for all the pride, and pomp, and gratification which float between the cradle and the grave.

I wish those members of Congress who think the

officers of the navy sufficiently compensated for their hardships and sufferings, would just take one voyage to sea. It is an easy thing for a man to rock on to Washington, getting fifty cents a mile for his smooth circuitous passage,—to take there a snug room, with its cheerful fire, easy chair, and sofa,—to retire to rest at what hour he pleases, without even a mouse to disturb his repose,—to rise sometime along in the morning, and, in gown and slippers, sip a bowl of coffee covered with rich cream,—to ride up to the Capitol at eleven o'clock, and take his arm-chair, in a hall warmed to a mild and congenial temperature,—to open his mail, and peruse a sweet letter from his affectionate wife; then unfold a newspaper and read the compliments of its editor on his last speech,—to ambulate in the lobby and talk over a little politics, while some younker is addressing the House about the complexion of the inhabitants of the moon,—to ride home to his quarters and dine on viands and vegetables, warm and rich, with a bottle of old wine to mellow them down,—to take a quiet siesta, and in the evening go to the drawing-room and exchange smiles with the ladies,—and, when the session is over, to draw eight dollars a day for services thus rendered the country!

All this is very easy,—very comfortable,—quite a desirable condition,—and I would not disturb its sweetness and serenity by one unnecessary care. But suppose this individual exchange situations with one of us, and ascertain what our amply compensated life of gayety and romance really is. Before he dreams of it, he is ordered off to sea, so peremptorily that even a new-married wife, or one that is dying, cannot plead him off an hour. He hastens on board his ship, looks back from the hurrying wave to his native shore, perhaps for the last time,—begins to feel the deck of his vessel spinning around him, and then enters on the agonies of sea-sickness,—lifts his faint and drooping head from this rack of straining torture, and hears a thunder-gale roaring through his shrouds like the summons of the last trump,—draws his nerveless form upon deck, and sees the tattered fragments of a top-sail fluttering on the distant wind, or a broken spar scudding away from his ship, like a thief from the gallows:—through night, and tempest, and torrents from the clouds, he must ever keep his regular watch, and feel in all his weariness and exhaustion that the safety of the ship, and the preservation of the lives on board, are at issue upon the wisdom and vigor of his conduct.

He is thirsty,—calls for a cup of water,—strains a liquid through his teeth, which has the name of that pure element, but which ropes away from his parching lips,—he is faint, requires sustenance, and thinks of a bowl of milk, so soothing and innocent, but it is far off in some farmer's dairy,—he thinks of fruit and vegetables, those fresh things of earth, which seen through a sea atmosphere, appear still more fresh and tempting, but they too are far away in some market which he may never see again,—and so he sits down with a dry crust, and hacks away at a piece of salt junk, at which a shark, in any remarkable degree fastidious, would turn up his nose and pass on.

While cruising around in chase of pirates, he falls in with a vessel just from his own country, and boards her with the eager expectation of finding letters from home, but he finds only a newspaper or two, containing a brief notice of the death of some esteemed friend or relative, and the remarks of some members of Congress on the romance of his life and the prodigality of his pay. At length, from some less healthy clime, he enters a salubrious port, but is put under a quarantine of forty days, and cannot even get a note to the town, without having it first steeped in fire and brimstone. This is intolerable,—he weighs anchor, puts to sea, and in his cruise reaches another port, and enters; but the yellow fever or cholera enters his ship. It is now too late to fly, and death to remain. Through the wearisome night, he can hear only the moaning of the sick, and the passage of the dead over his ship's side,—the fatal symptoms are upon him,—he orders his coffin to be made,—dictates a brief letter to his wife,—bids his messmates adieu,—and dies!

If there be romance in such a life as this, it is not that kind of romance which takes one away from the toils and troubles of a real world, into a fairy region of perpetual smile and sunshine; and if there be a prodigal compensation allowed to such a life, it is not that prodigality of reward which enables one to provide for the wants of his widow and orphans. The testament of an officer in the navy, who has no means of accumulation except his pay, has usually as little gold at its disposal as the last article in the will of a Palestine pilgrim. He can bequeath his good name —the memory of his virtues—and it is only to be regretted, that these cannot contain the essential elements of life.

Ye that are on land, leave not the safe, substantial earth; and when the pitiless storm raves around your snug dwelling, turn a thought to the poor sailor, tost on this howling waste, with only a plank between him and eternity; and in your evening devotions, commend him to the protection of that Being who "rides on the tempest and directs the storm," and who can say to the chainless ocean, "Hitherto shalt thou come, and no further, and here shall thy proud waves be staid."

It was past mid-day when the rock of Lisbon broke from a mass of clouds that hung densely over our larboard-bow. There was nothing remarkably bold or towering in the aspect of this rock, and yet to me it was full of thrilling interest. It was my first glance of Europe,—the first object seen in that old world, whose nations had risen to power and splendor, and gone down to their mighty sepulchres, while America was yet a stranger to the map of the globe, and before it had even floated on the dream of a conjecturing Columbus.

Owing to the faintness of the breeze, it was several hours before we could require or obtain a pilot. A signal-gun at length brought one on board; but he was a meager, narrow, and ghastly looking fellow; if old Charon be dead, he should be his successor; for he would appear much more appropriately occupied in ferrying the dead, than piloting the living. He at first refused to take us in that evening, declaring the night too near at hand, and the wind from the wrong point of the compass; but threw out a blunt hint, as he passed below, that a glass of brandy would enable him to overcome these obstacles.

Thus braced and conciliated, he returned to the deck, ordered sail to be made, and manifested the craft of his profession by an affected escape of difficulties which never existed, and an exhibition of knowledge for which there was no possible demand.

Moving up the Tagus, we found the U. S. sloop-of-war John Adams, commanded by Capt. Storer, lying at anchor, in quarantine. The crew, as we passed, gave us a hearty cheer,—a welcome which our tars cordially returned. We came to anchor opposite the royal palace Ajuda, about two miles below the town.

The Tagus is a noble river, deep and broad, and its wave has that rich yellow tinge, which has made poets sing of it, as ever "rolling its golden sand."

The heights on the right bank, as you look up the stream, are broken into conical hills, and covered with a profusion of quintas and villages; on the left stands Lisbon, coming down with its white dwellings, churches, and convents, on an easy sweep, to the lapping waters.

Around the quay shot up a forest of masts bearing the flags of different nations; while a little more remote, reposed at this time three ships of the line and two frigates, under the "proud ensign of Britannia;" nearer to us lay two frigates, bearing the tri-colored banner of chivalric France; and two ships of the same class, with the white field and central crown of the King of Portugal; while the light feluccas of the natives were in all directions cutting the broad stream.

As the shadows of evening deepened over us, the frequent rocket was seen darting through its pathway of flame, and now and then a long, loud cheer came floating on the wind. These demonstrations of pleasure were in honor of our arrival, and conveyed a compliment equally unusual and unexpected. It seems we are in great favor with the multitude, who threw up their caps for Don Miguel; this is in consequence of having so early recognized their king, but our acknowledgments of this kind, if rightly understood, would go but little way in establishing a man's title to the crown. We never sift the question of right, but give in our diplomatic adhesion to whatever may be on the throne, whether it may be Don Miguel or the devil. This is undoubtedly our true policy; for if we, with our republican education, were to attempt to settle the question of legitimacy, we should soon find ourselves in the predicament of the school-boy, who attempted to solve a problem by the rule of three, without having first made himself familiar with the simple rules of multiplication and division.

No one left the ship last evening. This morning, at an early hour, Mr. C. and myself landed down the stream, at Belem Castle—an old, feebly mounted fortress, and took a cabriolet for Lisbon. Every thing around convinced us at once that we were in a foreign land, and among a people where the march of improvement had long been pausing. The vehicle in which we were trundled along was one of those rude contrivances which might be classed among the first triumphs of civilization. It was a clumsy affair, moving on two heavy wheels, with a massive body, hanging stiffly down to the creaking axle, and a ponderous top, supported by rough iron stanchions, with a window on each side, and a thick movable leather curtain in front. It was drawn by two old worn-out horses, moving abreast; one in the long beamy thills, the other outside, mounted by a postillion, whose appearance was quite in keeping with his charge.

His large dingy hat was cocked up closely over

each ear—his straight, pendulous cue hung far down his shoulders—his coat was pinched and high in the waist, while its little narrow flaps struggled hard to reach the stern of his saddle; and his japanned boots, armed with a pair of enormous spurs, mounted so high up the lank leg as to let the knee well into the gaping top. His whip, which made up for the brevity of its stock in the length of its lash, he ever cracked ahead of his animals; and on such an occasion, he usually cocked his eye around to us, with that peculiar look in which one expresses his sense of the dignity and importance of his occupation.

On our asking him, if these were the only vehicles used here, he replied, with rather an offended air, " It is the only one in which a gentleman rides," and then gave his whip another crack far ahead. So, being satisfied our establishment was not as ridiculous in the eyes of others as our own, we moved on. Passing through a long series of narrow, dirty streets, with here and there a huge convent towering above the visible poverty below, we reached Buenos Ayres, a suburb of Lisbon, possessing some claims to neatness and comfort.

We here called on our Charge d'Affairs, Mr. Brent, whose long and successful services have given him an eminent station in the confidence of his country. He is almost the only diplomatic agent who has not been displaced by the spirit of change that has of late fallen upon our public counsels. Having delivered the dispatches of our government, and made a few inquiries respecting the political features of Portugal, we took leave, and jogged along into the city, meeting in almost every street an armed patrol, who were universally civil on detecting our American uniform.

Our next call was on our Consul, or rather his agent—the Consul himself being absent at Paris. Among other inquiries, we made one for the most convenient and respectable hotel; and were recommended to Madam Julia's, as possessing by far the highest claims. So, dismissing our knight of the cabriolet, we walked on in search of Madam Julia's hotel, the Dutch characteristics of which we soon discovered in the antic tricks of two monkeys, and the incessant prattle of a parrot, upon its porch. We found our hostess a thick-set, dumpy, Dutch woman, with a broad, red face, and a tongue equally voluble in a vast many languages. She assured me, within ten minutes after crossing her threshold, that she could speak the dead languages as well as the living.

I felt no disposition to test her knowledge of Latin and Greek, for I was already overwhelmed with her torrent of broken Engl'sh. I told her we would thank her for our dinners soon as practicable; but before I had finished my brief request, she broke in, by asking if I could speak the Hebrew—" that first great language of all the world." I replied by requesting our dinner, as we were in haste. She sug-

LISBON.

gested that I might, perhaps, speak the Arabic—" that language in which Mahomet wrote the Koran, —an excellent language, but a bad book." I insisted on the dinner first, and a discussion of the relative merits of the different languages afterwards. This partially satisfied her, and she waddled off through a large oaken door towards the kitchen.

In about an hour, which we lounged away upon a huge sofa, covered with venerable dust, our dinner was formally announced; and though neither of us ever had the character of being a gourmand, yet we were a little vexed upon discovering on the table, in meats, only a little poor boiled chicken; in vegetables, only a plate of hard peas; and in fruits, only three or four sour oranges. But the time even occupied in making away with these meager trifles, was evidently very long to Madam Julia, who was impatiently anticipating the classical discussion at its close. Nor could she wholly restrain herself till that time; but as we were picking some bone of the chicken, or sucking the acidity from an orange, remarked upon its peculiarities in some strange, unknown dialect.

On rising from the table, we asked for our bill. "Did you say," returned our hostess, "that the languages spoken now-a-days, are to be compared to those spoken by the ancients?" We replied, "We are now, madam, on our way to the very place where the ancients lived, where we shall pick up all the little notions we can respecting them; and upon our return, should we call at Lisbon, will tell you all we can gather about the matter, and in the mean, we will thank you for our bill." "My charge," she murmured, "is six dollars; Lord G. has lately been paying me two guineas a day for my table and some instructions in the languages." We handed her the moderate sum demanded, and bade her good-bye, while she followed us quite out the door, requesting us not to forget the literary hotel of Madam Julia.

The next place at which we called, was the store of a Portuguese merchant, where we inquired for a few ready articles; but before they were handed down, the keeper drawing close to us whispered in our ear, "Can you tell me any thing about the movements of Don Pedro?" We replied, "At our last advices, he was about embarking from St. Michel's with his collected forces." "And how strong does he number?" he whispered again. We told him, "From our best information, about seven or eight thousand." His countenance brightened. "And how long do you think before he will reach here?" he continued to whisper. We observed, "The wind is now very fresh and fair, and for matter of that, he may be here in a few days." "And have you come to aid Miguel?" he inquired earnestly. "No, that is no part of our business here." He grasped us by the hand, and expressed in his look a satisfaction, which language could not convey. We asked him,

"How stand the political parties in Lisbon?" He at first clapped his finger on his lip, and after a pause, breathed half audibly, "Very well for Pedro." We inquired, "How are the more wealthy, intelligent, and influential classes affected." He whispered mournfully, "Those who have not been put to death, are in banishment or the dungeon."

We purchased our articles, and bade him adieu; congratulating ourselves that we were born in a land where it is not treason for a man to speak his political sentiments. How miserable must be the condition of that country, where one man can tie up the very breath of millions! Freedom is the sacred birthright of man, and yet he is plundered of it by every petty despot that can reach a throne!

Mr. C., with myself, took a cabriolet this morning to ride out and see a celebrated section of the Alcantra aqueduct. Midshipman L. being present, we pressed him to take a seat with us; for these primeval machines can easily accommodate three, especially of our dimensions. This introduction of a third person roused the indignation of the postillion; he jumped from his saddle, and lustily swore he would not stir an inch. We remained firm in our seats, waiting for his choler to subside. After half an hour or so, he grumly remounted and moved off in a slow walk; but even this was not gained till he had been severely rebuked by one of the police, and we had promised an additional compensation.

The pertinacious obstinacy of these men is incredible. Two of our officers sent the other morning from Madam Julia's hotel for a cabriolet, and after waiting an hour and a half without seeing any signs of its coming, commenced their excursion on foot. Soon after their departure the vehicle arrived. The postillion was informed by the hostess that the gentlemen, wearied out with waiting, had left, and would not return till evening; but he remained firm at the door, declaring he would not stir till he had been paid for his services. Through the hot day he lounged about his horses, knocking off the flies, and at dusk, when the officers returned, peremptorily demanded his hire for the day.

For the sake of peace, they offered him half the price demanded, which he indignantly refused, and remained at the door till ten at night. Early the next morning he took his stand at the door again, and now demanded full pay for his second day's services. He remained there till noon, when, upon Madam Julia's suggesting that as she sent for the cabriolet she might be held responsible for its charges, the affair was settled by paying the whole price demanded.

To return to our team. Our sulky postillion would not move out of a walk. We threatened to leave him, and take it on foot; but it had no effect. I menaced his head with a massive stone; but he sat on his saddle with the most fixed, imperturbable obstinacy. I have no doubt he would have been killed, or "made desperate fight," sooner than put his horses into a trot.

This is a fair specimen of the mulish obstinacy of an offended Portuguese. When he can have his own way, he is remarkably kind and conciliating; but when thwarted, nothing can appease or coerce him. He is ardent in love, and terrible in resentment. Take him in a good humor, and you may coax him out of his life; but, offended with you, he would see you sink to forty graves without stirring a hand for your rescue..

We at last reached the object of our curiosity, the great aqueduct of Alcantra. It is truly a magnificent work, stretching across a deep valley of three-quarters of a mile, and sustained by thirty-five arches, the centre one of which is two hundred and seventy feet in height—the highest arch in the world. The aqueduct itself has the appearance of a majestic, substantial gallery, running along high in air, with its white walls, open windows, close roof, and frequent turrets; while the water sweeps through it in two sparkling currents, leaving a space between where three may move abreast. To the outside of each wall is attached another ample walk, defended by a balustrade, and supported upon the lofty arches.

The stupendous character of this work would lead one to suppose that the Portuguese, at the time of its construction, must have been ignorant of the first principles of hydraulics; but this was not the case. They were perfectly aware that water will recover its level, and that an aqueduct laid under the surface of the ground, would answer every essential purpose of one reposing on the most sublime sweep of arches. But they must have something that will strike the eye—something that will please the vanity of the multitude—something lofty and monumental. I was informed by a very intelligent gentleman, who has long been a resident in Portugal, that if this nation were now to construct an extended aqueduct, instead of using simple pipes placed in the earth, they would have it run from one height to another, upon a magnificent range of arches. But a nation, like an individual, will have its age, decrepitude, and folly.

On our return, we stopped at the Church of St. Roque, where we discharged our sulky postillion and his concern with three dollars. We found a priest at the porch ready to wait upon us. He conducted us slowly up through a dense multitude kneeling in the nave—for it was some saint's day—to a small chapel dedicated to John the Baptist. The embellishments of this sacred alcove, adorned by the treasury of John Fifth, display a rich profusion of precious marble, amethyst, porphyry, jasper, lapis-lazuli, and verd-antique. But the objects of greatest interest and admiration are three pictures, representing the Annunciation, the Baptism, and the Pentecost, in exquisite mosaic. They have a softness and warmth of coloring, a melting delicacy of tint and shade, which I did not suppose it possible for this kind of work, in its highest perfection, to reach. Three huge candlesticks of solid silver stand in front of the jewelled altar; and it is astonishing that they have escaped being coined, in the present disasters and poverty of Portugal. The rest of the church has nothing remarkably attractive or imposing. Handing our priest a crown for his politeness, we took our leave.

Our next resting-place was in the church of Coracao de Jesus, built by Queen Maria First, in the form of a cross, of small dimensions, and surmounted by a dome. This crazy queen believed she had come in actual possession of the heart of our Saviour; and reared this church as a monumental shrine befitting the last deposit of this precious trust. The pope discountenanced this article in the creed of her religious insanity; but as he could not " minister to a mind diseased," permitted her to indulge her fanatical whims. It is not strange that in a church, where every thing spiritual is materialized, and embodied, and worshipped, that these wild aberrations from truth and reason should occur. It is a greater wonder that heaven itself is not mapped in some quarter of the globe, and laid down to feet and inches in fixed lines. But pluck the beam from thine own eye.

Our next call was at the church of St. Domingo,

which, in architectural display, is perhaps the finest in Lisbon. The walls with their marble pilasters, unbroken by a gallery, and sweeping up to the lofty ceiling, have an imposing effect. In the centre of the nave is a representation of our Saviour fainting under the cross. Of the many who came and went, while we were there, most of them kneeled and kissed the foot of this statue. The paintings over the altars are some of them happily conceived, and executed with a tolerable degree of taste. In this church the royal family attend mass, which they do once a year on Corpus Christi day. Their piety cannot, therefore, be said to be of the most ostentatious kind; though the extensive orchestra is now being fitted up for this annual occasion. Kings and their subjects, masters and slaves, find a common level in two places—the foot of the cross, and the grave.

The next place at which we brought up, to use a professional term, was the Placo de Commercio, in the centre of which stands the equestrian statue of King Joseph. The attitude of the statue is excessively extravagant: it looks like ambition overleaping itself; and the clumsy allegorical figures, grouped around and beneath the feet of the horse, add to this Hotspur expression. I wonder an equestrian statue cannot be tolerated, without having the fore-feet of the charger raised as high as if he were attempting to leap into the moon. Why not put him on his four feet, where nature puts him. But if this will not do, et him paw the ground ; and if any thing more is necessary to express his impetuosity, let him foam at the inpatient bit; but do not heave up his fore parts, till you are in the painful apprehension that he will land on his stern and crush his rider. This is not a horse rushing into battle, or out of it; nor is it one lightly prancing in the gay tournament.

From this place we rambled to that section of the city which was most disastrously visited by the earthquake. The remains of temples, palaces, and towers still totter over the fatal spot; yet amid these ghastly ruins, where every thing seems to portend disaster, many an elegant dwelling has been reared, where hearts are now gay over the graves of their fathers. Perhaps it is a felicitous provision of our nature, that we can feel secure and be happy, where others have perished unwarned. The earth itself is but one vast sepulchre; every thing that regales the taste, or animates the eye, springs from corruption. The very breeze, that is music on our ear, has been loaded with the groans of millions. We should recollect, in our exulting pride, that we are not exempt from the laws of mortality, or that gloomy forgetfulness which hovers over the realms of death. Though we should sink in the ingulfing shock of the earthquake, or the burning flood of a volcano, yet thousands will live and smile amid the frightful monuments of our ruin. The sounds of merriment and revelry have gone up for ages over the tombs of Herculaneum.

The catastrophe which destroyed the fairest portion of Lisbon, would have been less destructive of life, had the population remained in their dwellings, or fled to some more open places, instead of rushing into their churches. These huge piles were the first to fall, and the escape of a solitary individual could have been little less than miraculous. If one is to die, it may be desirable, perhaps, to undergo the dread event within the sacred associations of the sanctuary. But if one wishes to escape destruction, in an hour when his own dwelling begins to heave to and fro, it is the last refuge he should seek. Yet in all Catholic countries, the first impulse is to get within the pictured presence of a patron saint, or of the blessed Virgin, as if these dependent beings had the power to suspend the action of an earthquake.

Far be it from me to trifle with the sentiment which expresses itself in this form; ignorance, unless it will be wilful, is not a crime. But the disaster which befell this city, in all the ruin of its work, had one alleviating feature, it sunk the Inquisition—that upper hell of intolerant bigotry and fanatical vengeance! Let a man's creed rest between his conscience and his God. Give him all the lights of information in your power, but do not torture him into a confession of your particular tenets. There are no engines of belief in heaven, nor in the world of untold sorrows. The arch-apostate finds no redeeming creed awaiting his burning signature. Compulsion in a man's faith is like force in his will, they both violate our most sacred rights; and the assent which they compel is as destitute of virtuous merit as the yielding of one's purse to a robber. Such violence will always in the end react on its source—the robber will be sent to the gallows, and the inquisitor to the devil.

But enough of this rambling. We called at Madam Julia's at six o'clock, where we had bespoken a dinner, and sat down to a plate of pea-soup, a slice of broiled veal, and a few poor oranges; for which we paid eight dollars. It was in vain to question the equity of her bill, unless you were prepared to carry on the dispute in all the languages into which our great mother tongue was split at the tower of Babel. If it be wondered why we patronized Madam Julia in her barren table and exorbitant demands, the true answer is, that there is not a respectable hotel in all Lisbon. Hers, with its monkeys, parrot, and confusion of countless dialects, is after all the most decent. She followed us again quite out the door, descanting on the profusions of her table, the beauty of her parrot, and the freshness of the classics, and enjoining it upon us not to forget her and her hotel.

Forget thee?—dear woman!—not till all the dead languages have been forgotten, and the living have ceased to be spoken!—not till a chicken that has perished of inanition be nutritious as one fattened at the tray!—not till an orange, eaten up of its own acidity, be palatable as one with its sweet juices gushing through its yellow rind! Forget thee? never!—

> I'll think of thee, thy parrot, and hotel,
>   Whene'er I see a lank, voracious shark,
> Darting about all day from swell to swell,
>   And missing everywhere his flying mark;
> Till—finding his last hope and effort fail—
> He turns upon himself, and eats his tail.
>
> I'll think of thee, thy parrot, and hotel,
>   Whene'er I see a starving crow half dead—
> Rattling his bones, and willing now to sell
>   His very soul—if soul he had—for bread;
> And croaking his despair in every tongue
> That grief or madness from the lip hath wrung!
>
> I'll think of thee, thy parrot, and hotel,
>   Whene'er I see a haggard miser die,—
> Half feeing him who is to toll the bell,
>   And narrowing down the grave where he must lie;
> Nor caring whether his departing knell
> Follow his spirit's flight to heaven or hell!

CHAPTER VIII.

> Lo! Cintra's glorious Eden intervenes
> In variegated maze of mount and glen.
> Ah me! what hand can pencil guide, or pen,
> To follow half on which the eye dilates,
> Through views more dazzling unto mortal ken
> Than those whereof such things the bard relates,
> Who to the awe-struck world unlocked Elysium's gates!
>
> CHILDE HAROLD.

EXCURSION TO CINTRA—SCENERY—MARIALVA VILLA—PETER'S PRISON—PENHA CONVENT—ROYAL PALACE—VISIT TO MAFRA CASTLE—ITS EXTENT—RICHNESS—SINGULAR ORIGIN—RETURN TO LISBON—ITS STREETS AND DOGS—DON MIGUEL—HABITS OF THE FEMALES—FRIARS AND MONKS—PERILS OF NIGHT-WALKING—IMPOSITIONS ON STRANGERS—A BLIND MUSICIAN—POLITICAL DISASTERS.

A PARTY of us left the ship this morning for Cintra, that little paradise of Portugal. We chartered for the occasion three cabriolets, provided with stout mules, and four saddle-horses. Thus seated and mounted, we left the city by the Alcantra suburbs, and soon emerged into a country of an extremely light soil, with here and there a conical hill, upon which was posted one of Don Quixote's windmills. It was not, after all, so strange that this valorous knight should have waged mortal combat with these formidable things of earth and air, for they look vastly more like brandishing giants than machines merely for grinding corn. I will defy any one to look at them for the first time, throwing their strong arms about in the mysteries of twilight, and not feel for the hilt of his trusty blade.

And then, it should be remembered, that the Don was just establishing his character for courage and chivalrous devotion, and felt it incumbent on him to attack every thing that came in so questionable a shape. Let Don alone; he was not so great a fool as some of his self-styled betters would make him; he was a little on the extreme; but one-half the fighting in the world hath a less show of reason in it.

On our way we passed Queluz, one of the royal palaces, standing near the road, with extensive and cool gardens in the rear. The building itself is long, low, and without any architectural pretensions. A number of troops were paraded in front, who showed, in the promptitude and crankness of their movements, that they were defending the person of their king. A soldier guarding a monarch, and a boy in charge of a baboon, are always full of pomp and circumstance.

A few miles further brought us to a wine and bread shop, where our postillions brought suddenly up, declaring it impossible for man or beast to go further without refreshment. Our horses were baited on coarse bread, saturated with wine—their grooms on the same articles; rather a dainty provender, whatever it may have been as a lunch. We now resumed our seats, urging to a quicker pace our anti-temperance team.

The heights of Cintra slowly appeared in soft romantic relief on the sky; and the country, as we advanced, gradually assumed an aspect of richer verdure. As we wound around a steep, obstructing elevation, the sweet village of Cintra appeared nestled in the drapery of a wild woodland, about half way up the "mountain of its home." The very look of its freshness seemed to melt into one's heart. It was like a green bower, on an arid waste, under a scorching sky. We stopped at the hotel of Da Costa—a house finely in keeping with the place. We had been over five hours on the road, though the distance is but eighteen miles. This is a fine specimen of Portuguese rapidity.

After an hour's repose, and a grateful refreshment, we rambled to the palace of the Marquis of Marialva, —an elegant and spacious structure, with grounds rather confined, but concentrating a good degree of beauty and variety. This Villa is celebrated for the Convention in which the French stipulated with Wellington to evacuate Portugal. The ink which Junot scattered in his indignant reluctance, as he put his hand to the instrument, still stains the floor. Silence now reigns unbroken in its spacious halls; the Marialva line, so celebrated in Gil Blas, has become extinct. Nobles in death have but one advantage over their vassals, and that is the unenviable privilege of living in the sarcastic wit of an author.

We now ascended to the Penha Verd Quinta of the celebrated Don John de Castro, who only asked of his sovereign this elevation, in consideration of all his privations, perils, and conquests in India. So his tombstone on the summit declares; and this sentinel of death for once, I believe, speaks the truth. We have in the present case no great occasion to doubt its veracity, for of all situations in Portugal, this is universally acknowledged to be the most beautiful and enchanting. We paused for a moment in a sweet garden of lilies, tastefully distributed in parterres of box.

We were then taken to what our guide called St. Peter in prison. The dungeon is here a cool grotto, lined with variegated shells, and refreshed with a sparkling fountain. The saint is represented in marble, with the chain still clinging to him; but so quiet, romantic, and wildly attractive is his situation, that no one of any taste would think of running away from it. Instead of a sentiment of commiseration, you cannot repress the desire to exchange conditions with the captive.

Higher up, a thick forest of cork, pine, elm, myrtle, orange, and lemon cast their deep fragrant shade. We here lost ourselves in a labyrinth of paths, and a dense maze of underwood, cut by these irregular alleys into every variety of shape. We emerged at the tomb of the hero, which stands on a high airy rock, overlooking Cintra, and commanding an extensive view of the ocean as it rolls its world of waters beyond.

Upon the very summit of the range we found the conspicuous remains of a Moorish Castle, with the noble tank still in a state of high preservation. Near by, on the same height, stands the Penha convent, which one might suppose must have got here as our lady's chapel got through the yielding air to Loretto; or its materials must have been taken up before balloons became the frail and feeble things that we now find them. This convent was plundered by the French. Nothing in height or depth seems to have escaped their rapacity; yet these gentlemen of love and pillage robbed with such an exquisite politeness, that even their victims appear to hold them in the most gentle recollection. In our descent, upon arriving at a more even and thickly shaded spot, we encountered three lusty beggars, who had come with two guitars and a fiddle, to give us a concert: we paid them in advance, and passed on. At six, we reached our hotel, and sat down to an excellent dinner.

Upon rising from the table some took to the luxury of the siesta, while a few of us improved the lingering light in a visit to the old Royal Palace. We found here no guard, no king, not even a sprig of nobility, but a polite old porter, happy to show us every thing, for the sake of his fee. He pointed out the room where Sebastian held his last counsel previous to his fatal expedition to Africa, and seemed unwilling to believe that he would never return! He pointed out the room where King Alonzo Sixth was imprisoned, and the pavement in which his solitary steps have left a deep track, and then descanted upon it with a sorrowful earnestness that almost flooded one's eyes. On our return to the hotel, we found the yard full of women and children, with a thousand little articles of their own fabrication to sell. We purchased a multitude of them, not from any want of the articles, or that they could be of the slightest use; but a man is always more charitable in a foreign country than he is in his own.

The evening passed off in easy pleasantries, and we retired at a late hour to rest,—Captain Read, as the Agamemnon of the party, to that chamber which Byron occupied on his visit to this place. It was here the youthful poet nourished those feelings which subsequently flowed off in the sorrowful harmony of Childe Harold, a poem which, unlike much that he has written, will keep its place in English Literature till the story of grief and melody shall have ceased to affect mankind. The chain of sympathy which binds him to the profound sensibilities of our nature, can never be broken. He had all the elements of poetic power in the most exalted degree, but failed of reaching his noblest destiny, owing in part to that singular fatality which often attends a consciousness of great force and originality of genius, but more to the want of a deep abiding sense of the responsibility which such rare gifts and such a sway over the human heart impose. Had he possessed this, it would have saved him—sustained him in his lofty career, nor left us as much to weep and shudder over as to admire:—

> He might have soared, a miracle of mind,
>   Above the doubts that dim our mental sphere,
> And poured from thence, as music on the wind,
>   Those prophet tones, which men had turned to hear,
> As if an angel's harp had sung of bliss
> In some bright world beyond the tears of this.
>
> But he betrayed his trust, and lent his gift
>   Of glorious faculties, to blight and mar
> The moral universe, and set adrift
>   The anchored hopes of millions:—Thus the star
> Of his eventful destiny became
> A wild and wandering orb of fearful flame.
>
> That orb hath set; yet still its lurid light
>   Flashes above the broad horizon's verge;
> As if some comet, plunging from its height,
>   Should pause upon the ocean's boiling surge,
> And in defiance of its darksome doom,
> Light for itself a fierce volcanic tomb!

The morning of our second day at Cintra found us mounted upon a pack of hugely saddled and cushioned donkies on our way to Mafra Castle.

The distance is nine miles, over a road as intolerable as one can well imagine; we were more than three hours getting through it, but were amply compensated, in the end, for all our back and leg breaking toils. Mafra has been justly called the Escurial of Portugal; its proportions are all upon a lofty and magnificent scale. It contains a splendid palace, an extensive convent, and a church of cathedral dimensions. I can almost believe, as Murphy informs us, that from fifteen to twenty thousand men were employed for thirteen years in its erection and completion.

The church is lined and paved with marble; it contains nine altars, of a reflecting polish, glowing with jewels and surrounded with statues; and six organs, the beauty of which is equalled only by their richness of tone. I was never so sensible of the aid which devotion may derive from external realities, as when standing in the vast solitude of this church, with its lofty dome, its twilight gloom, and the solemn anthem of the organs filling and moving the whole with a profound majestic melody.

The palace is as magnificently ample, as one would suppose an emperor of the world might desire. We were shown the luxurious couch, upon which the monarch may seek in vain that repose which the cabined slave freely enjoys. The marble font, which almost invades the regal couch, can contain no purer w··· than the peasant finds in the brook that murmurs past his humble cottage; and the mirrors, with their smooth, broad expanse, which line the royal apartments, cannot present more perfectly one's second self, than the tranquil stream into which Eve first looked and "timidly withdrew."

The convent is sufficiently ample to contain all the monks of a moderate realm; but the stillness of the apartments is broken only here and there by the steps of the solitary. The library, in its spacious hall of some hundred feet, casts at once its fifty thousand volumes on the eye. The spectator stands literally overwhelmed with the learning of the dead. Few of the books are in English; most of the ancient classics may be seen, while a great many of them are on ecclesiastical subjects, whose authors have long since gone to the realities of their devout conjectures.

On ascending to the top of this vast edifice, we found an area wide enough to furnish footing for a military force adequate to the defence of the whole. While here, we were favored with a concerto from fifty of the one hundred and twenty bells which swing in the towers. The music of these rolling organs might awaken the multitudes of a slumbering city to their matins: but there is no such city near, to be thus musically aroused. Mafra stands in the midst of a desert; a few humble huts only break the sterile solitude.

This vast pile, in all its richness and magnificence,

was reared and furnished on the sanctity and force of a conjectural dream. The king was informed, in his desponding hopes of an heir to his throne, that his wishes might be realized by founding and endowing a convent here. Thus were the foundations laid; the future monarch soon made his appearance, and the king, regarding this as a divine interposition and sanction, the work went on, till the stupendous whole, with convent, church, and palace, were completed.

Never did the prediction of a monk cost his sovereign more. Whether, as scandal reports, the prophet was concerned in the fulfilment of his own prediction, is more than I can say; but surely it was an expensive babe to Portugal. The castle, with all its appendages, is as much lost to the realm and the world, as it would be if it were located in the desert of Sahara. It is here visited only by the curious traveller, and it would there catch occasionally the glance of a passing caravan.

After the refreshments of a crust of bread and a glass of sour wine, furnished in a sort of hovel—the only inn-accommodations of which the place can boast—we started in a drenching shower for Cintra. Mrs. R. had fortunately been able to get the loan of a large coarse cloak, in which, with the courteous assistance of Lieutenant C., she wrapped herself into the semblance of a sister of the strictest order. Her transformation was so sudden and entire, as she appeared thus hooded and swathed, and holding on in the drifting rain, to a little sorry donkey, not larger than a good-sized sheep, that I could not at first, though in a most pitiable plight myself, preserve my gravity of countenance. Nothing but the irresistible force of this sentiment of the ludicrous, saved it from an appearance of rudeness. But the value of a diamond is not the less for being sprinkled with dust, or dashed with mud.

Cintra never appeared more sweet and beautiful, than as we approached it on our return. Some portions of its ascending range were covered with the shadows of a passing cloud, while others smiled out in the clear light of a warm sun. The cascade, now freshly replenished by the shower, came leaping down from cliff to cliff, with life and joy in its motion and voice. Here the bold rock broke into stronger relief, with its moss-covered front; there the elm and cork threw out their giant limbs; while upon elevations of a gentler genius, clusters of neat cottages were seen, embowered in vines. Higher up, and more in keeping with the majesty of the spot, the princely villa, surrounded with forest-trees, presented a portion of its stately walls, or the white range of its gleaming pillars; and over the whole, a warm, soft tint was sprinkled, which seemed to blend itself into the varied beauty of the scene. Cintra is the Eden of this realm—Mafra a stupendous monument of its superstitious folly.

The morning of our third day at Cintra was overcast; and frequent showers determined us to defer our return to Lisbon till the evening. In the mean time we formed a passing accidental acquaintance with two Portuguese officers of rank and accomplishments, who were temporary lodgers with our excellent landlord. They were gentlemen of the lyre as well as sword. One of them touched the guitar with the hand of a master, and the other had eminently the sweet gifts of a melodious voice. They played and sung at intervals for an hour or two, in compliment to Mrs. R., who returned the obligation by a few Italian airs in her best style.

We invited them to dine with us; and among other topics which floated around, was one calculated to detect their political leaning. They were asked with a profound affectation of ignorance, what could be the object of the English in sending, at this particular time, so large a naval force to the Tagus. One of them promptly replied, that the English were remarkably fond of the comedy, and, understanding that one was to be acted at Lisbon, they had come to witness it. Never was there an answer upon which a man's life may perhaps have depended more quick, or guarded, than this. Such men will never lose their heads, whatever may be the result of the quarrel between Miguel and his brother. And they are right; I would as soon peril my life upon a question of the comparative strength of the square or triangle construction of a cob-house, as that of legitimacy in sovereigns.

Taking leave of our worthy landlord, whom, with his ever-cheerful wife, agreeable house, and well-furnished table, I would recommend to all travellers, we started on our return to Lisbon. We arrived quite late in the evening, and put up at Madam Julia's hotel. The monkey had ceased his pranks, the parrot was silent, and even Madam Julia herself did not seem to speak in so many languages as usual.

The servant boy of Captain Read, whose horse had run away with him, and whom we had not seen for hours, now rushed in, and by way of apology for his absence, told how the animal had fallen him three times; while another proverb in Arabic, from our hostess, settled the point, that it is safer to walk than ride, inasmuch as the pedestrian has four the less legs to take care of. So, having established this great truth in probable accidents, we retired to rest. But Cintra was all night in my dream!—

> It floated there, as some sweet fairy land
>   Of fragrant flowers, for birds and bees to sip,—
> Where crystal streams glide o'er the golden sand,
>   And fruits of nectar greet the gushing lip;—
> Where life's a careless round of rest and play,—
>   A childhood mid the merriest things of May.

Approaching Lisbon from the opposite side of the Tagus, it has the appearance of a truly magnificent city. The lofty buildings, with their white walls, and airy turrets, stretch far up a finely ascending plane. But as you approach it more nearly, and wander through it, your admiration ceases, and you become excessively disgusted with the rags of the rabble, and the narrowness and filth of the streets.

The inclined position of Lisbon would render its cleanliness perfectly feasible; but no attention is given to the matter, except what exists in some municipal regulations, which affect the canine portion of the community. Dogs are the only authorized scavengers, and for their services in this respect, they are granted certain rights and immunities. They swarm through the streets, especially at night, and so obstruct the narrow passages, that you are continually stumbling over them.

The French, while here, bayoneted these scavengers by the hundreds, and compelled those who move on two legs to take their place. The effect, of course, was a more clean and healthy city; but the French are gone, and the dogs are reinstated in their ancient rights. I have seen no personal violence offered to any of them, except by the king. His majesty is in the habit of riding through the city upon a very fleet horse, and carrying in his hand a prodigiously long wand, with which he exhibits his muscular power, and brachial dexterity, in knocking over these poor Trays. His aim is sure, and his blow certain death. I saw him in the course of a few minutes knock several of them entirely out of existence, and that too—which made the case rather a hard one—while they were picking the filth out of their monarch's path.

But the dogs are now becoming extremely shy of their king, and are manifesting their sagacity by a timely escape from the reach of his wand. They detect at a distance the rapid sound of his charger's hoof, and instantly take to flight, after the true old maxim—let those escape who can, and the devil take the hindermost.

It is not safe for one who respects his olfactories, or his apparel, to be in the streets of Lisbon after ten at night. The goddess of Cloacina begins to reign at that hour, and her offerings are cast down indiscriminately from every upper window. Her altars, which in every other city are under ground, are here the open pavement; and woe to the luckless wight who happens to be passing at the time of oblations: he will think of any thing but the sweet scents of Araby and the pure waters of Helicon. How the ungentle worship of this goddess should be thus fashionably tolerated, is inconceivable; it is enough to drive all romance and knight-errantry out of a city!

I wonder not that poetry has ceased here—that the harp is unstrung and the minstrel gone. How Love should linger under the embarrassments and perils of such a dodging existence, is a mystery.

But this little fellow of the purple wing and laughing eye is somehow the last to leave any community. He manages to remain, whatever may betide, else he would have long since taken his departure from Lisbon, and left its daughters to their desolate hearts, their silent tears, and worse—their broken guitars!

Political disasters and jealousies here have nearly broken up those little intimacies, which used to prevail in families of the same rank, and upon which depend the social enjoyments of every community. Ladies are now seldom seen in any considerable numbers, except at worship; and here they meet at all hours of the day. You may pass from church to church, and find in the nave of each, large groups of well-dressed females. The most young and fashionable assume a position in advance of the others; coming in, they first kneel, cross themselves, move their lips for a few minutes, and then assume a sitting posture on the clean marble pavement, with their small feet drawn up under them, something after the Turkish fashion.

They sit here by the half day together; and when there is no public service going on, which is usually the case, they amuse themselves in whispering over to each other those little things of which ladies are prone to be fond. To the young gentlemen, who are probably attracted here more by the worshippers than the worshipped, they never speak, except with their eyes; but these organs with them have a language more true to the instincts of the heart, than any dialect of the lip.

These whispering and glancing assemblages are more excusable here, than they would be in our country. Ladies with us may meet when and where they please, and almost whom they please; but here these social indulgences are not known; and it is a very natural consequence that the ladies should avail themselves of the facilities which the church and balcony afford, for evading these irksome restrictions.

A lady who does not dare to afford you a passing look as you meet her in the street, will, in the church, knock aside her mantilla with her fan, and divide her glance between you and the image of the blessed Virgin; or, if you are passing near her balcony, she will dart upon you all the sweet attractions of her unveiled face. Unreasonable and indiscriminate restraints promote neither the cause of religion or virtue. They convert the sanctuary into an ogling room, and the ballustered window into an amatory bower.

The friars and monks of Lisbon are, apparently, the best fed people in it: they have a majestic corpulency of person, which reminds one of the good cheer which Sir Jack, of sack memory, so much admired. You meet them at every turn, in their black flowing robes, sandals, silver-buckled shoes, and hats of enormous brim. They move along with that gentlemanly, good-natured, slow pace, which heeds not the flight of time. They have none of that thin, thinking, anxious look, which converts the closet and pulpit into a befitting refuge for ghosts; but they have that full, fat, jolly cast of countenance which lets the world pass for better or worse, and which well becomes a man, who knows that he can shrive a Sodom of its sins in a minute, or exorcise the devil out of as many millions as there are sands on the sea-shore. There is something in this full, well-fed look of unconcern about this world and the next, which makes a man's conscience set easy upon him, and he begins to feel the flesh thicken upon his own bones.

The vow of celibacy in these fat, easy men, does not—if there be any truth in scandal—seriously interfere with their domestic pleasures. They have no wives, it is true, but the Foundling Hospitals, which are extensive and liberally endowed, have within them, according to report, many a sacerdotal likeness; and these little fellows of ambiguous parentage, will, many of them, come forth one day to confess their betters, and run the career of their worthy fathers. The thing runs round in a rich voluptuous circle, far above the intrusions of an impertinent conscience, and the insulting terrors of a threatened hell. Such a life is worth having, and branded be the heretic that questions its sanctity.

It is not, to be sure, in exact accordance with the habits of the Apostles; but those men of leathern girdles were foolish martyrs to their self-denying zeal. They lived in times when the absolving functions of popes and priests were not known: why, then, should their example be quoted in these good easy times, when there is no ignorance to be enlightened, and no depravity to be restrained? Let the world turn round on its axle, and let us all jog quietly along into heaven. But enough of this! The sentinel who sleeps on his post, forfeits his life, and the minister of Christ, who slumbers over his responsibilities, perishes with a double doom!

The dwelling-houses of Lisbon are, many of them, five and six stories in height: each loft has its family and restricted accommodations; a broad, dirty, common stairway leads up through the whole; and the rent decreases with the altitude. I wonder at this, for so intolerably filthy are many of the streets, which are continually sending up their noxious exhalations, that I would get, if possible, into the highest loft, though it reached the moon.

It is as much as a man's life is worth to attempt to get through the city by night. There are no lights, except here and there a glimmer from some casement, which only serves the more to bewilder; and you stumble along, through dirt, and dogs, and darkness, till you fall at last into some foul ditch, or bring up against some sturdy, black visaged fellow, who accosts you with a demand for your purse. Many a poor stranger, after having thus battered his shins, lost his hat, and bedabbled himself with mud, has ended the night's disasters by being robbed, and then perhaps murdered.

I experienced one night all but the last incident, and I should prefer being assassinated in any place to this, for I should not have even the miserable consolation of believing that my murderer would be detected, and made an example of warning to the rest of his nocturnal profession. Law here runs upon accidents; it is like a wolf plunging through a bramble—he may crush a snake, but he is much more likely to pounce on a lamb.

The traveller in Lisbon is imposed upon in every conceivable shape: he is besieged by beggars, pilfered by pickpockets, cheated by his hostess, and plundered by his cicerone. I inquired this morning of a cocheiro what he would charge to take me a short distance, to a place which I named. He stated his price in *rees*, a coin with which I was not familiar. A third individual, watching my embarrassment, touched his hat, and observed that the price named by the cocheiro was five Spanish dollars, and offered very kindly to take the money, pay him, and see he did his duty. But before he had finished his story, a fourth came up, and, drawing me slightly aside, said that the price demanded by the cocheiro was only four dollars, and that the man had stated it to be five, for the sake of pocketing one himself, and offered generously to take the sum, and pay it over, lest there should be some misunderstanding, and I should, after all, be cheated.

I hesitated, not liking the price, or the man's solicitude, when a fifth person drawing near, whispered that he had a word to say to me; when, turning away a step or two with him, he said that these two men were the greatest cheats in Lisbon, that they imposed on all strangers, that the price of the cocheiro was simply three dollars, that he would take the money, and perhaps he might be able to beat him down even a trifle below that sum. I was not, however, quite so *green* in the world as to be caught yet, and observing a Portuguese merchant, with whom I had become acquainted, passing, I got him to explain to me the amount of the price named at first by the cocheiro; and it proved to be only two dollars!

The reason the cocheiro did not interfere and rescue me from the friendship of these interpreters was, that they spoke very low and in broken English, which he could not comprehend; or there might have been an understanding between him and these kind souls, for, after all, I got cheated, and paid about twice as much as the usual price. A stranger here wants an eye in every hair of his head; and then, if his skull-cap be a wig, he will lose it!

The traveller will find but little choice between the hotels of Lisbon; they are all miserable, perhaps Madam Julia's the least so. If his linguistical hostess press him too hard on the subject of ancient lan guages, he must adopt a similar expedient to the one which I took refuge in last evening; for as this representative of all languages, especially the dead, came waddling to a chair near my side, commencing even before she had rolled into her seat, a dissertation on the relative force of Cicero and Demosthenes, I happened to look out at an open window, and discovering a blind man with a violin, led by a lad, who carried a guitar, dispatched a servant with instructions to invite them in.

Madam Julia declared a man must be out of his wits who could prefer such music as that to the eloquence of the classics, and that she was not accustomed to have beggars in her parlor. I told her the fiddle must come or I should go, and ordered two good suppers prepared for my new guests. The last order partially reconciled madam to the introduction of the strangers, and the sudden breaking off of the literary discussion.

My new acquaintances entered: one was a man of sixty, cleanly clad, and perfectly blind; the other was his son, a lad of twelve years, with a very bright, intelligent countenance. I inquired of the old gentleman how long he had been blind. He replied, "From my early childhood, sir." "And do you not find," I asked, " a consolation for this visual deprivation in this violin?" "It is the only thing," he replied, "that reconciles me to life." "And would you not," I thoughtlessly asked, " be willing to part forever with this instrument on condition you could recover your sight?" He seemed to hesitate a moment, and then said, "That, sir, is rather a difficult question."

After supper, in which the boy betrayed a truly filial and amiable disposition in assisting his blind father to the coffee and different dishes, they played for an hour; and I have rarely been more entertained. Nature seems to have made up in music to the bereaved man what misfortune had deprived him of, in the loss of his sight. His voice flows into the full harmony of his violin with expressive richness and force. I would exchange to-day the use of one eye at least for the musical gift of voice and the magical power over the violin which this blind man possesses.

In any country capable of appreciating and awarding merit, so far from mendicity, he would rise at once to affluence; but here the unworthy seem to prosper, and the meritorious to starve. The performance of the lad was astonishing for one of his years; but he had been trained, as his father informed me, almost from his infancy to the guitar. On parting with these new friends, I put into the hand of the boy what little money the extravagant charges of Madam Julia had left, and only regretted it was not more.

The resources of Portugal are now in a most wretched condition. She has squandered her wealth in the prosecution of schemes which have ended only in abortion—in the continuance of wars, which have terminated in her disgrace—and in the support of an overgrown ecclesiastical establishment, that now weighs like a crushing incubus upon the poor remnants of her strength. Her capitalists are deterred from investments by the insecurity of property; her merchants have lost their enterprise in the onerous restrictions of commerce; and her oppressed peasantry, discouraged and broken-hearted, have retired to their hovels to die!

Nor in a political aspect is she less degraded and miserable. Her throne is the subject of a violent fraternal conflict; her towns and villages are converted into lawless camps; and her more worthy citizens are sent into exile, to the scaffold, and the dungeon! Freedom of opinion, nobleness of demeanor, national pride, and self-respect have all perished from her soil, or survive only in some dark, indignant recess! These are the fruits of a doting, drivelling despotism, that has ever manifested its imbecility by the pursuit of schemes visionary and impracticable; that has long betrayed its ignorance, by confounding a calm difference of opinion with treason; and that still evinces its unrelieved tyranny by punishing with death an exercise of that intelligence which alone raises man above the abject brute.

But our anchor is weighed, and I must leave this

land of peril and sorrow. Adieu, sweet Cintra! thou art a green oasis in the desert of thy realm. Farewell, thou noble Tagus! would that those who dwell on thy fresh banks were more worthy of thy golden tribute: and Madam Julia, farewell to thee!— the tears are in my eyes!—farewell!

> Cherish thy parrot; and declare to all
>   That this serene, exquisite bird was given,
> Before the dismal discords of the Fall,
>   To bring to earth the dialect of heaven;
> The very bird from whose celestial stammer
> Our mother Eve first learnt the Hebrew Grammar.

CHAPTER IX.

> He is a child of more impulse and passion,
>   Loving his friends, and generous to his foes,
> And fickle as the most ephemeral fashion,
>   Save in the cut and color of his clothes,
> And in a set of phrases, which on land
> The wisest head could never understand.

PASSAGE FROM LISBON TO GIBRALTAR—DIVERSIONS OF THE SAILOR—HIS TACT AT TELLING STORIES—LOVE OF THE SONG—FONDNESS FOR DANCING—UNHAPPY PROPENSITIES—DUTY OF THE GOVERNMENT TOWARDS HIM—GIBRALTAR—A BEFITTING EMBLEM OF BRITISH POWER—ROMANCE OF ITS HISTORY—FORTIFICATIONS—TROOPS—MOTLEY POPULATION—SUMMIT OF THE ROCK—ST. MICHAEL'S CAVE—THE FIVE HUNDRED—MONBODDO'S ORIGINALS—PLEASURE PARTY—MUSIC AND A MERMAID.

WE are again at sea, with our canvas set to a fresh, fair breeze, that promises to take us to our destined port. The evening has come in bland and beautiful; the sky, nature's great dome, is yet unlit by the softer stars, but the light of the departed sun still lingers on the cloud, fringing it with golden fire. Such an evening as this more than reconciles one to the strange, adventurous life of the sailor; yet it brings with it, like the tones of recollected music, all the sacred endearments of home.

The ocean-traveller thinks if only that one being, who dwells so brightly in his memory, could be near him—could look at the same sunset, sky, and stars—

it would be all he could ask—he should be happy; and perhaps he would, for their hearts would imperceptibly become harmonized to the same tone of pensive sentiment, till, like the mingling note of two lutes in perfect unison, their spirits would become one, and the current of their thoughts would glide away as from the same fresh fount. In the solitude of their situation they would cling to each other, as all that this poor world contains, nor dream that either could survive a dissolution of this concentrated life. An hour of such confiding attachment as this is worth years of that heartless intimacy which obtains in the circles of the gay.

Such an evening as this, with its steady breeze, is a pastime to the roving sailor. He has no sails to reef, no yards to trim, and sits himself quietly down, while one of his companions, blessed with a more fertile imagination, spins a long yarn. These stories partake vastly more of fiction than fact, and are often, I have no doubt, the mere creations of the individual. They do not very nicely preserve the unities, but these are forgotten in a succession of marvellous, ludicrous, and tragical incidents. One of them will frequently be extended through several nights, and apparently increase in interest with its length.

I have just heard one resumed for the fourth night, and how much longer it will be continued no one can conjecture. The circle seated themselves in their wonted place on deck; a silence ensued: "And where did I knock off?" inquired the teller. "Just where the gale struck the ship and she was thrown on her beam's end," answered one of the listeners. "No, it was where she split on the rock, just as she was making a snug harbor," replied another. "That was not the spot, neither," interrupted a third; "it was where that strong swimmer, with a shark at his heel, made his way through breakers to the shore, and then dropped on the sand with his strength all spent. Don't you remember the beautiful girl who came down to the beach and held his head on her knee, when her blessed tears dropped on his cheek?"

"Oh! that was the spot," exclaimed the story-teller, "and a sweeter creature never lived: she knew nothing about that man, only that he had been wrecked, for she was standing on a cliff when she saw the ship strike the rock and go down; yet soon as he reached the beach, and was trying to get further from the wave, and kept fainting and falling till he couldn't rise any more, she came at once to him, sat directly down, and raised his head on her knee, and then—bless her sweet heart!—wrung all the salt water out of his hair, and watched his face like a sister, to see if he would breathe again. Oh! fellows, there is something in a woman you never meet with in a man. She never waits to be paid for her pity,—it comes at once bubbling right up out of her heart. This girl knew the man had nothing to give her for her kindness, for his landtacks had all been wrecked with the ship; she saw he was young, and handsome too, if he hadn't been so pale; but it wasn't that, that made her come to him." Here I was called away; the story, however, was continued, but of the end I know as little as the reader.

The song is another evening amusement among our sailors, when the breeze is steady and the sea smooth. They gather forward before the call of the first watch in a large group, when some one, more favored than the rest in melody of voice, is called upon for a song. With little ado, save adjusting his tarpaulin and dispensing with his quid, he strikes up,—it may be the Defeat of Burgoyne, the Battle of Plattsburg, the Star-spangled Banner, the Cherub that sits up Aloft, or Black-eyed Susan,—but whatever be his choice, or the selection of his comrades, he sings it with a genuine earnestness, and downright honesty of heart. The music, be the words what they may, has generally a touch of the melancholy, and might be classed, without any violence, among those airs to which the good Whitfield alluded, when he determined that the devil should not run away with all the fine tunes.

There was one among our crew, whose powers in the musical line were so far above his fellows that we often called upon him for a song. His favorite was Black-eyed Susan; and he sung it with a fidelity to the sentiment that reached the very heart. The national airs of the sailor ever breathe of battle, and burn with patriotism; they are intensely kindled with sentiments that flash through all the depths of his soul. Should the watch-fires of freedom ever be extinguished on our cliffs, there will still be embers in the breast of the sailor, at which liberty, exiled from the land, may light her torch.

Another amusement with the sailor in the still evening at sea, no less than among the diversions of the shore, is dancing. This elegant accomplishment, as it is generally termed, belongs, I think, of right to him; for without the least instructions, without having ever been taught a single figure, or step, or even told that he must turn out his toes, he goes ahead, and keeps time with a precision and emphasis of motion seldom met with in the saloon. There are with him no studied bows, no mincing airs, no simpering looks, no glances at one's own white glove, and light, elastic pump, no rivalries and jealousies, significant nods, nor quarrels about position, nor even about partners; for if Lucy is engaged, Mary is not, and that is enough for him. He unships his tarpaulin, dashes into the ranks and bounds to the music with an exulting life and heart.

Nor is the presence of the other sex, however desirable, indispensable to him in this frequent pastime; for, on the deck of his ship, and far away at sea, where women may have never been, if a lip or lute or string make the music, he is ever ready to move to it with his quick step and vigorous limb; and he may sometimes be seen, when the winds are frolicking and piping through his shrouds, keeping fantastic time to their wild notes. Alas, those notes! they are too often the pleasing, deceptive precursors of a gale, that is on its way to wreck that ship,—to sink it there with all its happy hearts, and leave over the spot where it went down, only the dirge of the passing wave!

> Our life is but a tale, a dance, a song,
>   A little wave that frets and ripples by;
> Our hopes the bubbles which it bears along,
>   Born with a breath, and broken with a sigh.
> Then fix, my heart, thy trust in faith sublime,
> Above the storms and tempest-wrecks of time!

Would that the diversions and excitements of the sailor never carried him more widely on the moral compass from his true course than he is borne when yielding to the vein of a song, or making the part of his story. But he is so entirely the creature of impulse and momentary feeling, and frequently finds himself so far out of his reckoning, that it costs him many troublesome tacks, and the most painfully close sailing, to enable him to bring up the leeway.

No one thing contributes more to this disastrous departure, than the stimulating bowl. This is his darling sin—his prevailing tempter—his flattering, false friend—his associate in joy, his refuge in grief,

—and the prime source of all the errors and evils that befall him. Will it be credited hereafter, that the government!—the kind paternal government which he serves,—presents this poisoned chalice to his lips? Yet this is the fact!—a fact that will fill those who may write the history of these times with incredulity and amazement!

The evils to the sailor, of which this vicious indulgence is the source, are of the most affecting character. There is not a wave or shore where our canvas has been spread that is not darkened with the graves of our mariners. There is not a circle from which these bold hearts have gone, that has not been filled with mourning for those who are to return no more. Could the wave that has been the winding-sheet of the sailor speak; could the lonely shore reveal the secrets of its frequent mounds, there would be voices on the ocean, and bones on its strand, to tell a tale of death, more wild and dark than any that ever yet knelled its terrors through the most tragic dream! It is not the tempest, casting the proud ship a naked hulk on the deep, nor the rock, strewn with the fragments of its perished strength, that has wrought this scene of desolation, and filled so many hearts with unavailing sorrow. It is that cup of insidious poison, mingled and mixed, and still placed to his lips by the government! Yes, by the government!

Nor were those who had a short time since the

humanity to propose, in our national legislature, a discontinuance of this criminal conduct, able to shield themselves even from an insulting levity. The senseless jest reached them, entrenched, as they were, behind this appalling mass of misery and death. Numbers, with whose names I will not dishonor this page, cast upon the earnest, impassioned appeal the mockery of their sneers! Such men might consistently trifle with the despair of the dying, and sport among the bones of their ancestral dead! They are a burlesque upon the solemnities of the legislative hall. They are as unfit to lay their hands upon the ark of power as a buffoon to administer incense upon the altars of the sanctuary.

But I forbear. Let the invective light only on the guilty. It is the imperative duty of those who hold the restraints of national law in their hands to legislate on this subject,—to withdraw the countenance and sanction which they have given,—to dash to the earth the fatal cup which they are holding to the lips of the sailor,—and to cut up, root and branch, this deep evil in the naval service. If, by any strange perversity or recklessness of heart, they fail to do this, they betray the trusts confided to them—they betray the interests of the navy, the interests of the country, the great cause of humanity; and the blood of thousands will be found in their skirts in that day when men shall give to God an account of their deeds.

As we floated around the rock of Gibraltar to our quiet anchorage, this morning, I found my anticipations of its formidable strength, and lofty, uncompromising look, fully realized. It rises, bold and majestic, some fourteen hundred feet above the water, and seems to cast its stupendous scorn upon the menacing violence of the two oceans that rave at its base. These oceans may roll on, and cast against it, through ages, the shocks of their undecaying power, but it will still stand firm, undaunted and unshaken. The unbarred convulsions of the final day will, indeed, heave it from its foundations, but with it will fall the pillars which support the vast fabric of nature.

This towering and unshaken Rock is a proud and befitting representative of the moral and political power of the sea-girt isle; and so long as that power is wielded with the dignity, moderation, and benign effects which now characterize it, I trust it will prove as indestructible as this mountain mass. It is filled with a central energy, which binds to itself the confidence of all nations that revere virtue and respect the sacred rights of man. Were this empire to sink from its present commanding elevation, there is no community that would not feel the shock, and no good man who would not weep over the ruin. God grant, that in my last vision of mortal realities, I may see the unimpaired power of this noble realm blended harmoniously with the spreading influence of my own country, penetrating every clime, and pervading all lands.

The lofty look of defiance which nature has stamped on this rock has been rendered still more formidable and threatening by the work of man. As you turn your eye to it, you are met below by a sweeping series of batteries, bristling with their engines of destruction. As you raise your eye higher up, you discover the fearful embrasures of long-connected ranges of ordnance, ready at a breath to convert the stupendous pile into a blaze of terrific thunder. A thousand hostile fleets, even before they had time to display their impotent strength, would sink here, like the bubbles that break around their chafing keels. If this impregnable citadel ever passes from the possession of Great Britain, it will not be by force. The giant of Gaza was despoiled of his strength by stratagem; and in this form, if ever, will England be deprived of her Gibraltar. But Britannia is too wakeful, too full of caution, to lay her head on the seductive lap of any Delilah.

The history of this mountain fortress is in keeping with its native wildness and singularity. The ancients, ever fond of connecting the origin of the most striking objects in nature with the virtues of some of their fabled heroes, ascribed the existence of this rock to the might of their Hercules. There was something in its solitary grandeur, its fearless, self-relying aspect, and the depth and darkness of its caverned womb, that roused their imagination; and they cast over it the mysteries of a deathless romance. This dream of wonder and worship came down with a dim and thrilling interest upon later times; and whenever a prince wished to distinguish himself in some perilous, romantic enterprise, he seems to have laid siege to this rock.

Thus, for ages, the gallant and brave of all nations appear to have regarded its possession as a sort of triumph, that could set the highest and brightest seal upon their adventurous valor. At length Britannia, in one of her wandering excursions over the ocean, being struck with the wildness and strength of its bold features, determined to possess it, as a sort of gorgeous and solemn outpost to her spreading power. She challenged its proud occupants to mortal combat, and won it, and gave her banner to the breeze upon its highest peak. The beleaguering strength of nations has since been exhausted to pull that banner down; but it still waves on, pointing in triumph and pride to the sea-girt isle.

Every part of Gibraltar, even that which has been most affected by the subduing power of human ingenuity, has still upon it a cast of the romantic. The town itself is reared upon parapets cast against its less precipitous side, and scarcely furnishes room for one jostling street; while higher up, as if half suspended in air, hundreds of toppling habitations may be seen fastened to the face of the rock. Thus fifteen or twenty thousand dwell, looking down upon the roof of their nearest neighbor in a series so steep that even the shrub, in its fear of falling, strikes its roots with an unwonted pertinacity.

Where the side becomes too nearly perpendicular to admit the construction of a support for the artillery, the rock has been entered, and long tiers of galleries cut in its solid recesses. The heavy guns, as if they might be rendered giddy by their elevation, scarcely look from their dark ports, except when an enemy may heave in sight, and then they will speak to him in a voice which the timid never mistake, and even the fearless can never withstand.

There is also something strikingly picturesque in the varied aspect of the population: almost every nation is here appropriately represented. Here is the Briton, in the substantial pomp and circumstance of office; the mercenary soldier, who perhaps never knew his parentage, or knew it only to run away from it, going through his evolutions with a crankness and precision which mocks the automatons of Maelzel; the stout Moor, with his broad benevolent face, and his turban still true to the prophet; the bearded Jew, peddling his false jewels, and expecting the day of his deliverance; the Greek, with his restless air, and the cunning of his ever-flashing eye; the Italian, living upon a crust of bread, and drawing from every instrument you may name the tones of its slumbering melody; the Frenchman, polite in his last shirt, and whistling over his misfortunes; the German, silently and snugly amassing a fortune for some unborn nephew; the Irishman, drinking his last penny in a health to the Emerald Isle, and vowing, by St. Patrick, that it is the sweetest *continent* in the world; and the Spaniard, with his dark piercing eye, his sinewy limbs and trusty blade, ready for any enterprise that the gallows and grave have attempted to obstruct.

These are only a few of the more prominent figures in the picture; more retired are groups where one might speculate for years. Indeed, if I wished to take to a distant planet a just specimen of this world, in the most condensed form, and had the Herculean power requisite, I would carry off Gibraltar. I should find, in my gregarious wallet, some of the best and worst specimens of human nature, with most of the intermediate links. All religions, trades, professions, and pursuits are tolerated and thrive here.

There is no pope, it is true, but the mass is said and sung with an emphasis; there is no high vicar of the prophet, but the Koran is read, and the houried paradise anticipated; there is no sanhedrim, but the chant of the synagogue is heard, and the promised Messiah still expected; there is no lecturing Esculapius, but the doctors nevertheless learn how to cure or kill; there are no tread-mills or entailed estates, but the lawyers still find fees; there is no water-fall, but the fabric still goes on, under human hands; there is no arable earth, but the delicious plant is still reared into maturity; there is no protection for commerce, but the din of a bustling mart is incessant on the ear; there is no court, but the trappings of nobility are constantly flashing on the eye; there is no Draco, with his bloody code, but the bailiff gets his fee, and the hangman is fed!

The large and well-selected library of the garrison, in its elegant, commodious building, with its reading-room supplied with periodicals from the different quarters of the world, was a retreat from which I reluctantly forced myself away. A stranger, who expects to spend any time here, should by all means get introduced to the library.

Another object of interest here, at least as long as its novelty lasts, is the beautiful Parade-ground, retired a little to the south of the bustling town. You may here listen to the music of a powerful military band; or witness, in the exact and simultaneous motions of the troops, how entirely a creature of system and position an English soldier is; or you may see the dark Genoese darting by, and only casting a furtive glance to see how her man of the red coat shows on parade. Near by you will find many snug cottages, picturesquely cast into the airy nooks of the rock, shaded by the spreading fig-tree, or the more majestic palm, or the ambitious vine dropping its festoons around the slight corridor; while the varied flowers of many climes cast up from their small parterre the perfume of their mingled sweets.

Another excursion of interest is to the excavations. We were taken through these by Mr. H., our late consul at this place, a gentleman of polite bearing and of extensive information. The galleries were sufficiently high for Mrs. R. to ride through their whole extent without once dismounting her donkey. They are cut at some depth from the face of the rock; their gloom and darkness is relieved only by the light which struggles past the muzzle of the guns, as they look out menacing the world below, with the heavy metal which lies hugely piled around them.

Looking from these lofty galleries, you feel perfectly secure from the utmost violence of a besieging enemy,—which to me would be not at all disagreeable,—and, at the same time, you feel that every thing beneath you is at your mercy. If it be a fleet, you see that you can send the plunging ball through the deck, while not a shot can mount to your position; or if it be a breastwork, you can strike it as the eagle, in his rushing swoop, strikes his prey on the exposed plain. These excavations are a perpetual monument of the enterprise and hardihood of the English.

From these central regions we ascended a spiral stairway to the top of the rock, and from thence on to the signal-tower, upon its highest summit. Here a corps of observation is stationed, who communicate the arrival of ships in the straits, and who announce, from a small battery, the rising and setting of the sun. From this elevation your prospect is eminently commanding. You see Africa, stretching away with a gloomy aspect that well comports with her history of strife and disaster. On the other hand, you discover the nearer coast of Spain, sending the glad tribute of its waters to the sea, and the wild ranges of its more distant mountains, heaving into the blue sky the glittering pinnacles of their eternal ice. Far over the intervening land rolls the broad Atlantic; while less remote lies the Mediterranean, in all the brightness and beauty of that hour when the morning stars first sang together over its unveiled face.

From this position we wandered to St. Michael's cave, whose winding depths lead down among the foundations of the rock. You enter by a small aperture, half concealed by shrubs, and which really promises but little in compensation for your pains. But when you have got fairly within, and see the outline of objects dimly revealed in the light that strays through the narrow opening,—the stalactites descending in columned beauty from the fretted vault to the well-formed pedestal,—the arch, sweeping from pillar to pillar with architectural symmetry and precision,—the dark portals of other caverns leading down to regions unknown,—you are as much surprised at the inward as outward structure of this singular mass.

It was here that the devoted five hundred concealed themselves through a long anxious day, till the shadows of night again concealed their invading movements from the enemy. They had vowed never to return, till they had won back this Rock to the Spanish crown. They had taken the sacrament, been shrived by their priest, and were thus doubly armed—not having before them the fear of this world or the next. They succeeded during the first night in climbing to this cave, where they remained undiscovered through the succeeding day. Upon the following night, they drew up, by the help of rope-ladders, other bold companions to their aid, and were now ready for the decisive blow.

But a trifling misunderstanding occurring at this critical moment, they were discovered,—attacked by a powerful detachment from the garrison,—driven over the precipice, or slain on the spot—battling it to the last breath. I could not but feel, as I stood on that spot, an indescribable sentiment of sympathy for the disastrous fate of those gallant men. The question of their success, or failure, appears to have been suspended upon a hair. But valor in this world seems to be destined to an early grave, while skulking cowardice lives out its lengthened life of shame.

Monkeys in considerable numbers, at certain seasons of the year, make their appearance among the heights above. They come, as report says, from the African shore, under the rushing straits, in a tunnel,

—probably less magnificent than that beneath the Thames—and reaching some of these lowest caverns, mount through them to the upper regions of light. They manifest such a degree of sagacity and cunning, that I should advise any one, who thinks of adopting Monboddo's theory of man's original formation, to come here and strengthen his incipient convictions.

These gentlemen of the tail are sometimes pursued by some of their two-legged neighbors; and on such occasions, when hard pushed, they are prone to turn a quick, short corner, upon the giddy verge of the rock, and let their eager pursuer, who is unable in like manner to arrest his momentum, plunge off the fatal steep. Though this is not exactly destroying an adversary by giving him battle, yet it is killing him in a much handsomer way.

I recommend, also, all molesters of society to come here, and learn how easy it is even for a monkey to out-wit a disturber of the public peace. Say what we will, the monkey has many of the traits which belong to a modern-cut gentleman. He carries, it is true, no quizzing-glass; but then he keeps looking and winking and staring, just as he would, were he using that elegant ocular aid. His tail, to be sure, is rather an embarrassment, but this is no fault of his; and I always feel, when surveying his person, a pitying regret that nature should have thought it necessary to afflict him with this most singular, and wholly superfluous appendage!

On the day of our departure from Gibraltar, we were favored with the company of an engaging party of ladies and gentlemen, who came on board at the invitation of Capt. and Mrs. Read, with whom they dined. In the course of the day we sailed across the bay to Algeciras, where we obtained a clean bill of health from its kind governor, for the purpose of evading the quarantine laws of Malaga.

There is a sort of family understanding here, that a ship passing from one port to another of the same nation, shall be exempted from all lazaretto embarrassments. It was an amiable act in the governor, and I wish it were in our power to return it. The company appeared in excellent spirits, and the occasion passed off with unusual animation. Mr. P., our present consul, and his lady, to our regret, were absent. But we could scarcely grieve over the absence of the best of friends, while listening to the music of a Spanish lady who composed one of the company. Her deep and elastic voice, full of sweetness and energy, passed through the wide compass of its powers with a thrilling force. In its lowest tones, it had a singular fulness and strength, and yet appeared to lose none of its expressive melody, even in that light and vanishing strain in which the music seems to linger when the lips have ceased to breathe. Her light and easy hand would now just touch the strings that answered in soft unison; and now sweep them as if calling up their harmonies from some profound slumber. I could have listened till another sun had risen; but the one now setting compelled our friends to think of the shore; and so we parted—they to their cheerful homes—we to the winds and waves of the Mediterranean.

Whether it may be ascribed to that apprehension of disaster, which we ever experience on parting with friends, or to the tragical cast of the music to which we had been listening, I know not, but—

> That night I dreamed while in my hammock swinging,
>   Our ship had suddenly become a wreck;
> The booming wave was in my dull ear ringing,
>   As I went downward from the parted deck;
> While far above, the hoarsely sounding surge
> Was murmuring to the rocks my funeral dirge
>
> A mermaid gliding from her coral cave,
>   And bearing in her hand a scallop-shell,
> Hovered around me in my sea-green grave,
>   And played the air, on earth I liked so well.
> It is an air which he who sings or hears,
> However gay, will find himself in tears.
>
> She breathed it through her sweetly sounding shell;
>   And as she reached that closing, tragic strain,
> Where wildly dies away Love's last farewell,
>   So long did her reluctant lips retain
> The parting sound in their melodious breath,
> I quite forgot the agonies of death.
>
> And there I lay upon my watery bier,
>   Enchanted by this minstrel of the deep:
> The strain had ceased, yet still she hovered near,
>   And seemed, as with a sister's love, to keep
> A tender vigil o'er the troubled slumbers,
> Which she had soothed with her celestial numbers.

CHAPTER X.

The morning stars, that hymned the Earth's creation
  In melodies which charmed the listening spheres,
Now fading into dawn, desert their station,
  But leave in dew-drops round their farewell tears;
While Cynthia pales at young Aurora's painting,
Like timid bride, at nuptial altar fainting.

MALAGA—COMING TO ANCHOR—CATHEDRAL—TOMB OF MOLIANA—FIDDLES AND ORGANS IN CHURCHES—CASTLE OF THE MOORS—HOURS OF A MALAGUENA—TRAITS OF A SINGULAR BANDIT—A SPANISH LADY—TWILIGHT AND THE PROMENADE—A FUNERAL.

WE dropped anchor in the bay of Malaga at a late hour last night, and fully experienced that illusion of distance, which objects discovered at sea, and especially by star-light, never fail to create. I would have ventured any thing on the conjecture, that we were not more than a good cable's length from the landing, when, as it afterwards proved, we were over a league.

This is a happy provision in nature, for otherwise we might, under a quick wind, a rapid sea, and perhaps a nodding watch, be carried against the rock before we had time to haul our wind, whereas we may now apparently strike it with our jib-boom, and still have room to wear ship. Those who are prone to regard the imperfections of man in a light that impugns the divine benevolence, may here find, even in our infirmities, the means of our safety.

One of the first objects to which we directed our steps upon reaching the shore, was the cathedral—a magnificent, stately pile—towering, in splendor and pride, far above the humble habitations around. The style of its architecture is a mixture of the Roman and Gothic—a union which has here been effected upon a colossal scale, with a happy and impressive effect. The interior presents an oblong spheroid, with a double row of Corinthian pillars, rising in marble richness and stability from the centre of the nave to the dome, which sweeps down in well-turned arches upon the lofty entablatures. The high altar and pulpit are of fine flesh-colored marble, and the choir of exquisite workmanship. It contains about fifty stalls, richly wrought in mahogany, and several statues of saints, by celebrated artists.

The monument of the late bishop Don Jesse de Moliana is well conceived, and tastefully executed. The dying prelate is represented on his tomb, in an inclined posture, leaning faintly on his hand, and looking calmly up with that serene confidence which triumphs over the terrors of death. The meekness and fidelity with which he is reported to have discharged his sacred functions, and his munificent donations to this church, might well secure for him a lasting memorial.

Though this cathedral is seldom mentioned by

travellers, yet it is well worthy of being classed among the marvels of modern architecture. The area embraced within its walls is four hundred feet in length by two hundred and sixty in breadth, with a hundred and forty to the height of its arches,—giving it dimensions approaching those of the temple which has brought so many thousand pilgrims to Rome.

The two organs, with their deep, rich tones, gave an air of solemnity and inspiration to the place more impressive than the spreading incense of the altar the majesty of the pillared dome, or the hallowing twilight, which softly bathed each object. While listening to these noble instruments, in the sublime part they bore in the anthem, I could not but feel a mortifying regret at the mistaken hostility with which so many in my own country regard these moving aids to the devotions of the sanctuary. In some of our churches even a sober bass-viol is not tolerated, and a wind instrument is looked upon as the very hornpipe of the devil. I do not suppose that our aspirations will be very much deepened or elevated by the trills of a reed or the quavers of a string. But this is no reason why an instrument, which can indeed " discourse eloquent music," and especially the organ, with its solemnity and power, should be expelled from our worship.

True, it has not an innate sense of its melodious vocation, nor a soul of conscious penitence or praise;

nor has the human voice; yet both may easily aid and express, in some degree, the fervors of our reverent homage. David, whose inspired harmonies still live in the church, and will while there is a grateful penitent upon earth, celebrated the "loving-kindness and faithfulness" of his benevolent Preserver "upon an instrument of ten strings, upon the psaltry and upon the harp, with a solemn sound." When our sanctity shall exceed his, it may perhaps be an additional indication of piety and wisdom to dispense with all these auxiliaries in our religious services.

Our next object of curiosity was a castle built by the Moors, on an elevation, from which it subterraneously communicates with the city, and commands the harbor. It is still in a state of good preservation, and from several inscriptions found on the blocks, of which its foundations are composed, evidently occupies the site of a Roman temple, and has been reared to some extent from the materials of that classic edifice. This is one of those strongholds in which the power of the Moors took its last stand; and where it was finally compelled to surrender to the superior force of Ferdinand.

The castle is now useless to its friends and harmless to its enemies, though a few appendages of modern fortifications might easily render it a source of safety to the one and terror to the other. But Spain appears to be satisfied with her past achievements; she is now impotent at a thousand points, where the least energy and enterprise might render her invulnerable. Nations, like individuals, when they have begun to fall, neglect the easiest means of preserving their tottering dignity and influence. The proud throne of the Ferdinands now exists only by the forbearance of many a power upon which it once looked down in contemptuous scorn. "How are the mighty fallen, and the weapons of war perished!"

In our rambles about Malaga we found all her streets narrow, but many of them preserving a decent regard to cleanliness. Her buildings are usually of two stories, with balconies, where pots of delicious plants and flowers cast their fragrance, and where sometimes the black-eyed Malaguena may be seen lingering around them with a lightness and gayety but half concealed by the lattice of the cool veranda. There she sits by the side of the rose, which is not more fresh and fair than is her cheek, and near her canary, whose musical voice is never hushed save when her own is heard; and she passes off her lightsome hours in casting the rich figure upon the embroidered veil, or touching her guitar to one of those strains which convert the dull realities of life into a sweet romance. She is not disturbed by your listening ear; her music still breathes on like that of the nightingale, which the hushed woodland catches and returns in mellow echo.

How different this from that unrelaxed gravity, that never smiles when it is pleased, and never weeps when it is sad! Give me the human heart with all its susceptibilities, sympathies, and emotions, unchained and unblighted, and then diffuse through its quick nature the hallowing and harmonizing influences of religion, and earth has not an object of more thrilling interest and beauty.

Malaga, though it embraces a population of sixty thousand, and in commercial importance is ranked the third city in Spain, yet it presents not many objects of curious interest to the stranger. But what it wants in objects which usually interest the traveller, it seems to atone for in the bold adventurous character of the outlaws who occasionally disturb the peace and safety of its borders. The most conspicuous of these freebooters is Jose Maria, whose history will hereafter, I doubt not, furnish the elements of some absorbing romance. He considered himself, as it appears, wronged out of that political position to which his talents and services justly entitled him, and in his indignant mortification determined to punish the neglect and ingratitude by assuming and enforcing an attitude that might set the prejudiced decisions and partial laws of the times at defiance. He collected a band of faithful, fearless spirits, and proclaimed himself general-in-chief of Granada and king of the roads. If a thorough maintenance of assumed authority can establish it in respect and approbation of mankind, then no one will feel disposed to question the titles of Jose Maria.

He is a chivalrous reformer, a gallant leveller of those invidious distinctions which the inequalities of property never fail to create. A fundamental principle in his innovating code appears to be, that as wealth is generally an adventitious circumstance, a participation in its benefits should not be denied to those who have been less favored of fortune. Accordingly, in his disposal of all the contributions which he levies upon the traveller and citizen, he manifests a scrupulous regard to the demands of the poor, reserving to himself only a sufficiency for the support of his hardy clan.

His mode of operation has none of that creeping, skulking meanness and cruelty about it, which so frequently disfigure the character of the outlaw. He rides in broad daylight into the neighborhood of some town or village, summons individually the more wealthy portion of its inhabitants to appear before him, and then names a definitive sum, which they must deliver to him in a specific number of hours. They do not dare to disregard the summons or refuse the amount demanded. This levy, reaching in some instances a very large amount, he distributes, with a slight reserve for himself, among the poorer classes of that community.

He has never been known to shed blood, nor is he often under the necessity of resorting to violent threats. The traveller discovers at once that resistance would be vain, and yields with as good a grace as he can. Yet the gallant robber will by no means deprive him of his last farthing, but leave him enough, with due economy, to reach his destination, or some place where he may replenish his funds. Sometimes, when the individual happens to be a wealthy citizen of Spain, travelling perhaps a short distance, without much encumbrance of specie about his person, Jose Maria furnishes him with pen, ink, and paper, and a suggestion—rather an embarrassing one, to be sure—for him to draw on his banker for a few thousands, and then politely entertains his guest till the draft has been presented and the funds procured; and even then he is not discharged without an allowance sufficient for his comfortable return home.

In this manner he detained, not long since, in his little encampment, even the governor of Malaga. The only consequence was, that his excellency returned from his morning ride with a pile or two less of doubloons in his drawer than what he possessed upon mounting his steed; and many widows and orphans had another donation to expect from their wild benefactor.

Another striking trait in the character of Jose Maria is his uniform courtesy to the ladies. So far from offering them the slightest indignity, it is an offence which he punishes in his ranks with death. He does, indeed, require them to aid him in the support of the numerous objects dependent on his bounty:

but he makes his demand with so much politeness, with such a gentlemanly bearing, that they could hardly have the disposition to refuse, even were it in their power. But when the intercepted lady proves to be destitute of funds, he generously supplies her with the means of pursuing her journey, and parts with her upon such terms that she will smile in her sleep as she dreams of him through many a night afterwards.

A lady of large fortune, wishing recently to travel from Malaga to Madrid, sent out to Jose and obtained a passport, for which she paid fifty dollars; but it so happened, owing to some very natural mistake on the part of the courtly king of the roads, that she was stopped on her route. She had, however, only to present her passport, when a handsome apology was made for the interruption, and she was allowed to proceed on her way with many kind wishes. The gallant freebooter never violates his word.

Several Englishmen, recently travelling through Spain, were intercepted by this gentlemanly robber, who exercised considerable liberty with their heavy purses, but allowed them to retain sufficient to take them to a town where they could draw on their bankers. Upon parting with them, he good-humoredly remarked, that as English travellers were in the habit of writing and publishing journals, he trusted they would speak of him in those terms of respect to which he was justly entitled. They might call him a robber, an outlaw: to these appellations he had no objections; but they must not write him down a bloody blackguard; for his reputation was much dearer to him than his life. John Bull then departed, in vexation, to be sure, for the loss of the money, but with an admiring astonishment at the open and courtly manner in which it had been exacted.

Another redeeming characteristic in Jose Maria is his ardent love of liberty. When a person has fallen under the ban for the freedom of his political opinions, this friend of the oppressed frequently effects his entire release. The expedients by which he accomplishes this are novel and various; but they all bespeak a singular shrewdness of intellect and energy of conduct.

A man of considerable distinction was recently condemned to the gallows, as entertaining sentiments too republican for the despotical nature of the times. Jose therefore just took into custody, as hostages, three or four monks, and informed the proper authorities, that in case the capital sentence should be executed on the prisoner, the heads of these monks should roll after him to the grave. The menace had the intended effect. The captive was released; and the men of saintly garb were allowed to return to their books and beads. Sometimes he even enters the place of execution, and rescues the noble victim while ascending the scaffold. His very name strikes a terror into tyranny, and disarms the miscreants that riot in its cruelties.

Many efforts have been made by the Spanish authorities to take Jose Maria, and bring him to an ignominious death; but they have proved unsuccessful. The mountain fastness, the blades of his trusty followers, the voice of the thousands he has fed, and, above all, his own exhaustless genius, have been his defence. He has his regular brokers in Malaga to facilitate his operations; and he has also a timid Medora here, whom he frequently visits in the stormy night, and with whom he talks over the perils of his present condition, and a hope of better days to come. It is presumed by many that her gentle influence will induce him at length to abandon his adventurous life, and accept a situation under a government that is already willing to purchase his alliance, at almost any price.

Before leaving this ancient town of Spain, I must pause a moment at the Alameda, the most attractive spot in Malaga. This green promenade, shaded with orange and oleander trees, occupies a spacious place in the most elegant portion of the city. It is ornamented with a superb fountain, ever showering its refreshing waters among groups of marble statues, which have all the frolic and garmentless glee of the bath! This fountain was a present from the republic of Genoa to the emperor Charles V.; and after having passed through the vicissitudes of being captured by an Algerine corsair, and of fortunately being retaken, was brought to this port, and finally placed where it now stands.

But the Alameda, at the purpling twilight, has a still lovelier sight than this. It is not beauty in the changeless representations of marble, but in the full pulse and play of real life. At this mellowing hour, the fair Malaguena may be seen, gliding away with the family group from the restricted corridor, to this more ample and animating promenade. Her mantilla falls in light flowing folds over the glossy clusters of her raven locks, and seems so attracted by the charms which it half conceals, that it scarcely needs even the delicate confinement of the jewelled hand that now and then adjusts its condition. Her basquinia, with its deep tasselled festoons, falls from the cincture of the slight waist, in spreading adaptation to the fuller developments of her form, down to an ankle, over which it scarcely consents to extend the obscuring veil of its drapery. Her small round foot, which seems at every moment in the act of leaping from its little slipper, leaves the earth, and lights upon it again, with most exquisite grace and precision. Her countenance, ever partaking more of thoughtfulness than mirth, has the carnation melting through the transparent cheek, the slumber of a smile around the lip, and the tender light of a full, black, overpowering eye.

As she floats along, she casts upon you, if an intimate, a look of the most glad and sparkling recognition; if a stranger, a look that lingers on your heart long after the beautiful being herself may have passed away. It is precisely such a look as one would wear who is pleased that there is just such a being as yourself in the world, and is happy in passing you this once, though she may never meet you again. It may, perhaps, be owing to my unfamiliarity with the world; but I did not suppose it possible for a person to find, in a land of strangers, that which could so allure him to the spot, and strike to his inmost sensibilities, as what one must experience who puts his foot within the sweet environs of Malaga.

But there are other engaging objects at sunset in this Alameda. Groups of sweetly clad children frolic hand in hand up and down its floating area; while the little miss of ten, under a less reserve than her senior sister, smiles up to you with a countenance full of light and gladness. You feel half disposed to recognize this infantine pleasure in the liberties of a kiss, but not venturing so far, you pass on, only to encounter again the same captivating scene. You meet also, at every turn, a cleanly clad individual, ready to help you to a glass of fresh water, a rich ice cream, or one ready, with his little flambeau, to light your cigar.

Under the shade of the orange and oleander you pass social groups, on their circling chairs, holding their free tertulia, where every topic takes its light and transient turn. From every thing that you see, your impression is, that the little embarrassments imposed by adventitious superiority are here laid aside; that artificial restraints are forgotten; that heart meets heart, and that many, without being the less wise, are rendered the more happy by such pastimes.

We had taken leave of these gay groups, and turned to depart for our boats which were waiting at the beach, when another scene, and one that strangely contrasted with those around, arrested our steps. It would seem as if it had come only to remind us of the fleeting nature of the objects that we had been admiring, to tell us that all this brightness and beauty, which our feelings had almost exempted from tears and decay, must pass down under the cloud of the grave! It came nearer, and now with a step mournful and slow entered the Alameda. This place, but a moment since so full of life, voices, and mirth, was now hushed, while every ear was turned to the low anthem of the dead.

The youth and drapery of those who numerously followed the bier, told that it was to a sister's worth that they were paying these last sad rites. It seemed as if I had known that young being,—as if I had often encountered her youthful face, heard her voice, and seen her die.

> But yésterday, and thou were bright
> As rays that fringe the early cloud;

Now lost to life, to love, and light,
    Wrapt in the winding-sheet and shroud;
And darkly o'er thee broods the pall,
    While faint and low thy dirge is sung;
And warm and fast around thee fall
    Tears of the beautiful and young.

No more, sweet one! on thee, no more
    Will break the day-dawn fresh and fair;
No more the purple twilight pour
    Its softness round thy raven hair;
No more beneath thy magic hand
    Will wake the lyre's responsive lay;
Or round its rings the wreath expand,
    To crown a sister's natal day.

Yet as the sweet surviving vine,
    Around the bough that buds no more
Will still its tender leaves entwine,
    And bloom as freshly as before;
So fond affection still will shed
    The light on thee it used to wear,
And plant its roses round thy bed,
    To breathe in fragrant beauty there.

CHAPTER XI.

> No breath from mountain, cloud, or cavern creeps
> Along the water's hushed expanse; the wave
> Unbroken in its tranquil aspect, sleeps
> Serene as Beauty in her sunless grave;
> Nor moves a tide, unless its silent flow
> Be through the caves and coral halls below.

PASSAGE FROM MALAGA TO MAHON—TEDIOUS CALMS—RELIEVING INCIDENTS—VISIT OF A BIRD—CAPTURE OF AN OMINOUS SHARK—INTRUSIONS OF A GHOST—UNFAIR TAKING OFF OF A BLACK CAT—PETTED HEDGE-HOG—MORGAN'S SPECTRE AT NIAGARA—MAHON—HARBOR—FORT ST. PHILIP—ADMIRAL BYNG—LAZARETTO—NAVY-YARD—HABITS OF THE MAHONESE—EFFECTS OF A CERTAIN VICE ON MAN—GRAND ORGAN—SAILORS ON SHORE—JACK AND THE OPERA—ENTERTAINMENTS.

WE have been fifteen days on our passage from Malaga to Mahon,—a distance frequently run in less than three. Most of the time we have been encountering a light head wind, or have been lying in a motionless calm. The sun has been intensely oppressive, and we have had nothing to temper its burning ray except a sight of the snow-clad mountains of Granada. I have sat by the hour together, looking at these icy pinnacles; and as my fancy ranged among their shapeless halls of frost, I have felt, or imagined that I felt, the palpitating pulse become more calm and cool. Philosophers may say what they please, but a man's imagination has nearly as much influence over the temperature of his body, as it has over the habitudes of the mind. Who ever in his dream of the avalanche cast another blanket from the covering of his couch?

A calm at sea, on board a man-of-war, is not utterly unrelieved by incidents. It is indeed devoid of the peculiar excitement which a storm brings with it. No spar is broken—no shroud is rent—no sail casts its tattered form upon the wind; but some novelty of a lighter and less perilous character is constantly occurring. Some wandering bird will rest its weary wing on the mast; or some hungry shark that has been hanging around the ship for days, will at last come within the deadly reach of the harpoon; or some evil genius that has haunted the ship in the shape of a ghost, or the less imposing form of a black cat, will be detected in the mysterious windings of its iniquitous errand. We have experienced these incidents, trifles in themselves, but which, with many others of a similar nature, tend incredibly to relieve the monotony of a calm at sea.

The bird lighted on one of our spars just at sunset, and wearied with its long wanderings, sunk instantly to sleep. We sent up a sailor, had him brought down into the cabin, where he was hospitably entertained through the night, and in the morning, after attaching a small silk thread to him was permitted to depart, with many warm wishes for his safety. But the next day, at sunset, he lighted again on one of our top-gallant yards; we received him with a cordial welcome, and parting with him the succeeding morning, we attached to him a slight label, upon which was delicately printed the name of our ship, with her latitude and longitude.

Thus intrusted and commissioned, he winged his way off, with the directness and speed of an aerial envoy; and when we next heard of him, he had lighted at an immense distance on one of our armed ships; conveying on the label information equally strange and unexpected. I would travel leagues to see that bird again; but it has gone, like most of the beautiful things of this earth, which only seem to cross our path, and then vanish away forever!

>They flutter round in airy mirth,
> And pour their little stave,
>As full of glee, as if the earth
>   Contained no grave.
>
>And thus when I shall sink to rest,
> The crowd will still move on,
>And be as gay above my breast,
>   As naught had gone!
>
>But He who hears the raven's cry,
> And marks the sparrow's fall,
>Will ne'er forget me, though I die
>   Unmourned by all.

The shark shared none of these feelings of hospitality and friendship. His very company is regarded as an extremely ill omen; especially when there is a person sick on board. Sailors believe that this fearful fish has what they term the instinct of death, and that his appearance is good evidence that the body of some one is about to be committed to the deep. They also look upon him as in some measure instrumental in bringing about the melancholy event; and are therefore as anxious to secure his destruction, as a threatened city to arrest the invading progress of the cholera or plague.

A favorite of the crew was now apparently lying at the point of death; and this shark had been hanging around our ship for several days. The harpoon had many times been poised to strike him; but the wily fellow had ever managed to escape the plunging steel. At length an old seaman, who had been accustomed to strike the whale on the coast of Greenland, and who still betrayed the characteristics of his rude profession, in the peculiar fierce fixedness of his eye and the muscular energy of his arms, taking the harpoon, stationed himself on the ship's bows, and declared he would never quit his post till he had "backed the topsails of that lurking devil in the water."

He had not been long on his watch before the wished-for opportunity arrived; and never went an arrow to its mark with more directness and celerity, than the harpoon to its victim. It struck him directly between the fore-fins, and with such desperate force, that extrication and escape were impossible. A shout of satisfaction and triumph announced the victory. The sick man soon became convalescent; and it would be difficult to persuade many of the crew that his recovery is not attributable to the destruction of this ominous shark!

The ghost appeared in a still more mysterious character. One of the young gentlemen who slept in the cock-pit, was observed rapidly to waste away in his strength; while his countenance suddenly assumed an aspect of melancholy wildness. He was naturally of a taciturn temperament, little disposed to obtrude his private fears and apprehensions upon the attention of others. Perhaps a silence on the present occasion, was the more strongly suggested by the philosophical habits which he had early and devotedly cultivated. He was often questioned as to the cause of the wasting illness, which had now become alarmingly apparent in the sunken, pallid expression of his features, and the fitful nervousness of his frame. But no reply could be obtained, except what might be conveyed in a mournful look or an involuntary sigh.

At last, however, he acknowledged that something appeared nightly before him, the most unearthly in its shape; and which, in spite of his utter disbelief in supernatural appearances, struck a chilling terror to his heart; and that on such occasions the hammock in which he reposed was violently agitated, and swung against the bulk-head with a force which no motion of the sea could create.

The rush of the hammock against the bulk-head had for several nights awakened the alarm of his companions in the cock-pit. This fact, together with the known character of the individual for veracity and sound sense, induced us to set a watch to detect, if possible, the mysterious agent of these alarms. This watch, consisting of three faithful and intelligent individuals, in the first place, searched the apartment in which the invalid slept, carefully closing and securing every door which led into it; and then waited, with dead-lanterns in their hands, for the nocturnal visitant. As the clock struck the hour of twelve, a low, vacant moan was heard; and the patient, who had till now remained composed on his pillow, starting up, exclaimed,—"There it is!" "there it comes!"—"Merciful heaven, protect me!"

His hammock, at the same instant, rushed against the bulk-head with a violence which no mortal arm could impart. Large drops of cold perspiration stood on the forehead of the patient; his eyes were starting from their sockets, and every nerve in his frame was shaking with a strange, unnatural fear. Search was immediately made, but no vestige of any living thing could be discovered, nor any clue to the convulsive movements of the hammock, or hollow moan of the voice, or ghastly form of the apparition.

The watch was exchanged for many nights in succession, and the same mysterious phenomena witnessed by each, till even the most skeptical regarded incredulity no longer an evidence of superior sagacity or philosophical wisdom.

Nor were these strange appearances confined to the cock-pit; but the men stationed in the tops observed a singular form, in a dress of spotless white, moving among the rigging—now pausing upon one of the yards, now ascending to mast-head, and then again balancing itself upon some of the lighter tracery of the ship. The unsubstantial movements of this spectre among the shrouds and loftier appendages of the ship, awakened in the susceptible mind of the sailor the most alarming apprehensions.

You would see him, as he was ordered to take his watch aloft, squaring off towards the ratlines with the looks and attitudes of one doubtful of results, but at least resolved to die manfully. "Let him come," Jack would murmur, "like something that has common honesty about him, and smite my timbers, if I don't knock daylight out of him; but this jumping about on the ropes, half the time in the air, and half the time on nothing, is foul play, and bodes no good." The imaginations of the crew soon became so excited, that nothing was thought or dreamt of among them but ghosts, spectres, hobgoblins, and blood! These alarms not only gave rise to many frightful stories, but they called up, from the smothered graves of memory, tales terrific enough to startle the dead in their shrouds!

The incantation, from which these ghostly terrors emanated, has now been sufficiently traced to remove all apprehensions of a supernatural agency. It was the jugglery of a young man, the apparent artlessness of whose disposition had subjected him to many a ludicrous hoax from the junior officers and some of the crew. But he has enjoyed a most ample retaliation:

> The luckless subject of the merry trick
> Became himself the master of the spell,
> And rolled the laughter back.

The fate of the black cat was one which the admirers of the tabby tribe will sternly disapprove. This restless domestic is looked upon by the sailor, especially when afflicted with a black visage, with no kindly or tolerant feelings. There is no bad luck about the ship which is not ascribed to some evil influence which she is supposed to exercise. Hence, in a storm or dead calm, poor tab has a tremendous responsibility. Our unfortunate puss had been taken on board at Malaga, and since her embarkation we had not been visited by one favorable breeze. This calamity was attributed to her universally among the crew.

There needed no language to tell what their sentiments were, for as puss came upon deck, so far from being petted, she encountered everywhere looks of the most threatening aversion. "Never," said an old tar to me, " did any good come to a ship that had a black cat in its concern. I have sailed," he continued, "on every sea and in every kind of craft, and I never yet knew a ship make a good voyage that went to sea on Friday, or had on board one of these black imps. These are facts, sir; land-lubbers may laugh at them, but they are facts, and true as my name is John Wilkins."

It was of no use to question the convictions of the old seaman's experience; he was as confident and deeply earnest, as a man testifying to the indisputable evidence of his senses. It was for this reason that he, with some others, formed that shocking purpose so fatal to poor tab. For on that very night, in the middle watch, a quick plunge was heard in the calm sea, and the next morning puss was missing! They had attached to her a heavy shot, and she sunk at once to the centre of the great floating realm, where she remains unapproached by the animosity of man, or the footsteps of the reckless rat!

Sterne would have written her epitaph in tears; but I am not penning a sentimental journal, nor am I now in the lachrymal vein; yet I would not have purchased by such a deed even the fine breeze which visited us the next day, and which was regarded by the tabby-cides as a sanction of their sanguinary conduct. We should never forget that many a man has atoned by his death for a life of crime, which commenced in the destruction of a harmless insect. We should also bear in mind the irremediable deprivation of life and happiness which even in these trifling instances we inflict; for

> "The poor beetle, that we tread upon,
> In corporal sufferance finds a pang as great
> As when a giant dies."

Though the antipathy of the sailor to the shark and black cat is so unqualified, yet his friendship and affection are extended to objects nearly as numberless and ill-favored as those to which the superstitious Egyptian paid the homage of his promiscuous worship. The favorite pet on board, at the present time, is a hedge-hog; who moves about with an air of freedom and independence which is truly enviable. Notwithstanding his bristling quills and inimical attitudes, he is cherished by the crew with as much solicitude as if he were a cherub, destined one day to herald their spirits to a brighter and better world.

They have already initiated him into some of our earthly sciences; and though he may not be able now to solve a deep mathematical problem or sing an exquisite song, yet he appears to be daily taking observations of the sun, and setting his organs for a melodious burst. He will not probably at first do justice to some of the more touching strains of a Rossini, yet he will doubtless far surpass many of our ladies, who affect a contempt for all music except these difficult compositions.

I return to ghosts: not that I would intimate the presence of any on board our ship at this time, or maintain, by an introduction of stern evidence, the credibility of their existence. I consider this question as settled conclusively among all enlightened unprejudiced minds. A few, indeed, may still withhold their assent, but their skepticism evinces only their want of philosophy, their weakness and vanity. They refuse their belief, as they inform us, because no one of these mysterious beings has ever appeared in the daytime. Now, what a fool a ghost must be to make his appearance in broad daylight, subjecting himself not only to the impudent curiosity of mankind, but to the riddling rays of the sun, when even the moonbeams cast through him their sickly light.

But it is not a fact, as stated, that no one of these spectres has appeared in the daytime. When Morgan was put to death on the strand of Niagara for his treachery, and his body sunk in that stream, there appeared hovering around the place an uncorporeal being, so like him in every look, that no one questioned the identity or doubted the tragic deed. The discovery filled everybody with consternation, and the whole land shook like the bones of a skeleton under a galvanic battery. Thousands not only abjured masonry, but renounced their political faith. I made myself a palpitating pilgrimage to Niagara. Ay—and I never shall forget that vision!

There walks o'er steep Niagara's wave
A ghost, whose form hath found a grave,
   Deep in those whelming tides;
Its feathered footsteps scarcely seem
To bend the surface of the stream,
   O'er which this phantom glides.

Around it there is cast a shroud,
That seems more like a folding cloud,
   Than aught that mortals wear;
Its downcast eye, its faded cheek,
Its pale and trembling lips bespeak
   A spirit of despair.

It moans a hoarse and hollow wail,
That mingles with the gusty gale,
   And with the rumbling flood;
It points toward the crimsoned shore,
And shrieks, as if it felt once more
   The knife that drank its blood.

Its wail is echoed wild and wide,
From rock, and steep, and bounding tide,
   Around that haunted coast;
And fearful mothers, trembling, tell
Their little ones how Morgan fell,
   And of this wandering ghost.

Along that fatal shore is heard
No more the song of merry bird,
   Or sound of hunter's horn;
The faithful watch-dog seems afraid
Of every sound that stirs the shade,
   And bays till peep of morn.

> No more can sun, nor lunar beam,
> Erect a rainbow o'er that stream,
>   From which the fish have fled;
> But there a little cloud appears,
> And sheds its unregarded tears,
>   Like one that weeps the dead.

We are now riding at anchor in the harbor of Mahon. This harbor cuts its narrow way between bold and broken shores for several miles into the island; affording through its whole length a most secure anchorage. The waters in this deep channel lie as still as the fabled river of Death, but they are much less gloomy than the tideless flow of that sullen flood. They are relieved by a picturesque shore—by the frequent ship reposing proudly on her element, and the traversing speed of innumerable boats, leaving behind their hastening keels a long train of phosphoric light. Nothing can surpass the sentiment of quietude and security which one feels riding here at anchor, while the chafing ocean is fretting against the rocky barrier without. It is like a snug seat by the side of a cheerful fire in a cold winter's night, while the storm and sleet are driving against your secure casement.

On entering this harbor you pass upon the left the ruins of Fort St. Philip; a fortification that, in the day of its pride and strength, might have looked with scornful defiance upon the menaces of any invading foe. The enduring parapet, the winding galleries cut in the solid rock, with the heavy bastion above, may still be traced, though they are but the dim and broken outline of ruined strength. This work of demolition is not the effect of time, but the condition of a treaty founded in weakness and folly. The once impregnable character of this fort owed its existence to British skill and hardihood; and in the possession of that sagacious power, it would have preserved this character, but every thing was lost by a lamentable want of judgment or courage in Admiral Byng.

The French, in their war of conquest, had fixed a determined eye on this spot; they had hovered around it with their fleet, and cut off all foreign supply of provisions. The islanders, with a most unaccountable insanity, withheld the few supplies which it was in their power to afford, and consequently the garrison was reduced to a state of starvation; still the besieged held out with incredible self-denial and perseverance. At last the fleet of Admiral Byng hove in sight, bringing with it the relief for which so many were famishing and fainting in death. But how appalling must have been their feelings, their despair, when they saw this fleet, after manœuvering in sight of an enemy to which they were superior in force, bear off and leave them to their melancholy fate! It is no wonder, that in their mortified pride and indignation at this desertion, and in the extremities of their famishing condition, they surrendered.

They were compelled to yield to the enemy or the grave. In the excitements of a desperate conflict men may prefer the latter, but without this absorbing passion, there are but few who may not be slowly tortured by famine into a surrender of temporary power. For this act of seeming treachery and its disastrous consequences, the Admiral atoned by an ignominious death. I can never think of his last end, however, without some sentiments of compassion. Perhaps his conduct flowed less from cowardice than irresolution, and that strange bewilderment, into which the minds of some men are cast, by the impetuous approach of a trying and perilous moment. If penalties can atone for indiscretion or crime, the memory of this unfortunate man should be allowed to rest without reproach.

Upon the opposite bank are the remains of Fort Marlborough; but there is now no terror or majesty about it except what lingers in its name. How are the most formidable works of man cast aside, like weeds which the wave sweeps from the rock! If man, in the phrensy of his passions, does not destroy his own works, Time soon comes with his levelling wand, and leaves only enough to puzzle the antiquary.

Not far from the relics of this fort stands the Lazaretto, a noble monument of wisdom and humanity. In the extent and convenience of its apartments, it is surpassed in Europe only by that of Marseilles. It is about fifteen hundred yards in circumference, and so arranged in its interior construction, that the most malignant or contagious diseases cannot spread from one ward to another. Its accommodations are sufficiently ample to meet any emergency that may arise among the squadrons which frequent this sea. How much wiser is it in a nation to expend its treasures in the construction of establishments of this kind, than in the erection of sumptuous monasteries for the accommodation of indolence and infamy!

Higher up the harbor, and near the right bank, emerges from the wave the quarantine island. Around this may be seen, moored in security, the ships and craft of various nations undergoing their purifying penalties. Directly opposite stands the village of Georgetown, whose kindly inhabitants, it is said, extend their hospitality even beyond that line where virtue should pause, and beauty veil the winning aspect of her charms. Still ascending, we pass, near the right shore, Hospital Island, with its infirmary; where the diseased may be fitted to join the living, or the innumerable dead.

Higher up still, on the same shore, and near the head of deep water, we find the navy-yard, with its small octagonal islet, warehouses, and the countless facilities which the mutable habits of a ship's exterior render so desirable. Here you may see the majestic ship reduced in a few hours, as by the demolishing stroke of a wizard's wand, to a mere hulk; and then, as if by the same magical influence, suddenly assuming again all its wonted stateliness and beauty. The dexterity and force of nautical science is nowhere more strikingly displayed than in the extent and rapidity of these metamorphic exhibitions. I would as soon attempt to construct a world as to return a tenth portion of the disengaged upper works of a ship to their puzzling places.

Opposite the navy-yard stands the town of Mahon, with its narrow quay, scarcely affording a foundation for the range of storehouses which wall the low shore; while far above, in giddy elevation, the more advanced dwellings of the place appear to nod from the toppling crags. Ascending to their airy position by paths cut in the rock, or secured among the spiral clefts, you find yourself in a quiet town, with clean streets, unambitious but neat dwellings, and a population characterized for their industry, honesty, frugality, and amiable deportment. I have seldom been in a community where there is so much to pity, and so much to admire.

Their poverty is attended by a simplicity and self-relying struggle at alleviation, which move your heart. It is not poverty in a cottage, surrounded and alleviated by rural delights. There are here no rushing streams, no waving forests, no flocks that skip the hills, or luxuriate in the vales; no lay of nightingales to charm in the purple evening, or song of early birds to usher up the rosy morn. It is poverty unrelieved by any of these romantic incidents.

It is poverty in a city; in a confined town, and among a people whose commerce has been crushed; whose resources have been cut off by a despotism that disgraces the age in which it is permitted to exist. Mahon, with its due privileges of trade, might be a place of great enterprise and wealth; but under its present onerous and prohibitory restrictions, it is doomed to languish on in a life of hopeless poverty.

Though the encouragements to industry here are miserably slender—such as in our country would be regarded as a mere mockery—yet I have seldom been in a community of more active habits. I have seen the mother rising with the earliest dawn, assiduously plying her task till a late hour of rest, and gaining but a few farthings, scarcely sufficient to purchase a loaf of coarse bread for her helpless offspring. There was about her, in her toil and deprivations, a cheerfulness and alacrity, which affected me far more than all the dismal complaints and solicitations of indolent mendicity. It may be a weakness, but I could cheerfully divide my last penny with such an individual. I never before so deeply regretted the narrowness of my means. I could hardly wish for a greater earthly felicity than being placed in a population of this description, with the power of relieving their wants, and making them happy.

If, in the more dependent sex, aberrations from rectitude here are too frequently to be met with, it is ascribable, in my apprehension, less to the want of virtue than the yearning instigations of want. Poverty in this frail world is a prolific source, not only of wretchedness, but of moral turpitude; and though it cannot sanction guilt, yet perhaps it ought to soften down the severity of our denunciations. We know not what we are made of till tried in the furnace of adversity; we should all probably come forth from such an ordeal, with a vast diminution of pride and self-complacency. When we leave our plentiful boards for the crumbs of a precarious subsistence, we may then speak of temptations and the force of virtue.

Competence is one of the strongest securities against crime. Treason to the wholesome institutions of society, and the moral sense of mankind, is seldom a wanton act. A wise legislator aims to make men happy, and thus to make them better. Would to God that those intrusted with the dispensation of law, might realize the extent of joy or sorrow, good or evil, that must flow from an exercise of their prerogatives. Acting under an adequate sense of their responsibilities in this respect, they would lay the foundations of a fame which time could not impair, or marble monuments prolong. Their memorial would be the transmitted happiness of millions.

Though the consequences of a ruined virtue in the other sex may be more immediately disastrous than in our own, yet in the latter case they are of a most destructive character. They benumb and destroy all the finer sensibilities of the soul. They convert the heart into a grave, in which its delicate emotions lie blighted and dead. The soft being that could once move and melt it by the moral charm which rested on her beauty, cannot now quicken its perished sympathy.

Purity is not only indispensable to the more refined susceptibilities of our nature, but also to that quietude of conscience which is the sunshine of the soul. I envy not that man his dreams, who seeks his pillowed repose while he has left another to blush and to weep. He may indeed be callous to his crime—and for a time slumber on in his remorseless guilt, but his hour of sorrow and shame will inevitably come; nor will its anguish and bitterness be mitigated by its delay. If there be pangs which strike deeper into the soul, they must be his portion who has betrayed the confiding and ruined the innocent—who promised only to deceive, and cherished only to destroy.

Nor is purchased, advised, and consenting criminality without its fearful penalties. A man who yields himself to vice, even in this form, nourishes a plant whose fruit will be wormwood and gall:

> And partake of this fruit, though he loathe it, he must,
> Till the world has his shame, and the grave has his dust.

But I was speaking of Mahon. There is another feature in the population of this place, which betrays their kindly dispositions. Sailors here are allowed to go upon shore on leave,—and on such occasions, they are apt to float widely from salutary restraint. They make merry, pass round their social circles the wild glass; promenade the streets, break out in the jovial song, or address the passers by with as much familiarity as if they were all shipmates on board the same craft, and bound to the same delightful haven. Instead of resenting this freedom, or construing it into insolence, I have seen the most respectable citizen take the proffered hand of Jack, wish him a prosperous voyage, and a happy home wherever it might be.

How different this from the treatment which the unceremonious Tar would meet with in one of our cities!—He would probably be knocked down, or, at least, thrust aside with a rebuking severity. Not so here: if too merry, it is excused; if impertinent, the best construction is placed upon it; if unfortunately out of his reckoning, he is taken within-doors till his senses and his gratitude return. I do admire, beyond the power of language to convey, this kind, forbearing, and hospitable disposition. I would not exchange the feelings and reflections of such an individual, for all the importance which wealth and power can bestow. The consciousness of having restored the wandering, and relieved the distressed, will commend the dying man to the grateful remembrance of his fellow-beings, and even the mercy of his final Judge.

The amusements usually indulged in here, are the opera, the masquerade, music and dancing. Among these, the officers of our navy are prone to while off some of their long winter evenings. They are seldom carried to excess; they are occasional escapes from the tedium vitæ incident to winter-quarters, and are secured, in a measure, from abuse, by the mediocrity of their splendor and attraction. Entertainments of this character, to possess an enduring interest, even for the gayest heart, must be sustained by an expense incompatible with the restricted resources of Mahon.

How an intelligent community can be fervently devoted to objects of this nature, and find in them their principal excitements, is to me inconceivable. I would much sooner sit down in a chimney corner with some scarred veteran of the field, who has survived the continental wars, and listen to his tale of conflict, rout, or victory; or with some old sailor, who has unfurled his canvas in each sea and clime, and whose thoughts run on the breeze, the gale, or wreck; or with some prying antiquary, who has sifted the dust of a perished city to find an unintelligible coin; or most especially with some village mate unseared by the world,—

> Whose thoughts run warmly back to early childhood;—
> The airy swing, the nested bower, the wild-wood,—
> The stream, the darting trout, the little boat,
> With mimic guns and mariners afloat;
> The bounding ball, the balance on the rail,
> The dog that watched the sport, and wagged his tail;—
> A sister's bird that came at break of day,
> Carolled its merry song, and flew away.

The entertainment of the opera is too refined for the rude taste of the sailor. A company of fifty or sixty were permitted, not long since, to attend one of these musical performances. They cheerfully paid the highest price for their tickets, and took their seats, expecting a rich treat. But it was soon evident that they had mistaken their port. You might see them glancing about for a moment when they would be less observed, and then skipping out as one escapes from the presence of a person whom he would not offend, and yet in whom he takes no interest.

In less than an hour they all disappeared. In the porch and court some of them ventured their criticisms on the performance. "Did you ever hear such singing as that?" said Jack, "such backing and filling—such veering and hauling—such puffing and screaming—there is as much music in a boatswain's whistle! And then the language—such a jingling jargon—such a hanging on, and spinning out in each word—it had no more meaning in it than the sound of the water behind a ship's keel." So they agreed to put up the helm; and striking up one of their old nautical songs, steered by many ambiguous tacks for the ship.

But the theatre, in the tragic or comic, seldom fails to affect or amuse this singular class of men. A number of them went to see Othello acted; they detected at once the diabolical deceit of Iago, and muttered their indignation. They became at length so absorbed in the performance, especially in the character and fate of Desdemona, that when the jealous Moor came out to murder her in her sleep, they instantly sprang upon the stage, crying out "Avast, there, you black, bloody rascal;" and were in the act of seizing him, when the curtain dropped, amid confusion and applause.

This incident did not occur here, or under my observation; but the anecdote was related to me by an eye-witness. It discloses striking traits in the character of the sailor—his credulous propensity—his quick and deep susceptibility—his electrical promptitude in rescuing the helpless. He would throw away forty lives to protect an innocent being, and even an enemy he scorns to injure, when taken at a disadvantage.

There is here, however, one source of entertainment —if that term may be applied to any thing belonging to the sanctuary—which must ever arrest the most careless ear, and which, though it make man no better, it surely cannot make him worse. It is the splendid organ of the cathedral. I could cheerfully sit on the cold pavement of that church, and listen to it till the highest candle that ever lit the shrine of the blessed Virgin flickered in its socket. In compass, power, and richness of melody, it is said to have no competitors, except one in Haarlem, and one in Catania. Almost every musical instrument is here represented, and so closely do some of its tones resemble the human voice, that when it was first set up, many of the audience, in their sudden wonder, rushed out of the cathedral.

From the solemn and stately anthem, it passes with melodious dignity and ease through all the varied expressions of the dramatic chorus, to the national ode, the capricious song, the vanishing air. At one time it astounds and overwhelms you with a burst of thunder; you involuntarily look up, and expect to find the bolted cloud blackening over your head; and then again, in the terminating range of its matchless transitions, you imagine yourself listening to the dying strains of an Æolian harp.

I could not accuse Lord Exmouth of a foolish prodigality in his offer of a hundred thousand dollars for this noble instrument. But it was not thus to be obtained. An Arab and his barb, a devotee and the auxiliaries of his devotion, are seldom parted. But it needs not pride or superstition to make one unwilling to part with such a treasure as this. I would almost as soon relinquish some inborn source of happiness and hope.

We were concerned on reaching this port to learn that the health of Commodore Biddle had not improved since our last advices. The duties of his station, as Commander-in-chief of the Squadron, require a degree of physical activity and energy which it is difficult to dispense with, even where, as in his case, there is found great elasticity and vigor of mind.

But though oppressed with these outward disabilities, he is not unmindful or negligent of the interests confided to his care; for we had scarcely let go our anchor, when an order came for us to get ready to proceed to sea with all dispatch. In the mean time, he honored us with an entertainment, where the choicest luxuries and delicacies of the island were served, and where the light and terse remark went sparkling round, accompanied by many endearing recollections of home.

There was at this table dignity without reserve, and ease without a gregarian license;—there was also an unabused Idomeneusan privilege extended to each guest, such as Homer thought not beneath the melody of his muse:—

———ηγεῖον δέπας, αἰεὶ
Ἔσυγχ', ὥσπερ ἐμοὶ, πιέειν, ὅτε θυμὸς ἀνώγοι.

The compliment of this dinner was handsomely returned by Capt. and Mrs. Read, who well understand how to impart interest and pleasure to such occasions. I can never leave one of these entertainments without a boding thought of the time when these interchanges of sentiment will be intercepted, the gratulations of friendship cease, and this breathing frame, inanimate and cold, be laid in its last sad receptacle, to mingle as it may with its native dust. The slight memorials that may remain, and the few who may remember and grieve, must soon follow;

while the thronging multitudes of earth will move on, indifferent to what is gone, as the mighty forest to the silent lapse of a solitary leaf. Then what is life! and what its pursuit!

> "An idle chase of hopes and fears,
> Begun in folly, closed in tears!"

But no, better than that, and more in the spirit of Christianity was it said by the grave poet of the "Night Thoughts:"—

> "This is the bud of being, the dim dawn,
> The twilight of our day, the vestibule:
> Life's theatre as yet is shut, and Death,
> Strong Death, alone can heave the massy bar,
> This gross impediment of clay remove,
> And make us embryos of existence free."

CHAPTER XII.

"ALL hands unmoor!"—the captain's brief command—
The cable round the flying capstern rings;
The anchor quits its bed, the yards are manned;
The gallant ship before the quick breeze springs.
Three parting cheers the noble tars send back,
Ere yet the shore sinks in her foaming track.

PASSAGE FROM MAHON TO NAPLES—LIFE AT SEA—CHEST OF A SAILOR—POWER OF A POET—TRACK OF THE SHIP—NAPLES FROM THE HARBOR—UNREASONABLE QUARANTINE—GRIEVOUS DISAPPOINTMENT—PREMATURE DEPARTURE—EBULLITION OF SPLEEN—PASSAGE FROM NAPLES TO MESSINA—VOLCANO OF STROMBOLI—DEAD CALMS—UTILITY OF WHALES—PASTIMES IN CALMS—FARO DI MESSINA—CHARYBDIS AND SCYLLA—ANCIENT WHIRLPOOL—CURIOSITIES OF THE SEA—MESSINA FROM THE STRAIT.

THREE days since we weighed anchor from Mahon, in company with the Brandywine, bearing the broad pennant of Commodore Biddle. The breeze has been extremely light and baffling; and the passage, though relieved occasionally by an interchange of signals, has nevertheless been thus far unusually destitute of exciting incidents. No bickering ghost has appeared in the cock-pit, or on shroud, or spar; no mermaid has tuned her scallop-shell on the wave or rock; no water-spout has burst in deluge and thunder; no sea-serpent has troughed himself between the combing billows; indeed, there have been no bil lows that could for a moment shelter this mysterious monster of the deep—whose sworn existence has been a greater source of curiosity and wonder, than were all the discoveries of Columbus.

Where was it that he was last seen? Ay, I recollect; it was in the polar seas, where he was trying to split up an iceberg with his tail. Every stroke was followed by flashes of fire that lit the whole heaven, and were taken by those living near the line as the most splendid and extraordinary exhibitions of the aurora-borealis. Every astronomer through our land had his instruments newly cleaned, and watched the burning phenomena, predicting not only that the north passage would be reduced to one vast lake of fire, but that the north star, set in conflagration and motion at the same time, would rush this way for a cooler atmosphere, and, coming in contact with the earth, reduce the whole to ashes! It is astonishing what this Sea-Serpent may do with a few strokes of his tail! But—I was speaking of the calm and slow progress we were making towards Naples.

The sea has scarcely afforded a wave that would have dangerously rocked a log canoe; but then as a negative compensation for this delaying calmness, we have not had that ceaseless surging motion which afflicts the Atlantic, and which sickens a ship without helping her onward. We have had the bursting splendors of a sun, wheeling up in resistless energy from a crimsoning waste of waters that still slumbered and slept. We have had the soft beauty of twilight mingling its purple charm with the rosy depths of sea and sky; we have had, through the early watch, the song of the mariner, breathing in unpolished numbers a patriotic fervor that will kindle on, when all the set forms of speech are cold and forgotten; we have had also the frequent cloud, which, though it often disappointed us in its apparent promise of a breeze, yet reminded us in the evanescent nature of its own being, that the life of man itself is only a " vapor, that appeareth for a little time, and then vanisheth away."

Would that these delicate admonitions in nature might never pass unimproved. But few things, even of the highest moment, produce a permanent effect on the mind of the sailor. Even the gale and wreck are half forgotten, if they but leave him a good plank upon which he may reach the distant shore. He knows not what a day may bring forth, yet sings his jocund song, and sleeps soundly every night with but a plank between him and a fathomless grave.

Yet he is not incapable of being moved, strongly moved, on subjects of a religious character. His heart is not the impervious rock; it more resembles the element on which he moves, and like that, loses the impressions it may receive. He will listen to a sermon with an attention that might be a model to any congregation of Christians, and then within one hour, if some new impulse strikes him, he is off perhaps on another tack. He respects religion and its consistent professors; the good man has always his confidence and esteem.

The Bible is with him, what it ought to be with every person—the book of books. Yet I have seen him take this blessed volume from his clothes-bag, leaving there, close to where it lay, a grape-shot attached to a strong lanyard, with which he will, perhaps, the next time he goes ashore, knock over a dozen insolent Goliaths.

Observing a sailor one day overhauling his effects, I inquired, "Where, Smith, are those tracts I gave you the other day?" "Here they are," he replied, producing them, "all but that one on stealing; I gave that to Joe Miller—I never steal myself; but it struck him exactly between wind and water." "And what book is that stowed away there, Smith?" I inquired again; "Oh, that is my Bible," he replied, lifting it up, with a cordial shake of the hand, "given me by my mother the first time I went to sea, when I was only a youngster; I promised her I would read it every Sunday on shore, and every day when out sight of land. You see I have steered as close to my promise as any fellow can with squalls, and a head sea knocking him off; but I hope I shall yet make that blessed port where she has gone. For she was the best mother that ever had such a wild chap of a son as I have been." He had evidently been pretty true to his word; for the traces of his fingers were upon nearly every page of the book, while the leaves of the more historical parts had been thumbed over, till they were scarcely legible.

"And what is that thing stowed away down there, Smith, next the tracts?" I inquired. "Oh, sir, that is a gouger." "But you do not take out a man's eyes, I hope?" "Not unless a rascal is after mine, and then I blind one side of his face; but I always leave him one eye standing." "Yes, but you take away the other, and what good can that do you?" "Why, sir, he will have one the less to look after me with the next time." I persuaded him at last to throw the unseemly thing overboard; but it will probably be replaced by something else, not a whit the less objectionable. Such is the mixture of shrewdness, filial regard, higher hopes, and moral obliquities which enters into the character of the sailor. He is an ocean which no one can fathom, unless he is able to sound the lowest depths in human nature.

I know not why it is, but somehow, the moment I get on the deck of a ship, and am out at sea, it seems as if I had suddenly been introduced into some element rife with poetry. If any thing could reconcile me to a sea life, it would be the enjoyment of this sentiment. I reverence in the profoundest emotions of my soul, the gifted poet. He is intellectually, in my opinion, the most interesting object in the world. He awakens and wields at will, all the finer feelings and master passions of our nature. His art is of a

NAPLES.

far higher and more effective order than that of the sculptor or painter. He not only represents, but he imparts life; and this, no one can so thoroughly effect with the pencil or chisel.

We may, to some extent, animate the canvas with the features of one we love; we may cast upon the changeless brow, the calm sunshine of her gentle nature;—we may elicit from the expressive eye, the speechless tenderness of a confiding affection—we may curl around the lip the smiling pledges of reciprocal fondness—we may spread behind her glowing cheek, the richness of her flowing tresses—we may cast around the symmetry of her form, the softness of her graceful drapery; and we may give her the air in which romantic devotion ever beholds the angel of its vows. We may represent, near at hand, the favorite glen in which she strayed—the moonlit arbor in which she sung—the silvery lake on which she sailed. We may look on this representation of life and nature, and deem it reality. We may gaze till bewildered sense reels in rapture. But look again—the floating vision becomes more calm—the associations less vivid—the emotions in our breast subside. But look again—here and there a new shade may be developed, here and there an unfamiliar expression be caught. But look again—it is what you have seen before—it is a mass of changeless, pulseless shadows!

But give this glowing subject to the poet, surrender

it to the magic of his genius—the changeless object lives—the motionless object moves—the silent object speaks. The heart where quenched existence had its grave is kindled, and renovated life gleams through its shroud, as the warm sun through its light vesture of clouds. The fount of feeling is stirred, and its currents come forth, fresh as the overflowings of a spring, when it melts away the icy fetters of winter. The features lose their fixed expression, and are radiant with a bright train of passing thoughts, and glad imaginings. Hope is there, mingling its colors with the shades of doubt;—confidence is there, banishing distrust;—affection is there, lighting up adversity. Every feature lives, every look tells.

We not only see the glen, but hear the soft whispers of the breeze, the mirthful voice of the brook;—we not only see the arbor, but hear the echoes, waking from their slumbers, repeat the favorite strain;—we not only see the lake, but hear the light drip of the suspended oar, and the soft murmur of the breaking wave. Every object is animated, and lives before us in palpable reality. We may gaze—and turn away—and gaze again—but new images, new sounds, new feelings, and new associations crowd upon us like stars on the steadfast vision of the astronomer.

Or we may shape the marble to the features of the man we venerate; we may render these features radiant with the qualities of his mind and heart; we may make the ruling passion brightly apparent upon the majestic brow; we may give the countenance that peculiar cast which calls up the lofty, and the tender recollection; and we may imagine the departed sage still existent and before us in undecaying strength; but lay our hand on this faultless resemblance—the clay of the grave is not colder—it is death with its icy chill!

But commit this departed saint to the gifted spirit of the poet: the veil of the grave is rent—the silent sleeper called up from the couch of corruption, and dressed in the garments of immortality. His actions are grouped around him in the brightness of their first appearance; his feelings recalled in the freshness of their infancy; his secret motives are revealed in the purity with which they were conceived; and his generous purposes, which perished in the bud, revived and expanded into fragrant life. You see the whole man, not in cold marble, not in awful abstraction from his fellow-beings, but within the warm precincts of friendship, love, and veneration, invested with the sympathies and attributes of real existence. Such is the power of the poet—such his mastery over life and death! He stands, prophet-like, over a vast ocean of thought, passion, and sympathy, that heaves and rolls at the stroke of his wand.

The breeze for which we have been long and anxiously looking has come at last. It is light, but fair, and promises to take us to our port; for before this watch goes out we are expecting to hear the cry of "land" from mast-head.

It is now one of those soft and brilliant days, which are no strangers to the clime of Italy; and our ships, under a light, easy sail, are passing up the splendid bay of Naples. This bay circles up bold and beautiful into the land; where it lies quietly imbosomed within a sweeping range of green and picturesque elevations. The city, from the shelving shore, ascends majestically this amphitheatre of hills, presenting at a glance its palaces, domes, temples, and towers, with all the fresher luxuries of the garden and the grove. More remote, and towering far above all, stands Vesuvius—a magnificent "pillar of cloud by day, and of fire by night."

All the nobler elements—earth, air, flame and flood—have mingled the romance of their richest triumphs, above, beneath, and around Naples. And then, as if to excite the last degree of admiring wonder and awaken an insatiable curiosity, the veil of centuries has been rent, and the embalmed remains of a Herculaneum and Pompeii brought up from their long mysterious repose! Thus the present and the past, the charms of the living and the hallowed beauty of the dead move before us, in the centre of a scene that might of itself almost induce an angel to pause on his earnest mission.

But it is our privilege only to look and admire; for all communication with the shore has been cut off by the imposition of a quarantine; though there is not the slightest disease, or scarcely a case of indisposition on board; nor have we been where it was possible for us to reach any exposure. There would have been as much sense in Adam's quarantining Eve, when he saw her first come in blushing beauty to his bower. And I have no doubt that our fair mother would have borne the restrictions, had our noble progenitor unaccountably imposed them, with vastly more good-nature than it is possible for us to muster on this occasion.

Our quarantine is for seven days; but before we can ride it out, we shall be obliged to leave for the Levant! This is a draft on a man's resignation, heavy enough to shake the self-complacent credit of any Christian or philosopher. Here we lie, only a few cables' length from the shore, seeing the picturesque multitude passing on their unknown errands—the pleasure party floating off for some rural retreat, in gayety and glee—the monarch and his court moving with all the ensigns of royalty—the wandering minstrel tuning his reed, and turning even his sorrows into melody—hearing through the long evening the loud cheers of some festive hearts, or the bursting chorus of St. Carlos, as it comes wafted on the wind; while the frequented gardens gleam with the radiance of their countless lights, and the flame of Vesuvius fringes with fire the wings of the passing cloud.

All these are to be left unrealized—unapproached!

and this, too, in compliance with the mockeries of a senseless quarantine! But this scene, so bright, so gay, and seemingly so full of happiness, I know full well is all an illusion—a fleeting phantom. It is a flower that springs from corruption—a laughter at the grave.

<pre>
How darkly changed this world since that first hour,
   When o'er its brightness sung the morning stars!
Time, death, and sin, and sorrow had no power
   Upon its beauty: man, who madly mars
His Maker's works, has swept it with a flood
Of tears and groans, and deluged it with blood.

It has become a Golgotha, where lie
   The bleaching bones of nations: every wave
Breaks on a shore of skulls; and every sigh
   The low wind murmurs forth, seems as it gave
This mournful tribute, unobserved and deep,
To millions—for whom man has ceased to weep.

It is a dim and shadowy sepulchre,
   In which the dying and the dead become
The hearse of all the living; yet the stir
   And sting of serpent-passion, and the hum
Of jocund life survive, with but a breath
Between this reckless revelry and death.

It is a rolling tomb, rumbling along,
   In gloom and darkness, through the shuddering spheres·
And filled with death and life, and wail and song,
   Laughter and agony, and jests and tears;
And—save its heartless mirth, and ceaseless knell—
Wearing a ghastly glimmering type of hell!
</pre>

Our anchor was again weighed, our lighter sails unfurled, and, swinging round near the Brandywine, we received the parting benediction of three cheers, which were returned more in sadness than mirth. All our canvas was soon spread to a light breeze which began to prevail from the northeast; and, passing out the ample bay, we held our course along the soft shores of Italy, for the straits of Messina. We met with no objects calculated to leave a distinct and abiding impression till we reached the lofty steeps of Stromboli. We passed the burning mount of this lonely island in the night; it was still kindling its magnificent watch-fire in the sky. It has been termed, with significant propriety, the lighthouse of the Mediterranean.

How triumphant is nature, in all her works, over the achievements of man! He lights his anxious beacon on the verge of some troubled coast, and, by unremitted watchings, is able perhaps, for a little time, to sustain its poor perishing ray. But nature, at once, without an effort, kindles up a beacon-flame that lights an ocean, and burns on through ages undimmed and unexhausted! The tempest may prevail above, the earthquake rock beneath, navies sink, and nations perish; but this flame burns on with a serene and lofty splendor—quenchless as the light of the sun!

We are again in a dead calm—like a politician in disgrace; but the misfortune is, we have not his facilities for getting out of it. He has only to go over to the other party, and his very blots become honorable scars. It requires, to be sure, a little flexibility of conscience; but what a fool a man is to be sticking to principles, when office, honor, and wealth lie in a different quarter! It is like keeping " Poor Julia's Ring," and watering the flowers at her grave, when living damsels with their beauty and their bowers invite one away. Remembrance cannot bring back to life the one that has perished from our bosom; nor can fidelity to principles that have become unpopular reinstate them in the humor of the age.

Most men seem to think the better way is to leave them to their fate, and take after those where something may be got besides the stale credit of believing this year what we did last. It shows no march of mind. It is merely repeating the past; it is chasing the rainbow in our gray hairs, because we did it in the sunny locks of childhood. Is the nurse's tale of the silver spoons always to be believed? No; the better way is for a man to change his creed, and his character too, when the times require. A coat that is often turned will outwear ten that never undergo this revolution; and, what is more, it will never be rusty. It may have in the end a variety of colors,— but so has the peacock, and who thinks the less of that bird for the numberless dyes which sprinkle the beautiful spread of its tail? But what have peacocks and politicians to do with our getting to the Levant?

We are still in this dead calm. I wonder that in this age of moon-touching balloons, steam shaving-machines, and patents for prolonging life, it has never occurred to any one that the whale may be turned to a most excellent account. I allude not to his blubber—I leave that to poets and all who burn the midnight taper; I refer to his strength—his power of going ahead. Just catch about forty of these fellows—by some process similar to that used in catching the wild horse of our prairies—and harness them, two abreast, to a man-of-war, with a taut rein in the hand of father Neptune, who, I have no doubt, could be procured as postillion, and then good-by to your steam, though it have a million horse-power, and a thunder-cloud for its safety-valve! I intend applying to Congress for funds to make the experiment, or at least for some special privileges on the subject. But the difficulty would be, if that body were to get upon a discussion of its merits, the Nantucket boys, seeing that in the event of my success, " Othello's occupation's gone," would harpoon every whale before Congress had finished their speeches, or I had obtained my patent. I must therefore hit upon some expedient that may expedite the delivery of these speeches. The thought strikes me—

To save at once this fatal waste of time,
    I'll get a gun that works by fire and steam;
And then let every member load and prime,
    With all the speeches he can write or dream;
For Perkins being right, this patent power
Will shoot off ninety thousand in an hour.

The steep rocks of Stromboli are still in sight: when they will sink in the distance I know not: we have not logged a fathom for several watches; our sails hang idly against the mast; our dog-vane has gone to sleep; we are in a motionless calm.

Sated with gazing on this sleeping sea,
    Some seek their lines and set themselves to angling;
Some take to politics, and, being free
    Of fact and full of feeling, fall to wrangling;
While some, reckless alike of soul and body,
Practise at fisti-cuffs, and drink their toddy.

While others, more sedate, lie stretched at length,
    Yawning on coils of rope, the deck, or cot;
A few while off their time in feats of strength;
    While here and there one, restless of his lot,
Thinks only of a distant eye and lip,
And rues the day on which he saw a ship.

Some look up to the sky and watch each cloud,
    As it displays its faint and fleeting form;
Some o'er the calm begin to mutter loud,
    And swear they would exchange it for a storm,
Tornado, any thing—to put a close
To this most dead, monotonous repose.

What if that oath were heard ? what if the gale,
  Rashly invoked, should lift the surging sea—
This noble ship be swept of mast and sail,
  And breakers lift their voice beneath her lee ?
Those lips might only breathe the strangling tone
Of one expiring gasp and bubbling groan.

Death is a fearful thing, come how it may—
  Fearful when it comes on like some repose
In which our breath and being ebb away
  As music to its mild, melodious close,
And where no parting pangs a shadow cast
On that sweet look, the lovliest and the last.

Not in this form the shipwrecked sailor dies,—
  A sudden tempest, or a latent rock,
And on the gale his fluttering canvas flies,
  Or down he sinks in one engulfing shock ;
While through the closing wave is heard his prayer
As now he strikes his strong arms in despair.

The breeze at last came, and Stromboli sunk in the horizon. On reaching the Straits—the Faro di Messina—we realized but few of those obstructions and perils which so threatened and impeded the navigation of the ancients. It is true, that what may have carried dismay and disaster to their frail galleys, which seldom ventured out sight of land, may be perfectly harmless to our keeled masses of daring and conquering strength. But still, it is inconceivable how even their diminutive ships, with their double banks of oars, and muscular arms to manage them, could have found such a serious source of difficulty and apprehension. The man who should now, like the hero of Virgil, circumnavigate the island of Sicily, to escape the dangers of these straits, would be an object of merriment. But Æneas must be forgiven; he not only followed the warning voice of an oracle, but Palinurus, his pilot, was little skilled in his profession, and had also an unfortunate tendency to slumber on his watch.

The oft-quoted proverb, which so briefly dooms a man to ruin, turn which way he will—

  Incidit in Scyllam, qui vult vitare Charybdem,

may flourish very well as a figure of speech in a younker's first oratorical display; but it has no foundation in truth. A log canoe, paddled with a decent degree of skill, may shun Charybdis without falling upon Scylla. Yet story relates how enormous ships have been dashed to fragments upon this mountain rock; or, in their escape of this disaster, have fallen within the sweep of the opposite whirlpool, where, after being carried about in helpless plight upon the absorbing circle, they have gone down and disappeared forever. If there be beneath these devouring waters mermaids of taste and a piratical conscience, doubtless their fair fingers are now adorned with many a jewelled ring that once flashed on the hand of Grecian beauty. What mysteries doth not the sea contain, which will never be unfolded or even conjectured!

I have often thought that of all revelations in nature, an exhibition of the secrets of the sea would possess the most thrilling interest. Were I permitted to explore but one untraversed realm, I should prefer that vast empire of curiosities which lies within and beneath the ocean. How little do we know of it! We catch a luckless fish and classify it, because it has fins like something which we have seen before; we draw up a lobster, and because he has wide claws, determine that he may either crawl or swim; we detach a bit of coral from its low mound or tree, and because it has cells, decide that some insect-bee of the water must have formed it; or we pick up a few shells which the returning tide has left on the beach as unworthy of its care, and because they are not found on the roofs of our houses, declare them most rare curiosities.

Thus ends our knowledge, but not our pride and prattle; for those who can utter the most absurdities about these strange things are dubbed philosophers; and the whole world is expected to do homage to the depth, extent, and minuteness of their learning. How entirely the greatness of one rests on the ignorance of another! Strike away the foundation and the fabric falls.

But I forget the straits and their poetical terrors. Homer describes Scylla as a steep mass of rock, towering so near the sky that even a thin cloud cannot shove itself between without having its drapery raked off; when in truth, it has scarcely an elevation of two hundred feet, with a little fort on the top, harmless alike to the bird that floats above and the ship that sails beneath. As for the monsters which Virgil or his muse heard howl so terrifically around the base of the rock, they are nothing more than the echoes of the waves entering rather unceremoniously a few low caverns; but which have not a fierceness of accent sufficient to startle a young duck from its slumber.

The whirlpool of Charybdis—from whose devouring vortex Ulysses escaped alone to tell the tale of his lost ship and perished crew—exhibits now only a broken disquietude of wave, without even a uniformity of circle, much less an absorbing centre. Brydone, to vindicate the nautical skill of the hero, and the sober veracity of the muse, would fain make us believe that a deluge of rocks has been carried into this vortex, and that thus it has become the tame thing we now see. This learned skeptic could not yield his faith to the reasonableness of the Mosaic history, and yet conceives that rocks may float around like slabs, and finally fill up a pit which was deemed almost bottomless! How admirably the creed of a man may adapt itself to his pride and prejudice! He creates a world from accidents to sustain a theory, and destroys it by the same agency to establish a conjecture!

On the projecting land, to which Charybdis is a

sort of threatening outpost, we observed a scattered collection of dwellings, the appearance of which would seem to intimate that the fabled horrors of this pass had still power not only to intimidate the mariner, but even to drive happiness and hope from the hearth of the peasant. But I do not wonder that men should hesitate to build there, or tremble over an hour's delay on that spot; for it was here that in the dreadful earthquake of 1783, two thousand perished. The waters of the strait were violently heaved from their bed over their natural boundary, and the returning surge left but here and there one, even to weep over the desolation.

But Messina, as we glided slowly up to it through the channel, mainly fixed our attention. It lies in the form of a crescent, sweeping up an easy elevation of hills, with a background of bolder eminences, and the clustering depths of forest shade. The harbor lies deep and tranquil, embosomed within the circling shore and a salient reach of land, whose falcated form stretches nearly round it, protecting it from the invading currents and rushing surge of the strait. The busy aspect of the quays, and the varied flags which floated above the anchored craft, showed that Messina had not yet lost its consideration in the commercial world. It has been the most unfortunate of cities. The earthquake and plague have alternately made it their victims. It has been the sad arena where, through centuries, foreign avarice and despotism have played their bloody game.

How fallen is Sicily! once the granary of Europe, now almost begging her bread; once giving laws to nations, now the veriest slave of a petty prince; once the source of science and freedom, now without light to discover her own rights, or courage to maintain them.

> Land of a past and perished greatness, wake!
>   Let sire and son now draw the battle-glaive,
> Their long-endured, disgraceful fetters break,
>   And strongly strike for freedom or the grave;
> Swear not to clank the chain, to blush and weep
> On those proud hills in which your fathers sleep.

MOUNT ÆTNA.

CHAPTER XIII.

O WHAT a glorious sight !—the sweet morn blushing
 Through drops of night, more beautiful appears
Than any damsel with the rich blood flushing
 Her modest cheeks, while they are bathed in tears :—
You little cloud, that spent the night in weeping,
Now upward soars, as into heaven creeping.

EXCURSION TO MOUNT ETNA—SLEEPING IN A CORN-FIELD—INCIDENTS OF THE ASCENT—STORM AT NIGHT—VIEW FROM THE SUMMIT—DESCENT—CATANIA—GAYETY OF THE LIVING ABOVE THE DEAD—MUSEUM OF THE PRINCE OF BISCARI—FRANCISCAN MONK—PASSAGE FROM MESSINA TO MILO—MURAT AND NEY—TIDES OF THE STRAIT—ISLAND OF CANDIA—ISLAND OF CERIGO—ASPECT OF MILO—HISTORIC INCIDENTS—GREEK PILOT—MEDICINAL SPRINGS—NATURAL GROTTOES—ANCIENT TOMBS.

WE were now on shore at Messina—not to survey and admire its monuments, or weep over its political degradation. We were chartering two vehicles of sufficient strength to take us to the foot of Mount Etna. Some of my companions suggested the propriety of first visiting the cathedral, as the stately columns which support its gilded roof once belonged to a proud temple of Neptune; but being in a state of negotiation with this aquatic charioteer to drive my whales as soon as I should get them fairly harnessed, and knowing how compliments in such cases always increase prices, I declined. Others mentioned a beautiful being in the nunnery of St. Gregorio, but the face of her who dwells in Santa Clara was yet too bright and perfect in my thoughts—that sweet image shall rest there unmixed and unmarred. I was for Mount Etna, though every leaf of the forests that stretch between should become a timid nun.

We left in two hackney coaches, and with Etna in our thoughts, took but little notice of objects by the way:—a man in pursuit of a whale never stops to harpoon a porpoise. We paused for a few moments to dine, but whether on fowl or fish, I know not; nor can I speak of the characteristics of the host or hostess: the huntsman tracking the lion, is not expected to notice the squirrel that chatters and cracks his nuts on the limb. Night came on, but we bade our postillion not to stop while man or beast could keep the road, or find it if lost. Yet, strange as it may seem, we fell asleep; but the hero of Marengo and Austerlitz slept before the battle of Waterloo:

> "He sleeps!—while earth around him reels,
> And mankind's million hosts combine,
> Against the sceptre-sword which seals
> Their fate from Lapland to the Line—
> While, like a giant roused from wine,
> Grim Europe, startling, watches him,
> The warrior lord of Lodi's field—
> O'er Jena's rout who shook his shield—
> Is hushed in slumber dim!"

We slept also!—not to awake like him, amid thunder, conflagration, and carnage, but to a situation seemingly as full of peril. Our horses had stopped; it was the hush of midnight; and what but the strong arms of robbers could be at the bit! One seized a pair of pistols, another an old broadsword. I levelled a blunderbuss—knowing its bell-muzzle to have a scattering faculty that must strike some one, however tremulously untrue the aim. We discovered, however, no enemy, no daring demander of life or purse. The fact was, our postillion had long since sunk to sleep; the reins and whip had fallen from his hands, and the horses, which had been hard pushed through the day, not partaking of our enthusiasm, had wandered—probably to look out for the feed which our impatience had denied them—far away into an old corn-field:

> "In a corn-field, high and dry,
> There lay gun-boat number one,
> Wiggle wiggle went its tail,
> And popit went its gun."

But our craft did not even wiggle; and my blunderbuss, so far from being in a condition to give notice of our distress, had no flint in its lock,—indeed, the lock itself was among the missing! How this fact should have escaped me, when I levelled at what I supposed to be a robber, is a thing which I cannot fully explain; but I did then suppose that a pull of the trigger would be fatal to somebody. I am thankful, on the whole, that there was no robber and no lock; for I never liked the idea of killing a fellow-being; I should prefer, but for the reflection it might bring on my courage, to be robbed. I always admired one trait in Falstaff—he never injured *living* man; even on the field of battle his assaults were upon those, who, without the least pang, derived from every blow he dealt only another evidence that they had fought bravely—he wounded only the dead!

Such indeed were his principles of humanity, his nice sense of honor, that sooner than draw his sword upon any living being, he would, where a reputation for courage required that blood should be drawn, wound himself. I present him to those who have renounced the rights of self-defence, as the best exemplar I have ever yet met with of their self-sacrificing nonentities.

Where was it we brought up?—ay, I recollect—it was in the corn-field. Our postillion with his head rolled over on to one shoulder, and his idle arms resting before him, was still in deep slumber; while his brutes were making, at drowsy intervals, their long and slowly recovered nods. Take them as a group, they were the very type of sleep. To rouse them at once and effectually, I determined, upon the impulse of the moment, to discharge the blunderbuss, kill whom it might. But then that want of a lock—it was a poser; besides, the barrel had no powder in it—a thing which, I am told, contributes considerably to the noise. At last I raised several tremendous whoops—a faculty which I acquired during my residence among the Potawattamies, on the shore of Lake Michigan. It had the effect—man and beast awoke from their sea of dreams, and even Night, starting from his ebon throne, let fall his leaden wand.

After boxing about some time among the bushes to find a substitute for our lost whip, we started—recovered the road, and though anxious to make up by a forced speed for the time lost in the corn-field, yet we did not reach Catania till a late hour of the morning. Here we took thirteen mules—five as substitutes for our own legs, five as sumpters, and three for the accommodation of the guide and muleteers. Thus equipped, with provisions for three days, and with greatcoats and blankets sufficient to protect us in a region of ice, we started a little before midday for the top of Etna. We were determined to see the next sun rise from the summit of that mount.

Our road lay, for fifteen miles, among the rugged reefs of lava disgorged in the last irruption. Every thing around had the appearance of a vast lake, tumbled in a storm, and suddenly changed to solid blackness. The sides of the mountain, as we approached it, presented features of a still bolder fierceness. The huge rock, the toppling crag, the protruding bluff, stood forth in frightful wildness from the channels and chasms which past torrents of fire had left behind. The summit, with its cloud of smoke and shaking cone, crowned the whole with a dark befitting **terror**.

At sunset, having reached the verge of the woody zone, we alighted for rest and refreshment. We here changed our summer apparel for that of winter; the greatcoats which had been put on our sumpters by our trusty guide, and which we should wholly have neglected, were now in eager requisition. Thus protected, and with spirits and strength renovated by the repast, we mounted again and renewed the ascent. Daylight had gone, but the sky was clear, and the light of the stars was sufficient for our practised guide. Our mules were sure-footed, and we had only to relinquish ourselves to their superior sagacity.

At a little before midnight, while approaching the foot of the great cone, where we were to part with our faithful animals, and where indeed we were to wait for the break of day, things began to wear a fearful change. Frequent clouds swept past us; but there was one at some distance which seemed more stationary—gathering in bulk and blackness. Our guide anxiously watched it, as it collected its strength and threw out its snagged flukes, and quickly leading the way up a steep ledge, called vehemently upon us to follow. We had only gained the ridge when the tempest came.

It appeared to me to be the last position one should seek under the tornado which now swept us, for we were obliged instantly to dismount and hold on to the sharp points of the rock. Our mules placed themselves instinctively in a posture presenting the least resistance to the rushing element. It was soon apparent why our guide had taken refuge on this unsheltered steep; for, as the cloud struck the side of the mountain, its enfolded lake descended in deluge and thunder. Rocks and large masses of ice, disengaged by its violence, rolled down on each side of us, and over the very track on which we were moving but a few moments before. Though separated from each other but a few feet, yet no one could make himself heard; the torrents around and the thunder above overpowered even the loudly vociferated admonitions of our guide.

There was at one moment a darkness that might be felt; and then at another the lightning, flashing down through the rifts of the cloud, would make the slightest pebble visible in its searching light. An hour of these dread alternations, while torrents and rocks were rolling on each side of us, and the storm went past. We were drenched to the skin, while our outer garments began to be stiff with ice, yet, with a shivering accent, we could speak to each other once more. It was the language of one spirit rallying and animating another. Capt. Read, with characteristic energy, was the first to mount.

Nil actum reputans, si quid superesset agendum.

The reader, without undergoing our fatigue, or being wearied with a detail of incidents, will now conceive us about two thousand feet above the point where we had encountered the storm—in a substantial shelter at the foot of the great cone—around a grate of coal, which we had brought with us from Catania—warming our fingers—snapping the ice out of our coats—toasting Etna in a bumper of its own wine—and watching for the break of day.

That hour comes: and now let him take his stand with us on the highest point of the cone, ten thousand feet above the level of the sea, and imagine the whole island of Sicily, with its peaks and glens, its torrents and valleys, its towns and forests, with the broken line of its bold shores stretched beneath in one vast panoramic view—the sun, wheeling up out of the distant sea—the heavens flushed with its splendor—the mountain pinnacles burning in its beam—the great cone shaking with the throes of the unresting element within—the crater sending up its volumes of steep cloud—and the central lake of fire flashing up through the darkness, like terrific glimpses of the bottomless abyss! But the reality overpowers all description! I drop my pen, and half accuse myself of rashness in having made even this brief attempt.

We effected the descent without any serious injury, though I had myself rather a narrow escape. My mule made a misstep—the only fault of the kind he had committed during the excursion. I fell over his head, and turned many somersets: on looking back, I saw my mule standing on the verge of the slope, and disregarding every thing else, directing his

MESSINA.

anxious look to me. There was sorrow and self-accusation in that look—I forgave him. Beckoning to him, he came down, snuffed about my mangled hat, and when I remounted, pricked up his ears, and started on with the most assured tread. From that time I have never seen this animal receive a stroke of the lash, without a feeling of disquietude.

We reached Catania at sunset, in fine spirits, and not the least so, Mrs. R., who had sustained all the perils and hardships of the expedition with wonderful courage and energy. That night we slept soundly, as well we might, for we had been up two nights without any sleep, except the nap in the corn-field, and that would have been less long had there been any powder in the barrel of my blunderbuss; for I have a wonderful tact at getting any thing off that is loaded. My first exploits in gunnery were with the pop-gun—the dear little thing!

> I do advise those who propose to fight
>   A duel, when they feel their honor pricked,
> To use this pop-gun—'tis so very light,
>   And what is more, so safe: none ever kicked,
> Or burst, unless it had too thin a shell,
> And then the little thing does just as well.

The Etna fever, which hurried us blindly past all other objects on our way to the mount, having subsided, we determined to defer our return to the ship, and glance at some of the features of Catania. This is a beautiful city, though built upon one vast field of lava, with the dead beneath, a volcano above, and the frightful monuments of the earthquake around. I know not why it is, but somehow in this strange world beauty, danger, and death are always in the same group. The sweetest violet I ever saw, bloomed among wreaths of snow on a sister's grave.

The amphitheatre, where the ancient Catanians held their sports, and where they may have been suddenly engulfed in a flood of fire, stands seventy feet beneath the gay promenade of the present town. This gigantic structure is built itself of lava, and for aught we can tell, may have been reared over playhouses, entombed in some eruption of a still earlier date. Thus it ever is in this world; on land, the votary of pleasure indulges his mirth over the bones of a perished race; and on the ocean, the mariner lightly hums his song on a wave, through which have sunk thousands to reappear no more. We present to heaven a picture of life and death, mirth and madness, over which angels might wonder and weep!

Nature often atones for the fierceness of present calamities in the beauty of remote results. The ashes that fall in the burning breath of the volcano, nourish plants which are to bloom above those they have buried; and the forest, which now encircles Catania, waves more luxuriantly than the one charred beneath. The vegetable life and bloom which followed the subsiding waters of the great deluge, were not less fresh and fair, than what had been swept away. But man covers the world with his slain—leaving their flesh to the vulture, their bones to the accents of the last trump, and his own guilt to the disposal of a final Judge!

We visited, while at Catania, the museum of the Prince of Biscari—the largest and most richly stored private cabinet in the world. I pass by the statues of the ancient deities, for time and disaster have been as fatal to their forms, as inspiration has to their worship. I pass by the collection of shells, for none, in all their vast variety, has the tone and rainbow beauty of the one through which the mermaid breathed my dying dirge. I pass by the vases which held the wines, and the lamps which lighted the festivities of the ancients; for who would gaze on the nail of the coffin in which youth and affection have sunk from light and life? I pass by the countless minerals and gems—they shed no rays of such living light as those which beam from the eye of the bright gazelle. I pass by the million of embalmed insects—others swarm the field and forest, happy in the life which these have lost. I pass by—no, I will not—the expressive statue of Cleopatra. The heart throbs beneath its beauty—the eye swims when lifted to that last look of suicidal despair.

Leaving the museum, we encountered an humble Franciscan in his simple attire—his uncovered head and sandals. He presented us with some flowers, and received in his thin pale hand our little charities.

Poor pilgrim! what is this world to thee? Thou hast renounced its wealth, its pleasures, its restless spirit of enterprise: thy home is not here—is it in heaven? Art thou indeed going to that better land, where the strife and vanities of earth never come? May the privations of thy lot atone for the mistaken virtues of thy creed.

If I determine to become a monk, I will come here and join the Benedictines. They have a splendid monastery, richly endowed—luxuriant gardens, sumptuous fare, nothing to do—they live like gentlemen. If any one questions the usefulness of such a life, I can only say, let him attend to his own business. What concern is it of his, if, like a silkworm, I wind myself up in my own web? Let him not attempt to wind my house on to his bobbin.

Cicisbeism prevails among the higher classes in Catania. It passes as a pure platonic affection—infringing no marriage obligation, no law of morality, no rule of rigid propriety—merely a chaste friendship, innocent as a new-born babe. It does, to be sure, encourage a peculiar intimacy, and may perhaps diversify the features of the younger members of the family; but what of that? No sentiment of delicacy has been publicly shocked, and no one dies before his time comes: let the exquisite arrangement alone. Never was there a charmer of the bird with so beautiful a skin, so bright an eye, and so venomous a fang! It is the devil himself disguised as an angel of light!

Leaving Catania—the excellent hotel of the attentive Abatti—and travelling the remaining half of the day and the succeeding night, we arrived at Messina at the break of dawn. The leaves were wet with the dew, and the first rays of the sun were among them, while yet the day-star could be seen over the hills.

> Lone star that lingerest still on yon steep height,
>   Dost not perceive that thou art wondrous pale?
> Why keep untiring watch in deep daylight?
>   Come, spread thy pinions on the morning gale,
> And haste away—thy sisters all are gone—
> Earth will not hear thee singing there alone.
>
> Sweet star, though morn hath blanched thy cheek and brow,
>   Thy glancing eye is full of tearful mirth;
> With thee my softened heart would meekly bow,
>   And own the Power that ruled thy heavenly birth—
> But, hark!—thy sisters call again to thee:
> Haste, haste away, and meet me on the sea.

Weighing anchor from Messina, we passed, on the opposite side of the strait, the small village of Reggio, which would have hardly arrested our attention but for its being the last retreat of the unfortunate Murat. There is over the whole career of this splendid officer a warmth of generosity, a depth of enthusiasm and romance, which should have secured him from the inhuman and unmerited death which his miserable foes decreed. His last look, as he sunk alone, unarmed and unbefriended, beneath the mortal aim of his executioners—and the last words of his brave companion in arms, the gallant Ney, as he kneeled down to die—may perhaps have been regarded by some with exultation; but a man of the slightest magnanimity would have turned away with indignant shame and regret.

The errors of such men meet with an adequate retribution when the reverses of the field divest them of their splendor and power; and let us not insult their misfortunes and human nature, by sending them to the hands of the common executioner, or chaining them, like their captive chief, to a desolate rock in the ocean.

But I have wandered unintentionally to St. Helena, and must come back to take a parting look at the strait. A current sets here alternately north and south, at the rate of three or four knots an hour. It is strictly a tide, influenced by the moon, with a strong ebb and flow, though the rise and fall are not great. When the current sets in from the north, it first encounters the point of Pelorus, which still perpetuates the name of Hannibal's pilot; it is here headed off, and sets towards Scylla, where it is again deflected in an opposite direction, and drives towards the isthmus, which protects the harbor of Messina.

On its return, it pursues essentially the same track, but rarely in either direction seriously annoys a ship, unless there be a calm, a strong head-wind, or one of those traversing gusts which frequently issue from the gorges of the mountains. But, like the renowned Argonauts, we have escaped the disasters of the pass; so adieu to its counter currents, whirlpools, and rocks. They have ever had more poetry in them than peril.

Our next sight of land rested on the island of Candia. Mount Ida, which claims the proud pre-eminence of being the birth-place of Jupiter, strikingly sustains its pretensions in its own lofty and solitary grandeur. It is a place befitting the infancy of one destined to reign over the hopes and fears of this poor world. It would seem that the infant Thunderer began to exercise his frightful functions even before leaving the place of his nativity; for Ida has all the blight and barrenness which the fiercest lightning leaves behind.

The presiding divinity must also, in some measure, have molded the character of the inhabitants; for they have ever been distinguished for valor and vice, skill and falsehood. They exhibited their courage and resolution in their resistance to the Romans, and in the memorable siege of their principal city by the Ottoman power in the seventeenth century. Their vices, aside from the passages of Strabo, live in many a lewd tale, and their piratical audacity still thrills through the story of the mariner. Their skill in archery aided Xenophon in his celebrated retreat, and assisted Alexander the Great in his conquests.

Their proneness to falsehood passed into a proverb, and even shocked the satirical muse of Ovid:

> ——Non hoc centum quæ sustinet urbes,
> Quamvis sit mendax, Creta negare potest.

The next island that we made was Cerigo—the ancient Cithera, and favorite isle of Venus. Near its sweet shore this goddess rose from the wave in the full perfection of her soft entrancing beauty. Her being, no less than her birth, betrayed her celestial origin. With a form molded in all its developments to the most rich and exquisite symmetry—a countenance lighted up with the earnestness of serene and passionate thought—a soul breathing through her very frame the warmth and kindling fondness of love—with a step that could dispense with the earth, and a look that could make a heaven,—it is no wonder that she filled and fascinated the human heart; and that the prince and the poet, the warrior and the sage, laid their richest offerings upon her shrine.

But her worship is now passed—her temples are tottering in ruins—her altars are forsaken—her fountains unvisited—and even this sweet isle where she once dwelt, has only the murmuring wave to mourn over the dream of her perished beauty. Some glimpses of her loveliness may linger still in the triumphs of the chisel and pencil, but her soul of surpassing sweetness and power is not there; and the spell of her charms will never return, while the spirit of a holier revelation continues to chasten down the voluptuous imagination of man.

Passing Cithera, we held our course for Milo, and soon came to anchor in its well-sheltered harbor. The first sentiment that occurred to me, in looking at the form and aspect of this island, turned to the injustice which has been done to it, in the purposes which it has been compelled to subserve. It appeared as if, from some motive of curiosity, it had merely looked up out of the wave, to see what was going on in this strange world—had been caught in that situation and detained, as an adventurous traveller peeping into an Arab encampment, is sometimes held there in lawless bondage.

Yet there is no cast of grief or violence upon it; indeed, it seems as cheerful as if it never had endured a compulsory servitude; though, so far from having escaped the ignoble task of contributing to the maintenance of man, it has at one time sustained a population of twenty thousand upon its own resources. It was first made a captive by a Lacedæmonian colony, and like a true knight, enabled them, for seven hundred years previous to the Peloponnesian war, to preserve their independence.

With more gallantry than selfish wisdom, it refused in that long struggle to aid the designs of the Athenians, who revenged this neutrality by visiting it with the heaviest desolation in their power. This wicked act has been sketched by Thucydides in one of his terse sentences. The men, it appears, who were able to bear arms were put to death—the women and children carried off into exile.

In the recent struggle between the Greek and Turk, this little isle saved itself from Moslem vengeance by its peaceful demeanor, and better served the interests of humanity in thus becoming a partial asylum, where the oppressed and despairing might recover strength and resolution. It is now what it was in earlier times—a sort of resting-place for the mariner. In weariness and storm, he has only to drop around into this quiet harbor, and then he may tune his reed, or traverse his deck, and let the tempest without rave, till it frets itself to rest.

But our object here was not to shelter ourselves from a gale, but to procure the aid of those whose knowledge of the intricate passes of this sea might perhaps save us from that last disaster which sometimes befalls a ship. The skill of the pilot here is very much confined to occasions when there is the least necessity for it. It is to be relied on when perils are distinctly visible; but when storm, and wave, and night mingle in conflict, the Greek pilot has no resource but to fall on his knees and supplicate the assistance of the blessed Virgin.

Could that sweet saint send out the light of those stars which once lighted her solitary path in Judea, it would be eminently wise to invoke her aid. Far be it from me, however, to quench the hope and trust which even a delusive confidence may awaken. Yet in a storm, I would sooner trust to a strong cable, or a good offing with a close reef, than to any miraculous preservation within the power of the compassionate Madonna. But enough of these heterodox sentiments.

Mounting some little stunted ponies, which were but a trifle larger than goats, we went in quest of some of the natural curiosities of the island. A short ride brought us to the tepid springs, which rise quite up the harbor near the water's edge. These springs are strongly impregnated with sulphur, and are much frequented by those afflicted with scrofulous diseases,—maladies which are often met with here, and which are ascribed to a noxious property in the honey with which the Cyclades abound. There is no sweet without its bitter—no rose without its thorn. But nature sometimes, as in the present case, furnishes an antidote for the ills which she brings. Would that man could do the same; but his wrongs strike so deeply, that a reparation is frequently not within his power. A broken heart can never be revived and restored; it may perchance smile again, but its smiles will be like flowers on a sepulchre.

From the springs we rode to a singular cave near the entrance of the harbor. After winding down a narrow and difficult passage, we found ourselves in a large hall, beautifully vaulted with crystallized sulphur. This mineral, in the hands of man, has a bad name, and a worse association; but left to nature, she converts it into brilliant gems, with which she studs the glowing domes of her caverned palaces.

Here was one of her halls in which even an Egeria might have dwelt, and sighed for nothing earthly, unless it were the footsteps of her mortal lover. And perhaps it was in other times the abode of some sweet romantic being, whose devoted love flew the crowd, to cherish in solitude and silence its fondness and trust. For there is something in the spirit of this mysterious passion which takes the heart away from the empty bustle and prattle of the multitude. It is this which sanctifies the private hearth, and garlands the domestic altar with flowers that can never die. One that looks away from the companion of his bosom for solace and delight, has mistaken the path to true happiness and virtue.

But I am again on a theme that has little to do with the present fountains and grottoes of Milo. We were struck, on riding over the island, with the number and variety of its caverns, and with the beautiful results of the chemical operations which are constantly going on in these natural laboratories. These singular results are produced from rich mineral substances, abounding in the hollow hills, dissolved and sublimated by the agency of a volcanic flame, which appears to live in the heart of the island.

Let this isle alone—it needs no forge, retort, blowpipe or galvanic battery, to aid its chemical experiments. To its lectures Pliny listened, and thousands since have wisely imitated the docility of his example. We observed in our rambles the constant occurrence of excavations, which were once immense reservoirs for the reception of rain-water,—there being no fresh springs in the island, and which, though now neglected and partially filled by falling fragments, attest the former denseness of the population.

We spent some time among the Catacombs, the most perfect of which are just being opened, and may be found near the site of the ancient capital. These chambers of the dead are cut in the soft rock, being eight or ten feet square and as many in height, with narrow cells opening around them, in which the bodies were deposited. In the cells are discovered the jewels and ornaments of the deceased, and in the chambers lachrymatory vases, in which the bereaved preserved their tears, as sacred to the memory of the departed. Among the ornaments a massive ring was recently discovered, which was purchased here for fifty pounds, and subsequently sold for five hundred.

The vases are some of them of glass, brilliantly colored in the material; others of an argillaceous substance, pencilled with a delicate and unfading force. They are now searched for and sold by the natives to the antiquary, or to any one who may feel or affect an interest in the arts and habits of the ancients.

How every thing in this world tends to ruin and

forgetfulness! We are not only to die—to be placed in the earth—but the violets are to be plucked from our graves—these narrow mounds perhaps to be levelled down to gratify the pride of a village, and furnish a promenade for the gay—and then, as if this were not enough, should the place of our burial in after ages become known, our ashes may be disturbed, and though the tearless grief of our friends may save the search after lachrymatories, yet our very dust may be sifted in search of a gainful trinket. What has been will be; for "there is nothing new under the sun." Then let me be spared all mockery of grief, all eulogies written and forgotten by the same individual—let my resting-place be unknown.

> When ye shall lay me in the shroud,
>   And look your last adieu,
> Ye shall not tell it to the crowd,
>   Nor to the friendly few;
> And when ye place me on the bier,
>   Ye shall not wail a word,
> Nor let your eyes confess a tear,
>   Or e'en a sigh be heard.
>
> Much less shall there be funeral knell,
>   Or roll of muffled drum,
> Or, when ye leave where I must dwell,
>   The peal of parting gun.
> Bear me away at dead of night,
>   And let your footsteps fall
> As soft and silently, as light
>   The moonbeams on the pall—

Till ye shall reach some desert shore,
    Or some secluded glen,
Where man hath never been before,
    And ye will not again;
Inter me there, without a stone
    Or mound to mark the spot,—
A grave to all but ye unknown,
    And then by ye forgot.

CHAPTER XIV.

> The early lark from out the thicket springing,
> Now like an angel lures me to the skies;
> The waking warblers from the hill-top singing,
> Hail the sweet morn—notes various as their dyes.

TOWN OF MILO—STEEPNESS OF THE STREETS—ADVICE TO DISTILLERS—STATUE OF VENUS—VIEW FROM THE TOWN—GREEK WEDDING—DRESS AND PERSON OF THE BRIDE—FICKLENESS OF FASHIONS IN DRESS—ANECDOTE OF FRANKLIN—PASSAGE FROM MILO TO SMYRNA—CAPE COLONNA—TEMPLE OF MINERVA—PROFESSION OF PIRATES—ISLAND OF IPSARA—ASPECT OF SCIO—MASSACRE OF THE INHABITANTS—CONDUCT OF THE ALLIES—GULF OF SMYRNA—ANCIENT CLAZOMENÆ—TRAITS OF THE SAILOR.

We left the ship this morning for the purpose of visiting the town of Milo, which is built around the conical summit of a mountain, and sufficiently elevated to look down on Mahomet's coffin, high as it floats even in the fanatical dream of a Mussulman. This giddy position was chosen as a refuge or protection from pirates; but the corsair has reached it—not in search of a Medora (I could almost excuse him for that), but in quest of a treasure far less lovely, though of deeper fascination to a sordid heart.

On our ascent, we turned aside to the remains of a theatre, which has been discovered within a few years past. The rubbish and earth with which it was covered have been partially removed; and the relic presents an entireness of preservation rarely to be met with even where, as in the present case, the material has the durability which belongs to marble. The theatre, soon after its discovery, was purchased by Baron Haller, under whose direction the excavations were vigorously prosecuted, until a treacherous wave, as he was crossing the harbor, terminated his career, and deprived the world of the fruits of his enterprise. The object of his munificent curiosity remains; and the rent cornice and column will long be surveyed by the stranger, as the touching emblems of his broken hopes and purposes.

On returning to our path, we passed the spot where the celebrated statue, the Venus of Milo, was discovered. It has since been purchased by the French government, and is now exhibited in the Louvre, where doubtless many a Parisian belle is studying its air and attitude, and endeavoring to mould her yielding form after its perfect symmetry. But corsets and studied positions will never make a Venus.

This peerless prototype looked and moved just as she came from the soft hand of nature; and those who would approach her, in the power of their charms, must listen to an oracle that talks not of airs and stays. Were Praxitiles to come from his resting-place, and a modern beauty to present herself before him, to stand for her statue, in all the narrowing and disorganizing appendages which fashion now sanctions, the astounded artist would drop his chisel and hasten fast as possible back to his grave!

But enough of this censorial criticism on the false taste of the ladies. They will, I have no doubt, regard my strictures as extremely querulous and impudent; but I can assure them I am one of the most modest and peaceable men in the world, and little disposed to give offence in that quarter, where I may perhaps one day be seeking the happiness which heaven has righteously denied to the cynanthropy and selfishness of the single state. I trust that this confession, if it fail to secure me their favor, will at least obtain me their forgiving tolerance; and I will engage not to offend again, though nature pants and dies under the constricting tortures of the cord and steel.

We recovered the path to Milo, from which we had diverged, by beating our way through several small plats of ground, surrounded with hedges of the aloe, whose lance-like thorns wound a man's flesh as much as scandal does his character. Our way now lay up in a rambling zig-zag line, rendered necessary not only by the steepness of the actual ascent, but the frequent occurrence of the insurmountable bluff and projecting crag.

It appeared to me, while twisting my sight and strength through the exhausting tortuosities of this path, that Satan would have never found his way from Tartarus to Paradise, on a road as crooked and laborious as that which we were threading. But here, I hope, will end all supposed parallel between the situation, climbing functions, and errand of his satanic majesty and myself. I was bound to Milo—he was in search of Eden; I went to bless a new-married couple, as will presently appear—he to make miserable the only wedded pair on earth; I was on, to say the worst of it, a fool's errand—his was that of a fiend. But to close this contrast, so severe upon Milton's hero, without perhaps being honorable to myself, we at last reached the town.

We found all its streets extremely narrow, for the want of room to make them wider, and decently clean, from their precipitancy; for the contents of a dish-kettle or wash-bowl would hardly stop till they had reached the harbor; and as for a stumbling drunkard, he would roll down with increasing momentum, plump into the wave. There are, consequently, no "Temperance Societies" here—no annoyances from those who will not allow others to drink, because they have ceased to drink themselves.

I would therefore advise the distiller, as he appears to be particularly obnoxious to these men who have forsaken their bottles, to come and work his worms here, where he will cease to be annoyed, not only by those who do not take a drop at all, but by those who take a drop too much. For instead of having the grounds about his establishment disfigured by an unseemly group, one trying to knock off another's nose, another blinking and sleeping in the sun, another zig-zagging a plain path, another casting his sickly smile on the stranger, another cocking his eye ahead, as if levelling at a partridge, and another looking as if about to assume the functions of a stool-pigeon—instead of this, the moment a fellow has taken a glass too much, and attempts his first step, he tumbles, and rolling downward about two miles, comes souse into the bay.

This cleverly cools him off, quenches all the burning rags on his back, and he is ready to mount again, fresh as a fish. The distiller, therefore, escapes all annoyance from those who do not drink, and all disgust from those who do; and as for that being who goes about as a roaring lion, seeking whom he may devour, if there be any virtue in friendship, any merit in good service, he has naught to fear from him.

The roofs of the houses, we observed, were all flat. This may have been from a prudential anxiety to present the least possible exposure to the violent winds which occasionally sweep these heights, or to lessen the weight, which only aggravates the toppling propensities of the dwelling; or, from motives of economy, which I do not assuredly know, as I never made the inquiry. But whatever may have been the inducement, they afford a good protection from all inclemencies of weather, and the only promenade of which this cloud-capped town can boast.

Under the guidance of an intelligent native, who had been engaged as a pilot for our ship, we continued our climbing till we reached the roof of the church, which rightly crowns the summit. The wide panorama of wave, and isle, and mount which now spread around us, would have rewarded much greater fatigues than we had undergone in the ascent.

Milo itself, with the soft oval sweep of its shores, the picturesque prominency of its hills, the green depth of its valleys, and above all, the slumbering beauty of the harbor, as it lay with the repose and brilliancy of an inland lake, was enough to chain the eye and fill the heart. But the charms of the prospect rested not here—a multitude of isles like this lay within the circling range of our vision, bright as the waves in which their shadows were enshrined, and soft as the skies that covered them. They seemed as if formed for the most fond, fraternal alliance, yet capable each one, in an hour of ingratitude or indignity, of leaning upon its own resources.

I like this self-relying aspect, both in nature and man; it imparts dignity, respect, and confidence, without detracting in the slightest degree from the obligations and advantages of friendship. In this selfish and treacherous world, a person should never place his happiness at the mercy of another; betrayal and ruin are too apt to be the consequence. This remark, however, must not be extended to that sacred alliance on which the marriage seal has been set, for the greater the confidence here, the less liable perhaps is it to abuse; and not only so, but without this unreserved confidence, love's lamp would burn dim, even before the first night had waned on its middle watch.

Since I have touched on this delicate theme, my narrative may as well descend at once under its light, from the roof of the church to the new-married couple, whose first day of a happy date hundreds had now come to witness and to bless. To this festival we had been invited, and though unable to discourse in modern Greek, yet we determined to see with what peculiarities Hymen might still hold his court in this ancient Melos.

We found the assembly about a third of the way down the declivity, on a small green, sustained by a bold range of rock, which served it as a natural parapet. The aged were seated under the fruit-trees, eating sweetmeats and drinking sherbet; the children were in scattered groups, wildly at play; the youth of both sexes were more in the centre, dancing the Romaika. In performing the evolutions of this oriental dance, the parties begin with a slow and solemn movement, and gradually accelerate the action as the music becomes more lively.

The conductress of the figures, who on this occasion was the bride, led the company by easy and natural gradations to the most rapid evolutions, involving them constantly in a maze of intricacies, through which they followed her, without once breaking the chain or losing the measure. The music consisted simply of the Balaika, which accorded with the rural and romantic aspect of the scene. Something like this, blended perhaps with still stronger fascinations of personal beauty, drew from the author of Evenings in Greece the passionate and sprightly strain commencing with the lines—

> "When the Balaika is heard o'er the sea
> I'll dance the Romaika by moonlight with thee :
> If waves then advancing, should steal o'er our track,
> Thy white feet, in dancing, shall chase them all back."

The dress and appearance of the bride were peculiarly native and striking. She was crowned with a wreath of white flowers, which contrasted beautifully with the jet-black locks of her hair floating behind in glossy ringlets; her dress was of white satin, with short sleeves, and cut low in the neck; over this appeared a stomacher of scarlet, richly embroidered, encircling and sustaining the round bust. Her dress, with its deep and well-adjusted folds, descended only a little below the knee, where it was more than met by a white silk stocking, that betrayed a small round ankle, and an instep that seemed bounding from the light shoe. Her necklace was of pearl; her ear ornaments and bracelets of cameo, delicately wrought and set in gold.

She appeared to be about sixteen years of age—

with a round cheek of deep carnation—a countenance of brunette complexion—eyes black, shaded with thick silken lashes, and of sparkling brightness—an upright forehead, though not high—a neck of smooth and graceful curve—a stature rather low—a form not slight but symmetrical—and a hand on whose tapering fingers glittered the tokens of love and friendship.

She had the air of one who has just passed that period of life where the lightness and gayety of the heart give place to sympathies of deeper tone, and feelings of stronger power. Her manner, costume, and person alike riveted our attention, and though she could not be said to reach the perfection of grace and beauty, yet I was not surprised on being told that the commander of a squadron in this sea had recently employed a limner expressly to sketch her picture. But to be rightly appreciated, she would require more than lies in the power of the artist. There was something in the flowing of the full soul, as it lighted and filled her countenance, which no pencil could express.

The bridegroom was a good-looking Greek, of twenty-three or four; slightly below the medium stature, with a compact muscular frame, and countenance that needed not the aid of the mustaches, that curled from the upper lip, to give it expression. His dress was the flowing Turkish trowsers of white, confined suddenly and closely about the ankle, and a coat of blue, in the form of the spencer, deeply embroidered in front. His manner was manly, frank, and affable. On being presented to him, he immediately introduced us to his fair bride, and invited us into his well-furnished house, which opened on the small green. We were here served with fruit, cake, sherbet, coffee, and the cordiality of the pipe.

Our conversation was carried on through an interpreter, which left the ladies, who composed a majority of the circle, quite at leisure to ponder the dress of Mrs. R., which they evidently thought very singular, wondering no doubt why it descended so low—why her head was protected by a bonnet instead of a veil—and how it was possible for her form to possess its symmetry, without the visible aid of the stomacher.

But they were not more surprised at a novelty of costume than we were; though, had the bride been mine, I should have anticipated with no pleasure, in any country or community, the necessity of an essential change in the style of her dress, bating the shortness of the petticoat. This dress, in its outline, is what it was two thousand years ago, and what it will probably be two thousand years hence.

What a contrast to the whimsical fickleness of taste in my own country! Our garments instead of being comely on some future generation, the caprices of fashion render ridiculous even on our own backs. Indeed, fashions change with such an electrical rapidity with us, that if the boy who brings a dress from the milliner's be slow on the leg, it will have to be sent back to be conformed to some new freak of fancy, or some more newly discovered model. Our taste in dress, so far from aiding a permanent nationality of character, is a mere bubble,

"Which a breath can break as a breath hath made."

It is a servile imitation of the fooleries and fopperies of some foreign metropolis; and worse than this, it is sometimes a serious submission to a quiz, played off for the merriment of others upon our aping vanity.

I have often admired the good-humored reply of Franklin to his daughter, on her request to be gratified with an article of fashionable inutility. While that philosopher was embassador to the court of France, his daughter wrote him that ostrich feathers were all the go in the head-dress of the ladies, and requested him to send her out some of the first quality. The honest Republican replied—"Catch the old rooster, my dear child, and take some of the longest feathers from his tail: they will answer, my word for it, every purpose." Were a parent now-a-days to tell his daughter so, she would probably fly into a nunnery, or die of grief.

But I ask pardon of the ladies, for I promised not again to offend; and I can say in conciliation, that they are not much more extravagant and frivolous in their taste than the men. And we have this disadvantage also, that we lie under the just imputation of imitating their worst vagaries. A close observer of the variations occurring in the style and shape of our apparel, cannot but remark, that we look to the ladies as truly as the sea in its ebb and flow looks to the moon. But I must hasten on, for at this rate my story will never get away from Milo,—it will die here, like a pilgrim that has never reached the shrine of his saint.

Taking two intelligent pilots on board, so that they might relieve each other in alternate watches, we weighed anchor, and, clearing the narrow entrance of the harbor, were once more running before the breeze. The next morning brought us close to Cape Colonna, on the southern extremity of Attica—a bold promontory—crowned with the magnificent remains of the temple of Minerva. We solicited Capt. Read to lie to, till we could visit these ruins. A boat was immediately lowered, and we were soon on shore, up the steep, and among the remains.

We found twelve columns of the purest Pentelican marble, with their entablatures, still standing. Others lying around, mingled with the massive fragments of the cell. The stateliness and Doric simplicity of these columns, with the extent of the foundations on which the edifice reposed, afforded a noble conception of its original beauty and grandeur. It required but little effort of imagination, with what was before us, to fill the broken outline, rear the prostrate pillars, extend the architrave, and perceive in the completion of the whole, a temple worthy of the best days of Greece, and deserving even the high encomium which Pericles is said to have passed upon it.

From the decisions of this artist there has never yet been found a just ground of appeal. His genius was an oracle to which nations listened; and we are even now disinhuming cities to recover the sacred sanctions of his taste and judgment. In architecture, sculpture, and poetry, the world has lost its richest specimens, and has not the power to restore them; nor will this power ever be realized, unless it shall awake in the regenerated Greek.

On one of the pilasters still standing, among a multitude of names unknown to song, I discovered one that was a brilliant exception, and well worthy of its place,—it was the name of the author of Childe Harold, engraven here under his own eye, in his pilgrimage to this relic. If any one could, without profanation, presume in this form upon the sacred remains of ancient art, it was this wandering, weeping, and admiring minstrel. He not only entertained himself a profound veneration for these remains, but he inspired millions with the same sentiment.

Each moldering fane, deserted shrine, and tottering column have found a tongue in the pathetic and eloquent spirit of his numbers. He kneeled amid the relics of a ruined race, and, in the eloquence of his admiration and sorrow, touched an electrical chain of sympathy that has kindled and vibrated in all lands. He finally set the last and decisive seal of the martyr to the sincerity of his reverence and grief. His name is now embalmed among ruins, on which his genius has cast the splendors of a fresh immortality.

Lingering around the relic, which now seems to sanctify Colonna, I found myself invaded by one deep and melancholy sentiment—a sentiment of utter desolation. I was standing where thousands once thronged to pay their festive devotions; where the ancient Sunium embraced its happy multitudes; where the eloquent Plato, with his serene philosophy, soared like an angel with his golden lyre to heaven. Now not a human being to be seen, not a solitary voice to be heard, and not even a sound stirring to relieve the unbroken silence of the place, except the hollow moan of the wave as it died on the desolate shore!

I could have sat down there and wept over the dark destiny of man; for if a people so inventive in monuments to perpetuate their power and splendor, become a blank, how soon will those spots, now the seats of refinement, opulence, and gayety, be changed to empty sepulchres! and the ruin will never stop, nor will it ever be repaired. Babylon is still a desert, and Palmyra known only to the wandering Arab. Other continents may perhaps be discovered, and other islands emerge from the ocean, but over all that now smiles in the light of the sun, the dark tide of ruin and death moves on with a slow but inevitable tread.

The only solace in our doom is the assurance that nature, in her salient and self-restoring power, may remain—that the same sun which gilds our palaces will gild our graves—that the same sky which pavilions our pomp and pride will canopy our dust. But this cannot benefit us, or serve to cheer the pilgrim who may ages hence wander to our tombs. What know the dead who were sepulchred here, of the surviving light and influences of nature? It is of no moment to them that the succession of morn and eve, the budding spring and mellow autumn, are still repeated. And the stranger who pauses here, only feels a deeper sadness at seeing the wave still sparkle on its strand, and the light, with its purple and gold, still fringing the cliff, while all else only bespeaks decay and ruin.

> The towers of Thebes, which millions toiled to rear,
>   In scattered ruins own the earthquake's shock;
> The fleets of Rome, that filled the isles with fear,
>   The storm hath left in fragments on the rock:
> But thrones may crumble, empires reach their goal;
> Their frailties reach not thee, thou deathless Soul!
>
> The mighty mound that guards Achilles' dust;
>   The marble strength of Agamemnon's tomb;
> The pyramid of Cheop's dying trust,
>   Now only give to doubt a deeper gloom;

But Plato's memory ages still shall find
Immortal mid the triumphs of the mind.

A signal-gun from the ship for our return, aroused me from the reverie in which my thoughts had been thus gloomily wandering. On reaching our boat, we passed over the memorable spot where Falconer was wrecked—a catastrophe which he has converted into strains of the most poetic and touching character. This hymning mariner found the elements of his poetry, his home, and his grave in the ocean.

The ship in which he finally left his native shore for the East Indies, never reached her port. She was arrested on her way: how long she struggled with the tempest, and with what feelings they whom she bore met their doom, are secrets which will never be revealed by the incommunicable sea. Could the harp of the poet have floated away with the sad story of his death, thousands would now be listening, weeping, and clinging with increased fondness to their hearths. There is over the fate of those who go to sea and are never heard from again, a tragical uncertainty and horror which must fill the most apathetic heart with emotion.

Having mounted the ship's side again, orders were immediately given to fill away, and we were soon moving up through the Doro passage, which lies between Negropont and Andros. This channel being the one generally preferred by merchantmen bound to Smyrna, became a favorite haunt for pirates—a class of men who took upon themselves the responsibility of collecting a sort of water-tax, for which they have been much scandalized in this censorious world.

They levy a contribution and exact it at the peril of their lives—kings do the same, but with vastly less hazard to themselves; for their majesties, in case of resistance to their exactions, have only to sit in their palaces and issue an order to some inferior agent for their immediate enforcement; while the corsair has to enforce his demands himself, and is frequently battling it, breast to breast, at a desperate odds.

If taken himself, instead of taking the gold of his opponent, he will scorn to crave a life as a suppliant, which he has forfeited as a pirate; whereas a king, the moment he becomes a captive, compounds for his personal safety by treasonably betraying his subjects, and forfeiting his realm. I think the advantages of dignity, courage, and self-respect, decidedly on the side of those who levy contributions on the water, upon the force of their own steel and valor.

Leaving Negropont on the left—a fruitful island abounding in the grape, olive, orange, citron, and pomegranate, and the largest in the Ægean, with the exception of Crete—we doubled the northern cape of Andros, which is much less in its dimensions than its

Negropontan neighbor, but equally fertile in its soil, and delicious in its fruits. The ancients owed this island an unaccountable spite, and christened two of its tutelary divinities Poverty and Despair; when, according to their own confessions, it had not only a beautiful temple dedicated to the jolly Bacchus, but a fountain near it, whose waters on the Ides of January tasted so very like wine, that the most exquisite connoisseur could not tell the difference.

Passing on, Ipsara soon appeared on our larboard bow, a small island of wild ragged peaks and rockbound shore. Its inhabitants, in their struggle for independence, exhibited a heroism that would not have disparaged the days of Leonidas. After contending with their swarming foes till every ray of hope was extinguished, they blew up their fortifications, whelming themselves and thousands of their enemies in instant death.

Those who were not within the works, to escape the vengeance or lust of the Mussulman, threw themselves into the sea. The mother was seen on every cliff, clasping her infant to her breast, and plunging into the wave, with her shrieking daughters at her side. Youth and beauty, maternal tenderness and infant sweetness, were seen for days floating around this isle on their watery bier; a sight which might have moved the very rocks with indignation and pity, but which the Turk looked upon with triumph and pride. The island is now a blackened ruin—thus let it remain, as a frightful and becoming monument of the desolating spirit of Islamism.

Close on our starboard beam lay Scio, once a flourishing and populous island, now another naked and ghastly memorial of Moslem vengeance. At the breaking out of the Revolution, the inhabitants, owing to their removal from the great scene of action, to the complicated character of their commerce, and being naturally of a quiet disposition, declined involving themselves in the confederation. They were in the enjoyment of privileges to which the other islanders were strangers, and they very naturally felt a reluctance in putting these blessings, small as they were, upon the hazard of a die that might consign them to utter ruin, without perhaps benefiting their brethren.

A suspicion at length, on the part of the Aga, or military governor, of a disposition in them to favor the spirit of revolt that was abroad, put an end to these privileges, and a system of the most oppressive violence was adopted. To these atrocious measures, however, they unresistingly submitted, till their wrongs, increasing with their forbearance, attained an aggravation and malignity that became at last insupportable. Their elders and opulent citizens were cast into prison as hostages—their fields and dwellings plundered by mercenary soldiers, and the sanctity of virtue wantonly outraged. Still they hesitated in adopting the desperate alternative of open resistance, and hung in torturing suspense till roused by the reckless zeal of a few wandering Samians.

They were without an organized plan of operation, without the advantages of discipline, or the implements of war, but arming themselves with such weapons as their forest furnished, they rose on their oppressors. Fortune, for a time, under all these disadvantages, seemed to favor their perilous determination; but the alarm having been given to the Admiral of the Turkish fleet, who was supposed at the time to be at a much greater distance, he immediately anchored in the bay, with a force of forty sail, and opened all their batteries on the devoted town.

The scene that followed has no parallel in the history of modern warfare. It was not the suppression of a rebellion, but the total extermination of a people, who had ever been characterized for their amiable and forgiving dispositions. The town was taken, sacked, and demolished—the priests and elders, who had been cast into prison as hostages, were brought out and impaled alive—and the inhabitants of every age and condition, without regard to sex, were hunted down in every retreat, and massacred in cold blood; till at last, the whole island, so recently teeming with life and beauty, became a Golgotha of groans and blood. If there be a God in heaven, such crimes as these will not go unpunished! The retribution may linger, but it will come in the end like lightning from the cloud.

> The frown of God will on the guilty fall,
>   Like volleyed thunder on the trembling sea;
> Despair o'ercloud them, with its sunless pall,
>   While bursts the wail of their wild agony,
> Like that of nations, when their cities rock,
> And fall in ruins with the earthquake's shock.

Let the man who can reproach the retaliating spirit of the Greek, or the conduct of the Allies at Navarino, visit this island. Let him plant his foot where the flourishing town of Scio once stood, and gaze on a mangled mass of ruins—let him stand where the Attic college rose, with its library of thirty thousand volumes, and its assemblage of seven hundred youth receiving the elements of a classic education, and be presented only with ashes—let him grope through the choked-up streets and call for the once thronging and happy population, and hear not a voice in reply—let him wander through the fields where innumerable vineyards once showered their purple store, and meet with only the bramble and the lizard—and then let him inquire why an island so populous and fruitful as this, has become a waste and a tomb. Let him ask what crime has been committed to draw down this desolating curse.

Let the dead answer: Because we offered resistance to wrongs and outrages, from which the grave is a welcome refuge!—God of my fathers! there was a time when enormities like these would have roused up a spirit, before which the guilty perpetrator would have sunk in shame and despair! But we coolly sit and canvass the policy of a measure that would prevent a repetition of these brutalities. In the name of humanity, what is religion worth, unless it lead us to defend the innocent, and succor the helpless? Let us cast off the name of Christianity, unless we can perform some of its most obvious and imperative duties. If we cannot show ourselves worthy of our calling, let us cast aside the mask, and stand confessed for what we really are. Let us cease to hug a profession which serves only to betray others, and must in the end expose us to the deepest humiliation and reproach.

I ought not, perhaps, to linger here, yet I cannot but ponder, as I pass along, and give vent to feelings excited by objects so full of interest. I cannot restrain the torrent of my soul, when passing a spot that has been thus steeped with the blood of the great and the brave. I wish the sighs, agonies, and despairing shrieks, of which this island was the scene, might float on every breeze through the earth, to sicken men's hearts with the hateful deformities of war.

Could the sufferings and sorrows of which the field of battle has been the source, be gathered up, and speak in their collected wretchedness, the horrors of a thousand earthquakes would be forgotten amidst the lamentations and wailings that would then sweep through the habitations of mankind. God formed man upright, and placed him in a world of beauty and happiness; but he has profaned his high nature, and changed his dwelling into a charnel-house.

But to resume the path of our ship. Leaving Metelin on our larboard quarter, we doubled Cape Karabornu, and entered the Gulf of Smyrna. This arm of the sea strikes up some fifty miles into the main land, and is invaded at several points by an abrupt termination of some mountain range, shouldering its way boldly forward with its stupendous steeps of forest and rock. At other points, a circular sweep of small islands, rising near the shore and bending into the gulf, subserve the purposes of a mole, and give an air of varied beauty to the whole.

On one of these islands, the first in a small chain that swell to the right as we pass up, stood the ancient Clazomenæ. In its day it had the aspect of a neat floating city; the dwellings rising over the oval curve of its form, with light and beautiful effect. The pier connecting it at a distance of one-fourth of a mile with the main, constructed by Alexander, is still standing, and though dilapidated, is sufficiently entire to subserve still the purposes of its original construction.

The Clazomenians, however, were in course of time forced to relinquish their isle of palaces, to escape from the annoying visits of the pirates of Tino. This was very wrong in the Tinoan corsair; his familiarity any where is a great liberty, and he should not extend his freedom to the land. It was a breach of good-breeding which can never be excused, especially as his obtrusiveness was ultimately the means of leaving to this island only the Mosaic pavements, which are still the wonder of the traveller.

Passing Clazomenæ, which now in its desolate beauty bears the name of him who once dwelt in Patmos;—passing near by the small town of Vourla, standing on its two hills, from which the Turks and Franks look at each other, with feelings and habits that will amalgamate when their hills rush together;— passing the excellent and convenient fountain where our ships replenish their exhausted tanks, breathing a blessing, as they depart, to that article in the Mussulman's faith which inculcates these hospitable provisions for the wayfaring and weary;—passing the neglected fortress which was posted here to command the pass, with its guns of ostentatious calibre, and huge marble balls piled around the low embrasure, but which, with all its threatening malignity, like our unfortunate Ticonderoga, may be overawed and silenced from a neighboring height;—passing the invading shoals, which the Hermus, in strange forgetfulness of its classic purity, is depositing, and which, if the sad prophecies of many shrewd observers prove true, will one day stagnate the gulf;—passing many woody steeps, where the huntsmen are still wont to chase the wild-boar and goat, and a succession of valleys, with their groves of the olive, the fig, the almond, the pomegranate, with the trailing grape,—we came at last in front of Smyrna, crowning the head-water, and giving that sort of plump satisfaction, which one feels in knowing that he has arrived indisputably at the end of his journey.

Yet, strange as it may seem, one week will not have elapsed, before the crew of this ship will begin to manifest some of their roving impulses.

> A sailor finds, where'er he goes ashore,
>   One whom he cherishes with some affection;
> But leaving port, he thinks of her no more,
>   Unless it be in some severe reflection
> Upon his wicked ways; then with a sigh
> Resolves on reformation—ere he die.
>
> He thinks his dialect the very best
>   That ever flowed from any human lip,
> And whether in his prayers, or at a jest,
>   Employs the terms for managing a ship;
> And even in death would order up the helm,
> In hope to clear the undiscovered realm.
>
> An order given, and he obeys of course,
>   Though 'twere to run his ship upon the rocks—
> Capture a squadron with a boat's crew force—
>   Or batter down the massive granite blocks
> Of some huge fortress with a swivel, pike,
> Pistol, aught that will throw a ball, or strike.
>
> He never shrinks, whatever may betide;
>   His weapon may be shivered in his hand,
> His last companion shot down at his side,
>   Still he maintains his firm and desperate stand—
> Bleeding and battling—with his colors fast
> As nail can bind them to his shattered mast.

CHAPTER XV.

Far in thy realm withdrawn,
Old empires sit in sullenness and gloom;
And glorious ages gone
Lie deep within the shadow of thy womb.
Childhood, with all its mirth,
Youth, manhood, age, that draws us to the ground,
And last, man's life on earth,
Glide to thy dim dominions, and are bound.
BRYANT.

SMYRNA—ITS SEAMEN—MOTLEY POPULATION—THE TARTAR-JANIZARY—MODERN WARFARE—ENCOUNTERS IN THREADING THE STREETS—FRUIT MARKET—BAZARS—GREEK GIRLS—TURKISH BURIAL-GROUND—THE CHILD UNACQUAINTED WITH DEATH—SMYRNA CONTINUED—RELIGIOUS SECTS—VISIT TO GOVERNOR—HIS PALACE—PIPES—HORSES—TROOPS—COFFEE-HOUSE SCENE—PRAYERS OF THE MUSSULMEN—MARTYRDOM OF POLYCARP—BIRTH-PLACE OF HOMER—PARTING WITH THE READER.

Our ship was now riding quietly at anchor, before Smyrna; and I was casting about to catch a few of the singular sights and incidents of flood and field. The quay was lined with vessels bearing the flags of different nations—clearly indicating the commercial importance of the place. It gave me feelings of peculiar pleasure, to see here in this "distant orient" the stars of my own country floating independently among crowns and crescents. A considerable portion of the craft were the Levantine feluccas—confining the utmost range of their nautical daring to the shores of the Mediterranean—seldom venturing out sight of land—and thus, by this strand-keeping anxiety, encountering a thousand perils from which the open sea is exempt.

The Levantine sailor is as constant and stationary in his habits as are the rocks on which he is so frequently wrecked. He constructs his vessel after the same model which was observed centuries ago, and navigates her as anxiously from island to island, or close along the coast, as did the Argonauts their crowded ship in search of Colchis. His craft, with its wedge-like stem, and triangular stern, has upon it every evidence of rudeness and haste—it is just such a thing as mariners, cast upon some forlorn coast, would drive together. Yet this ill-shapen waddler is made to float in the dream of the classic poet, gracefully as the motion of a swan on the breast of a lake. How poetic illusion vanishes, when the reality comes up!

Among nearer objects on shore, the Marino first attracts the eye. It is bordered by a range of Consular residences, and is constantly trod by a bustling crowd, with every variety of dialect and costume that have obtained since Babel was confounded, and Joseph's coat of many colors stitched together. Smyrna is said to contain a more numerous and vivid representation of national character and peculiarities, than any other city in the world—and I believe it; for I have never read or dreamed of any communities, except those in the moon, that are not appropriately represented here.

This motley crowd have also no tendency whatever to amalgamation. They are as distinct in feature, language, and habits of life, as if they had been but yesterday, by some tremendous convulsion in nature, thrown together from the four quarters of the globe. I have stood by the hour together, displaying my want of good-breeding, in laughing at the ring-streaked and speckled throng as they went by—each uttering a distinct language—and making in the whole a chorus, embracing every sound, from the whispering of the reed in the wind, to the crack in the thunder-cloud.

In appearance and movement the Turk is the most majestic and imposing. His frame is portly and muscular; indicating, in every look and motion, a life of ease and unconcern. His green turban rolls in rich pomp about his head; his blue embroidered spenser descends into a broad red sash, which encircles his waist, supporting at the same time his mounted pistol, and jewelled yataghan; his white trowsers flow full and free to the gathering ankle, where the green slipper receives the foot and terminates the variety. He moves on with a slow, dignified step, allowing to no object even the compliment of an oblique glance—with a countenance of imperturbable gravity, betraying in its composure that self-complacent confidence which leads you to suppose that he is confident of going, whatever may betide, to the seventh heaven of the Prophet.

Near him strides the Armenian, with his large brown calpec, snuff-colored gown, and red boot, meditating on some new banking scheme, or whispering to himself some unfamiliar terms, which he may have occasion to use in the office as dragoman. Then follows the Jew in his careless, promiscuous attire, without weapons, but ready to purchase out all Smyrna for you, at a trifling advance beyond the original cost.

Then darts past the Greek in his red cap, round jacket, and ample kilts, twisting his mustaches, or replenishing his pipe, and snapping his eyes around, as if some sudden peril, or new scheme of cunning had occurred to him. Now dashes by the Tartar-Janizary in his stiff capote, with his trusty weapons in their place, defiance and fidelity in his eye, and on a steed of quick hoof, leading some party of travellers to Sardis, Ephesus, Constantinople, or anywhere else that their curiosity or interest may require.

There is something about this wild being, that strikes the most careless observer. It is not his equipage so much as his bearing, and the fierce unalterable decision and energy which flash from his eye. He looks as one whom you could rely upon in an hour of peril and conflict—whom you would like to have at your side if waylaid by robbers—and who would resolutely deal the deadly blow, though but a fragment of his blade remained. An army composed of such men would make every disputed field and pass a Marathon, or Thermopylæ; and I am not sure but that the interests of humanity would be consulted by such inevitable alternatives. Wars would be more bloody, but they would be of less duration, and occur with vastly less frequency.

We have now so much marching and countermarching—so much scouting and skirmishing—so much shooting behind the bush, bramble, and breastwork—so much rallying and running,—the great and solemn "note of preparation" all the while sounding—that our wars are as long and doubtful as the siege of Troy. In the mean time hundreds are dying —some from random shots and sallies—some from disease and privations incident to camp life—some from having deserted, others from ennui, and not a few from potulency.

The difference is, that in one case men die at once, and in the mass—in the other they die singly and by inches; and I leave it for amateurs in gunpowder and gold lace to determine which involves the greatest expense of treasure and blood. For my own part, I am in favor of carrying the art of war to such a degree of perfection and dispatch, that the fate of a Waterloo or Austerlitz may be decided in fifteen minutes, and then let the survivors go home and attend to their domestic and civil concerns.

As for naval engagements, I have just now but very

little to say on that subject. It is not a pleasant thing to be sunk, and it is not a pleasant thing to be captured; but whether victory or death is to be the result, let it come at once,—no apprehensive manœuvering—no playing off and on—no wearing and tacking—no nice calculations of relative force: be the future a repetition of the past—lay the ship gallantly to her place—and then triumph, or sink, as the tide of battle may turn.

I did not think, when the Tartar dashed past me, that the daring fierceness of his eye would lead me into a lecture on military and naval tactics. But our thoughts are like the enchanter's birds, flying to whatever quarter of the earth or sea the wand is pointed. I should be willing to have mine wander almost anywhere, to get rid of the narrow and dirty alleys of Smyrna. I found myself, in threading some of them, in a predicament truly unbecoming a gentleman,—who, if Shakspeare's definition be good authority, is one that "holds large discourse, looking before and after." I had nothing to discourse to, unless it were dogs, and dirt, and dingy dwellings, —except now and then, when a form moved past me wrapped in a white sheet and close visor, but coming in such a "questionable shape," I could not speak it; for it required more nerve than it would to accost a spectre in the silence and gloom of a sepulchre.

I was told that each of these walking phantoms

was a Turkish female! "Angels and ministers of grace defend us!" If death himself had invented a garb, it could not have been more frightful! How the harem can need any protection beyond it, is inconceivable. Had the arch-deceiver on his first visit to earth encountered Eve in such a disguise, he would have run howling out of Eden. What a world is this in which we live! beautiful in its origin, replete in its resources, but darkened and disfigured by the jealousies and passions of man.

Another source of trouble in threading the narrow streets of Smyrna, is encountering loaded camels that come along in strings of one or two hundred, fastened together, and led by a little jackass, who appears not more foolish and sulky than you feel, in being obliged to squat down upon the first stone, to escape a worse fate from the sweeping range of their enormous sacks. There is no alternative left you, but either to retreat or squat: and if you determine on the latter, you must sit there till the whole interminable file have crept past.

You may then get up and move on, but before you have got ten roods, you will run a narrow chance of being knocked down by the poking end of some long plank, or beam, borne by a bent porter, whose distance from the projecting extremity of his burden, frequently prevents your hearing the dead moan which he gives as the only admonition of his coming. His untimely warning can be of very little service or consolation to you, picking yourself up from the filth of the street, after having ruined a coat, on which your tailor exerted the highest skill of his profession.

These porters are usually Turks, who pay a liberal bounty for the privilege of their occupation. The weight which they carry is incredible; it inclines one to some confidence in the correctness of Doctor Nisborn's theory—that the muscles of the human system are capable of being brought to such a degree of strength and endurance that a man might carry the globe on his back, could he only find a platform beneath on which to walk.

The most bustling and attractive spot in Smyrna is within the Bazars, occupying the centre of the city. These shops, forming a succession of low and convenient arcades, contain all the finery and foppery of the East; and are constantly thronged by the natives, who appear to find half their pleasures and excitements in purchasing trinkets and gewgaws.

Among the most interesting of these purchasers, are the Greek girls, chattering, as you often find them, to some old Turk, Armenian, or Jew, over the queer beauty of some trifle, and laughing with a glee that makes you good-natured with all the world. Their flashing eyes, and sprightly conversation, with the fresh gladness which fills each feature, affords you more pleasure than you can experience among the most refined circles.

I began to think that I had found nature once

SMYRNA

more, and that, too, where it was least and last to be expected. But the grave and demure manner of the Turk, seated on his small carpet, around which his glittering articles were exposed for sale, cooled a little my effervescing enthusiasm. He never smiled, he never looked up, nor appeared to take the slightest interest either in the fair purchasers or the bargain. "What a stupid block is this!" I exclaimed. "There is neither sentiment, civility, nor common reason in him! Why, I would part with the locks from my temples for the mere smiles of such sweet creatures! But this unconscionable fellow sits here as untouched and unconcerned as if he were speculating with gravestones."

I must not, however, be too severe on the Turk, as he atones in some measure for his want of gallantry, in never recommending his articles for what they are not, and never in his change cheating his young customers. This is more than can be said generally of the Franks; they are all smiles and deception, politeness and imposition. The Turk, though vastly less attractive and engaging, is the safer man to deal with. Yet among the shopping ladies of my own country, he would not sell the value of five farthings a year; for he holds no chat, exchanges no smiles, no glances, and pays no compliments. He coolly presents the articles inquired for: if you purchase, well; if not, it is a matter of your concern, not his.

Our ladies would undoubtedly call occasionally at

his shop, but it would be to look at his beard, disturb the slumber of his goods, vex his indolence, and laugh at his self-complacent taciturnity. But though ever so silent and supercilious, there are at least two things in which you may trust a Turk all lengths—money and malice: in both he will be sure to render you your full due, be the consequences what they may to himself.

The fruit-market forms another object of interest in Smyrna. It is the true temple of Pomona. You can scarcely name a product of the garden, field, or grove, that is not to be found here, with a delicious richness of flavor unknown to other climes. The grape, apple, orange, with the fig, pomegranate, and melon, seem to melt in the mouth, and flood the taste with a gushing richness, which lingers there, like the absorbing sensations of the infant receiving its nourishment at the earliest and purest fountain of life. Even the Turk—the solemn tranquillity of whose countenance is seldom disturbed by an emotion of pleasure—as the ripe peach of Sangiac, or the luscious melon of Cassaba, flows over the palate, will look up, as if he had already gained a portion of his future paradise.

There is one species of fruit here, than which the charm of the serpent is not more fascinating and deadly—it is the apricot, with its blushing beauty and tempting flavor; but he who eats it jeopards his life. It is called here by the natives the Kill-Frank, and so it nearly proved to me. I began to think that I had indeed reached the end of my journey—but its tumultuous agonies slowly passed off, and I am still living to stamp it, in all its hypocritical charms, with my unqualified denunciation.

There is nothing so deceptive and fatal, unless it be the mint-julep, which some of our giddy young men take before breakfast to reinstate their nerves, after the potulent excesses of the night previous. They are both fit only for those who have suicidal intentions; yet, if a man has really determined to destroy himself, perhaps the julep is the preferable instrument; for the victim, in his drunken delirium, will not be unavailingly visited by

> "The late repentance of that hour,
> When Penitence hath lost her power,
> To tear one terror from the grave,
> And will not soothe, and cannot save."

The Turkish burial-ground forms one of the most green and fresh features in the landscape around Smyrna. It lies in quiet retirement from the noise and empty parade of the town, and seems in its own stillness to intimate to man the vanity of those objects which so engross his cares, and fever his existence. It is densely shaded with the cypress—that appropriate and beautiful tree, which appears to have been given to guard the tomb, and furnish, in its unfading verdure, a type of our immortality.

The sepulchral monument is a simple column of white marble, surmounted with a tastefully sculptured turban, and bearing frequently a brief sentence from the Koran. No titles are recorded, no virtues proclaimed; it is what it should be, a touching memorial of our own frailty. No one can linger here through a still summer's evening—the soft wind sighing through the branches of the cypress—the moonlight touching the marbles of the dead—the wave of the bay dying with a melancholy murmur on the shore—without departing the wiser and better.

Standing here at this hushed hour of even with these memorials, and dying whispers of nature around me, the world, with its strife, and pride, and noisy pleasures, appeared but as the vanishing away of some troubled dream. Would that the years which remain might partake of the spirit of this scene. Why should life be exhausted in pursuit of that which is so soon to convince us that it is only shadow!

> Sweet Star!—I do invoke thy power
> To soothe and lighten my distress:
> O let thy tranquilizing beam
> Pervade this agitated breast;
> And let me be what thou dost seem—
> A sinless spirit of the blest.
>
> For I am weary of this shroud,
> This mortal shroud of guilt and pain—
> Where every hope seems doubly bowed,
> Beneath an unrelenting chain.

When shall my spirit leave its clay,
Refined from all the dross of earth,
And fit to dwell in that pure ray,
Wherein, sweet Star, thou hadst thy birth?

I know the night is waning fast,
But linger still, sweet one, with me,
And hear this once, as oft thou hast,
My early orison to thee:
O break this dark distempered dream—
This unavailing search for rest—
And let me be what thou dost seem—
A sinless spirit of the blest.

The burial-ground of the Armenian, like that of the Moslem, removed a short distance from the town, and sprinkled with green trees, is a favorite resort not only for the bereaved, but those whose feelings are not thus darkly overcast. I met there one morning a little girl with a half-playful countenance, busy blue eye, and sunny locks, bearing in one hand a small cup of china, and in the other a wreath of fresh flowers.

Feeling a very natural curiosity to know what she could do with these bright things in a place that seemed to partake so much of sadness, I watched her light motions. Reaching a retired grave, covered with a plain marble slab, she emptied the seed—which it appeared the cup contained—into the slight cavities which had been scooped out in the corners of the tablet, and laid the wreath on its pure face.

"And why," I inquired, " my sweet girl, do you put the seed in those little bowls there?" "It is to bring the birds here," she replied, with a half-wondering look—" they will light on this tree," pointing to the cypress above, "when they have eaten the seed, and sing." "To whom do they sing?" I asked—" to each other?—to you?" "Oh no," she quickly replied —" to my sister: she lies there." "But your sister is dead?" "Oh yes, sir; but she hears all the birds sing." "Well, if she hears the birds sing, she cannot see that wreath of flowers?" "But she knows I put it there: I told her, before they took her away from our house, I would come and see her every morning."

"You must," I continued, " have loved that sister very much; but you will never talk with her any more, never see her again." "Yes, sir," she replied, with a brightened look, "I shall see her always in heaven." "But she has gone there already, I hope." "No; she stops under this tree till they bring me here, and then we are going to heaven together." "But she is gone already, my child: you will meet her there, I trust; but certainly she is gone, and left you to come afterwards." She looked at me—her eyes began to swim—I could have clasped her to my heart.

> Come here, my sweet one—be it so,
>   That 'neath this cypress-tree
> Thy sister sees those eyes o'erflow,
>   And fondly waits for thee;—

>That still she hears the young birds sing,
> And feels the chaplet's bloom—
>Which every morn thy light hands bring,
> To dress her early tomb.
>
>And when they bring thee where she lies,
> To share her narrow rest—
>Like sister seraphs, may ye rise
> To join the bright and blest.

The mosques, synagogues, and churches of Smyrna are very numerous, but without any architectural pretensions. In the first, the Mussulman, after having performed his ablutions, lays aside his slippers, and bows himself with an air of profound veneration towards Mecca. In the second, the Jew chants with a deep and solemn tone his Hebraic harmonies, and kneels with mournful confidence towards Jerusalem. In the last, the Greek crosses himself, and looks with penitential solicitude to his patron saint, to the blessed Virgin, or to that great Spirit, the universality of whose presence none can escape.

In neither sect is there much tolerance towards apostates from their faith. The follower of Mohammed, who deserts his faith, loses his head; the deluded child of Abraham, who ceases to expect the promised Messiah, goes to the bastinado or the dungeon; and the unreflecting Greek, who may assume the turban, or turn away from the altar of the Madonna, forfeits the friendship of his relatives, and secures the scorn of his foes.

A convert from either sect is looked upon by his brethren as an apostate from truth, hope, and heaven He has no safety or repose, but in an escape to other lands, where the rights of conscience are recognized and respected. Yet, while this unmingled hatred and cruelty are visited upon apostacy, these different sects manifest towards each other, in their collective capacities, a forbearance and civility that is truly commendable. Their indignation appears to light simply on those who have swerved from their own faith.

The Turk, while he beheads his brother, who may have ceased to call on the Prophet, has apparently no objection that the Jew should still expect his deliverer, or that the Greek should still cross himself at the shrine of his saint. His tolerance flows not so much from that charity which "suffereth long, thinketh no evil, and is not easily provoked," as from a deep and settled contempt for the short-sighted beings who may differ from him in their religious creed. He looks upon the Koran as such a splendid and well-authenticated revelation, that a man who can refuse it his belief, and forego the pleasures which it promises, evinces, in his estimation, a stupidity and dogged obstinacy of character, which forfeits him all claim to consideration. He would seemingly regard it as a degradation in him to make a proselyte of such an incorrigible, miserable being.

Yet, in secular affairs, in business, in trade, the

Turk meets you with a civility, frankness, and honesty, which you are disposed to construe into a complimentary confidence and respect. But this is his nature,— he would be the same were he purchasing shells of a Hottentot, or furs of a Siberian savage. His respectful demeanor flows from an innate pride and dignity of spirit, and not from the suggestions of any flattering regard for you. He is above a mean trick— though unequalled in that duplicity of character which Joab revealed in taking his friend Amasa by the beard, kissing him, and ending the fraternal embrace by stabbing him under the fifth rib.

The most extensive and sumptuous edifice in Smyrna is the palace of the Musselim, or Governor. It is pleasantly situated near the harbor, in the southern section of the city, and is surrounded by an extensive garden. Our consul, Mr. Ofley, with Captain Read, and the officers of the Constellation, called on his Excellency, in accordance with an appointment previously arranged. Passing a mounted guard in the court, and ascending a broad flight of plain stairs, we were ushered into an extensive saloon, surrounded by a rich ottoman, in which the Governor was seated, with his feet drawn under him, in the true turco modo.

He received us with a courtly ease, and gratifying familiarity of manner; and immediately on our being seated, commenced a scattering series of questions, in which he betrayed both ignorance and shrewdness.

His mind ran incessantly from one topic to another, like a fox first confined to the grated apertures of his cage. Whatever the answer might be to any question, it appeared to excite little surprise, and sometimes he would cut it off, by putting another so foreign to the last, that the contrast would force an involuntary smile.

His questions were sometimes involved in a little mist, but they generally reached their most remote object with singular directness and celerity. The moment he spoke, his countenance lighted up as if some new thought had suddenly flashed on his spirit; and then again it would as instantaneously subside into its customary good-humored apathy.

He appeared to be about fifty years of age, and to possess a constitution impaired by anxiety and sedentary habits. His dress was a red velvet cap, with a rich blue tassel depending from the centre of the crown—a loose robe of the glossy angora—with full trowsers, and close vest of the same light and elegant material. His slippers were not seen, his feet being drawn up under him on the sofa, where he sat with a greater ease of attitude than I ever saw assumed on chair or tripod.

We had not been long seated when fifteen or twenty handsomely attired attendants entered with hands crossed in front, in token of submission; and each bearing a pipe, which he presented to us in a kneeling posture. The stems of these narcotic auxiliaries of Turkish luxury were of the native cherry, elegantly slender, and seven or eight feet in length, with a bowl of argillaceous substance, and a long mouth-piece of pure amber. One end rested on a silver plate near the centre of the room, and the other it was expected you would place to your lips with delighted suction. He that never smoked before with such a pipe as this, would be excused if he began the giddy experiment.

The first sensations of love, with the dilating heart and mysterious sympathy, could not be more sweet and inexplicably delightful, than the soft vapors of this aromatic plant, winding along through the cool and polished tube, and finally flowing through amber, into the mouth. Cynics and quacks may prattle as much as they please against the pipe, yet no man who wishes to be soothed when he is weary, or exhilarated when he is depressed, will decline the Turkish chibouque.

> Thy quiet spirit lulls the laboring brain,
>   Lures back to thought the flights of vacant mirth;
> Consoles the mourner, soothes the couch of pain,
>   And breathes contentment round the humble hearth;
> While savage warriors, softened by thy breath,
> Unbind the captive hate had doomed to death.
>
> Thy vapor bathes the Caffre's sooty walls,
>   And fills the mighty Czar's imperial dome;
> Rolls through Byzantine's oriental halls,
>   And floats around the Arab's tented dome;
> Melts o'er the anchorite's repentant meal,
> And shades the lightning of the Tartar's steel.

While enjoying the pleasures of the precious weed, the attendant kneeled before each with a few sips of coffee, in an extremely small and elegant cup of china, resting in a delicate stand of filigreed gold. It was taken without sugar or cream, and though but a swallow in quantity, it contained more of the real juice of the Moca-berry, than is usually found in our cups of much more promising dimensions. Coffee with us is frequently about as strongly impregnated with the berry, as the passing stream in which the native plant may happen to cast its shadow.

After having our pipes several times replaced by fresh ones, and filling the saloon with a cloud of floating fragrance, and drinking a glass of cool sherbet, and touching on all topics within the ranging imagination of the Musselim, we were to depart, when his Excellency informed us that his horses had been brought into the green, and the troops of the garrison paraded for our inspection, and he might have added—for the gratification of his own pride.

We found the horses well worthy of their princely master—plump, smooth, and playful—full of energy and fire, yet submissive to the bit—and prancing under their riders as if motion were a new, delightful sensation. Several of them were of the Arabian blood, with small muscular limbs—graceful and athletic conformation, with a flowing mane, free nostril, bright eye, and a curved neck, in which the very thunder seemed to lurk.

The Mussulman preserves his steed unmaimed and entire, just as nature formed him, and bestows upon him the most kind and constant attentions; and not without just reason, for a Turk without his horse would be almost as deplorably conditioned as a Catholic without his beads. The one would give up all hope of seeing his nearest neighbor, and the other of reaching heaven.

If a man proposes running away with a horse at the risk of being hung or decapitated, I should advise him to take the Arabian; for in the first place, he could not be overtaken except on a steed of equally astonishing fleetness; and in the next place, if overtaken and bow-strung, or made to swing so very awkwardly from the ground, he will have the satisfaction of knowing that he forfeited his life in an effort to avail himself of the noblest animal on earth. Still I would not, in this world of stern law and unforgiving justice, advocate even this kind of magnificent plunder, for there is no romance in the gallows—no racing or riding in the grave.

I wish I could say as much in favor of the Governor's troops as his steeds—for a more unsoldierlike body of men I never saw under arms. They reminded me of one of our backwoods militia trainings, where no two have coats or corn-stalks alike. The apology given for their appearance was, that they had just been driven in from the country.

The mode of raising recruits here, exhibits the true

genius of the Ottoman government; it is to send out a force sufficient to reconnoitre all the small villages,—where the youth, who cannot make their escape, are seized, tied together, and driven into the encampment, to fight, nolens aut volens. If they show a disposition to desert, they are pretty sure to be shot, or bastinadoed to death; and if they remain, their fate may be more slow, but it will come with equal suffering and certainty, in the charge of the enemy, the destructiveness of the plague, or the tyrannical authority and merciless inconsideration of their commanders.

Let those who would dissolve our Union, and render us in our scattered strength the prey of foreign avarice and power, look here and see what the loss of liberty really is, and take a lesson of wholesome admonition. These poor fellows have been wrenched away from their parents and homes, chained together as culprits, driven over parching sands to this garrison, and are now, in a few days to be marched off under their arms, with a prospect of a more precarious subsistence, into the burning plains of Syria, there to perish in battle, or wither away with fatigue and famine.

But whether the sands of the desert, or the field of blood be their grave, their homes will know them no more! They have left forever behind them all that the earth holds dear. The most foolish and frantic disunionist in our country who can look at this, and not feel compunctions of shame, and devote himself anew to the great cause of united liberty, is unworthy of the age in which he lives, and of the country that has given him birth.

But to return to Smyrna. Through the southern section of the city swells a very high hill, commanding a wide range of land and water, and bearing the name of Mount Pagus. It is surmounted by a Genoese castle, reared on the huge foundations of one constructed by Alexander the Great. The castle is now unfortified, and has only the frowning aspect of its gigantic proportions to strengthen its friends, or intimidate its foes.

In our ascent to the castle, we passed over the obliterated foundations of the amphitheatre, where Polycarp was martyred amid thousands who had assembled to wonder at his fanatical fortitude, or jeer his recanting timidity. But that great apostle of truth felt too deeply the responsibility of his situation, to consult the weaker impulses of his nature. He had heard the warning voice of the Son of God, calling to him, through the sainted exile of Patmos, as the angel of the church of Smyrna, to be "faithful unto death;" he stood untremblingly true to the confidence with which he had been divinely honored; and passed from the sorrows and agonies of martyrdom, to receive the promised "crown of life."

His devoted example inspired hundreds with kindred emotions,—it strengthened the weak, decided the doubting, and confirmed the wavering; it made the church of Smyrna one of those firm outposts of Christianity which no bribes could seduce, and no terrors or trials disarm. She stood simple, erect, and uncompromising—leaning upon an unshaken faith in the promises of her Redeemer, and looking forward to the day of her deliverance and triumph. That day came, and the humble cause which she had espoused, sweeping away the altars and fanes of idolatry, enthroned itself upon the affections and confidence of the civilized world.

From the battlements of the castle we could trace the Meles, winding through its fertile valley, and mingling its waters with the broad wave of the bay. We wandered down to the bank of this classic stream, and lingered around the green spot, which, it is contended, was the birth-place of Homer. The young, beautiful, and unfortunate Critheis—if the story be as true as it is full of scandal—fled to this secluded shade to escape the exposure and shame of becoming a mother; little thinking, in her solitude and anguish, that the offspring of her erring fondness was to string a lyre to which the whole earth would listen.

She sunk to an early grave, and left her boy, as most do who thus err, to wander destitute and forsaken. But nature was not denied him,—he strayed among her founts and flowers, visited her recesses of deeper beauty, listened to the tone of her thousand voices, caught the spirit that quickens through her mysterious frame, and poured forth his exulting sensations in a tide of imperishable song. Though unknown, except in his numbers, he has charmed the world into an immortal remembrance and affection. The posterity of those who left him to famish and die, have contended for the honor of his birth, and reared their richest monuments to his name. Soon or late the claims of genius must be acknowledged and felt. Time, while it levels all other distinctions, will leave untouched those created by the mind.

The prayers of the Mussulman at the rising and setting of the sun, and at mid-day, never fail to attract the ear and eye of the stranger in Smyrna. You hear at that hour, from all the minarets of the mosques, a voice uttering, in tones deep and solemn, the invocation—" Come to prayer—there is no God but God, and Mahomet is his prophet—come to prayer—I summon you with a clear voice." The faithful fall on their knees, and, with their faces turned towards Mecca, bow themselves three times to the earth; repeating between each prostration a brief prayer; then slowly rising, seem to carry into their occupation a portion of the solemnity which characterizes this scene.

Your impression is, that the follower of the Prophet, however erroneous may be his faith, is not ashamed of his religion—that he is not the being who will forego his prayers out of a shrinking, unbecoming regard for the presence or prejudices of others—and your respect for him, in this particular, is in proportion to his seeming want of it for you. Let those who put away the good old family Bible on some unseen shelf, and who go to bed at night without their domestic devotions—if a stranger be present—take a hint from the Mussulman.

The most silent spot in Smyrna is that which you would expect to find the most noisy; that is, the cafenet, or hotel. You will find here at every hour of the day thirty or forty Turks, seated under the trees which deeply shade the court—now and then giving a long whiff, and relieving the intervals by a sip of coffee, which atones for the absence of cream and sugar in its strength. All this while not a word is spoken; not a sound is heard, save that of the little fountain, and even this, in the faint lapse of its notes, seems falling asleep. On one occasion, and but one, I saw this silence broken up.

I had observed two Turks, seated on opposite sides of the court, casting at each other, between their whiffs, looks of rather a menacing character. No words, however, passed—no inimical motions were made—nothing indicated anger, except the occasional scorching glance of a deep, black eye; when, suddenly dropping their pipes, they sprang at the same instant upon their feet, and discharged their pistols: but neither took effect. I expected to see them rush at each other with a plunging yatagan; but what was my surprise, when I saw each leisurely return his pistol to his belt, and resume his seat as composedly as if he had merely risen to pluck the orange that depended from the branch over his head.

The company, so far from being thrown into confusion and uproar, continued silently to smoke their pipes; the affair appeared not to furnish a topic of conversation sufficiently interesting to relieve the silence that ensued. This feature of the scene I liked; it shows that the Mussulman, however irrespective he may be of other salutary injunctions, strictly obeys what sailors call the eleventh commandment—thou shalt mind thine own business.

Among the most pleasant rides in the vicinity of Smyrna, is that to Bournebat, leading through a succession of vineyards and olive-groves, with the tulip and ranunculus blooming around in wild profusion. The village is ornamented with many elegant mansions, belonging to merchants in Smyrna, who seek here a refuge from the heat, dust, and noise of the town. We were here introduced into the summer residence of Mr. Offey, the American Consul, to whose influence and hospitable attentions we were indebted for many pleasures, connected with our cruise in the Levant. His agency in establishing the relations which now exist between us and the Ottoman government, entitles him to the respect and gratitude of his country.

Nor should I fail to mention here the many tokens of assiduous kindness which we received from our worthy countrymen, Messrs. Clark and Stith, merchants of a character and standing that do honor to America. Nor should I pass by the cheerful hearth and benevolent efforts of the Rev. Mr. Brewer. His schools are diffusing a spirit of intelligence and inquiry among the Greeks, that will one day speak for itself.

The favorable position of Smyrna for commerce, is the main source of its wealth and political importance. It has been successively plundered by the enemy, overthrown by the earthquake, depopulated by the plague, and consumed by the flame; but it has risen again to increased opulence and power, on the force of its commercial advantages.

Alexander manifested his extraordinary shrewdness and judgment in its location. It would seem as if he intended to found a city that should survive all the hostile agents by which it could, in any possible event, be assailed. It has been for centuries without fortress or wall; and though often reduced, in its sad vicissitudes, to a ruin and a tomb, yet it now embraces the most dense and thriving population within the wide dominion of the Porte.

The female beauty which once brought to it the sculptor and painter for originals, may in some measure have disappeared; but its commercial facilities have assembled within it, from the most distant realms, another class of beings, whose enterprise contributes vastly more to its wealth and prosperity. It may look with composure at its temporary misfortunes, for it must stand and thrive, so long as the caravans of Persia can move, the vintage of the teeming year come round, and the ship hold its course over the deep.

Nor need any be deterred from a residence here by apprehensions of Turkish treachery and violence. The authority recognized in a Consular representative is nowhere held more sacred and inviolable. Heads may fall like rain-drops from an April cloud, but beneath the flag of his country the foreigner is safe. It is an ægis which the most profane weapon of the Mussulman dares not touch.

And now, reader, I must bid you adieu. But if you have not been too much offended with some of my hasty expressions, if you have been amused by the light incidents of my story, if over its simple pages your hours have passed with a less perceptible weight, meet me here again. That brilliant barge which rocks so lightly on the wave of this Bay is to take me and others to the strand of Ilium.

Join our company, willing to be pleased, and I will show you the palace of Priam, Achilles' tomb, and Helen's gushing fount. We will then pass up between the wildly wooded shores of the Dardanelles, on to the bright bosom of the Marmora, and watch the city of Constantine, emerging in splendor from the wave. Glancing at its domes and its delicate minarets, we will wind our way up the

Golden Horn into the valley of Sweet Waters; we will stray through the romantic dells of Belgrade—along the beautiful banks of the Bosphorus, catch the traits of those who dwell there in oriental gayety, and returning, mount again to the deck of our ship, sail to the purple shores of Greece, walk around among the magnificent ruins of Athens, and visit the sweet isles of the Ægean.

All this I promise you, if you will accord me your company, and then you will find me more attentive than I have been—less forgetful of your tastes, and less captious under my own slight provocations.

But before we part, come with me down to the beach of this moon-lit bay, for at this still hour of the evening we have nothing to fear—nothing can break on our solitude—and let me tell you here, under the light of these sweet stars, what I love.

I love to wander on the shore of ocean,
    To hear the light wave ripple on the beach;
For there's a music in their murm'ring motion,
    The softest sounds of earth could never reach—
A cadence breathing more of joy than plaint,
Like the last whispers of a dying saint.

I love to wander, on a star-lit night,
    Along the breathing margin of a lake,
Whose tranquil bosom mirrors to the sight
    The dewy stars; where not a wave nor wake
Disturbs the slumbering surface, nor a sound
Is heard from out the deep-hushed forest round.

The vesper-star sleeps in that silent water,
   So sweetly fair, so tenderly serene,
You fondly think it is the bright-eyed daughter
   Of that pure element, and, breathless, lean
To catch its beauty, as if bent above
The face of *one* you only live to love.

THE END.

THE SEA AND THE SAILOR.

CHAPTER I.

I LOVE the sailor—his eventful life—
　His generous spirit—his contempt of danger—
His firmness in the gale, the wreck, and strife:
　And though a wild and reckless ocean-ranger,
God grant he make that port, when life is o'er,
Where storms are hushed, and billows break no more.

THE OCEAN IN ITS GRANDEUR AND SUBLIMITY—THE OCEAN AS A THEATRE OF MAN'S POWER—TRIUMPHS OF SAIL AND STEAM—ITS EFFECT ON CHARACTER—THE TRAITS OF THE SAILOR—HIS GENEROSITY AND COURAGE—THE TAR IN THE CONSTITUTION—ON DECK AND ON THE PARAPET—OBEDIENCE TO ORDERS—INSENSIBILITY TO DANGER.

THE most fearful and impressive exhibitions of power known to our globe belong to the Ocean. The volcano, with its ascending flame and falling torrents of fire, and the earthquake, whose footstep is on the ruin of cities, are circumscribed in the desolating range of their visitations. But the ocean, when it once rouses itself in its chainless strength, shakes a thousand shores with its storm and thunder. Navies of oak and iron are tossed in mockery from its crest, and armaments, manned by the strength and courage of millions, perish among its bubbles.

The avalanche, shaken from its glittering steep, if it rolls to the bosom of the earth, melts away, and is lost in vapor; but if it plunge into the embrace of the ocean, this mountain mass of ice and hail is borne about for ages in tumult and terror: it is the drifting monument of the ocean's dead. The tempest on land is impeded by forests, and broken by mountains, but on the plain of the deep it rushes unresisted; and when its strength is at last spent, ten thousand giant waves, which it has called up, still roll its terrors onward.

The mountain lake and the meadow stream are inhabited only by the timid prey of the angler; but the ocean is the home of the leviathan—his ways are in the mighty deep. The glittering pebble, and the rainbow-tinted shell, which the returning tide has left on the shore as scarcely worthy of its care, and the watery gem, which the pearl-diver reaches at the peril of his life, are all that man can filch from the treasures of the sea. The groves of coral which wave over its pavements, and the halls of amber which glow in its depths, are beyond his approaches, save when he goes down there to seek amid their silent magnificence his burial monument.

The island, the continent, the shores of civilized and savage realms, the capitals of kings, are worn by time, washed away by the wave, consumed by the flame, or sunk by the earthquake; but the ocean still remains, and still rolls on in the greatness of abated strength. Over the majesty of its form and the marvels of its might, time and disaster have no power. Such as creation's dawn beheld, it rolleth now. The vast clouds of vapor which roll up from its bosom float away to encircle the globe: on distant mountains and deserts they pour out their watery treasures, which gather themselves again in streams and torrents, to return, with exulting bound, to their parent ocean.

These are the messengers which proclaim in every land the exhaustless resources of the sea; but it is reserved for those who go down in ships, and who do business on the great waters, to see the works of the Lord and his wonders in the deep. Let one go upon deck in the middle watch of a still night, with naught above him but the silent and solemn skies, and naught around and beneath him but an interminable waste of waters, and with the conviction that there is but a plank between him and eternity, a feeling of loneliness, solitude, and desertion, mingled with a sentiment of reverence for the vast, mysterious, and unknown, will come upon him with a power, all unknown before, and he might stand for hours entranced in reverence and tears.

Man also has made the ocean the theatre of *his* power. The ship in which he rides that element is one of the highest triumphs of his skill. At first this floating fabric was only a frail barque, slowly urged by the laboring oar. The sail at length arose and spread its wings to the wind. Still he had no power to direct his course when the lofty promontory sunk from sight, or the orbs above him were lost in clouds. But the secret of the magnet is at length revealed to him, and his needle now settles with a fixedness which love has stolen as the symbol of its constancy to the polar star.

Now, however, he can dispense even with sail, and wind, and flowing wave. He constructs and propels his vast engines of flame and vapor, and through the solitude of the sea, as over the solid earth, goes thundering on his track. On the ocean, too, thrones have been lost and won. On the fate of Actium was suspended the empire of the world. In the Gulf of Salamis, the pride of Persia found a grave; and the crescent set forever in the waters of Navarino; while at Trafalgar and the Nile, nations held their breath,

> As each gun
> From its adamantine lips
> Spread a death-shade round the ships,
> Like the hurricane's eclipse
> Of the sun.

But of all the wonders appertaining to the ocean, the greatest, perhaps, is its transforming power on man. It unravels and weaves anew the web of his moral and social being. It invests him with feelings, associations, and habits, to which he has been an entire stranger. It breaks up the sealed fountains of his nature, and lifts his soul into features prominent as the cliffs which beetle over its surge. Once the adopted child of the ocean, he can never bring back his entire sympathies to land. He will still move in his dreams over that vast waste of waters, still bound in exultation and triumph through its foaming billows. All the other realities of life will be comparatively tame, and he will sigh for his tossing element, as the caged eagle for the roar and arrowy light of his mountain cataracts.

But let us leave generalities, and look more closely at the distinctive features of character which an ocean-life impresses on the sailor. Among these, generosity is, perhaps, the most prominent. You may take the most gnarled and knotted heart that can be found, one where a kindly emotion seems never to have existed, and send it out on the sea, and it will soon begin to crack and expand.

This same being, who, if he had remained on land, might have seen orphans starve around him without a pitying impulse, and cheated the poor sexton out of his fee for tolling the bell at his burial, will, in the development of his ocean-life and character, be seen dividing his last shilling with an unfortunate shipmate; and when all is gone, show no dismay, or distrust of

> "The sweet little cherub who sits up aloft,
> And watches the life of poor Jack."

You never see a sailor, when he falls in with a

fellow-being in distress, no matter in what clime born, or what may be the color of his skin, play the Levite; he acts the good Samaritan, and as naturally, too, as the blood rolls from his heart to the extremities of his frame.

Nor does the sailor ever meet a national foe in a spirit of malice, or of personal hostility. He fights not for himself, but for his flag; not for his own honor, but the honor of his country. When the enemy has once struck his colors, he would consider another shot an act of cruelty and disgrace. If the enemy's ship be in a sinking condition, he dashes through the boisterous waves to reach her, even at the imminent peril of being carried down in the maelstrom of her disappearing hulk.

He scorns stratagem with an enemy, or any advantage which gives him the victory on unequal terms. He would hardly consent to engage a man-of-war in a steamer armed with a Paixhan gun, where he might quietly take his distance and riddle her at such a remove that her guns could not reach him. He would prefer throwing himself alongside of her in a ship of equal capacity, and then battling it out with her on what he would consider fair and honorable terms. I once asked an old sailor who had been in three signal engagements in the last war with Great Britain, and victorious in each, what he thought of the Torpedo system of blowing up an enemy. "Sir," said the old sailor, touching his tarpaulin, "I think it was a sneaking way of doing the business. It is only the assassin, sir, that stabs in the dark."

Courage is another feature of character strongly impressed on the sailor by his ocean-life. He is always in peril; he lives with but a plank between him and eternity. If the sea be smooth, and the sky free of clouds at the setting sun, still before his midnight watch is out, his spars may be falling in fragments around him, and the tempest roaring through his shrouds like the blast of the Judgment trump. The caverns of the sea are full of sailors, who have sprung from their hammocks and gone down before even one prayer could be uttered.

> O'er their dark unfathomed slumbers
> Wakes no human wail or knell,
> But the mermaid pours her numbers
> Through her wild eleginc shell.

Thus accustomed to danger in all the forms which the gale, the breaker, the lightning of the cloud, and the iron hail of the enemy can present, the sailor becomes a stranger to fear. Peril is his element as much as water is that of the leviathan that floats around him. He has, therefore, no new character to assume, when summoned to a work of desperate daring. The same strong muscles, the same unshrinking courage, the same indomitable resolution which are now to be tasked, have been tested in other life-suspending emergencies. He rushes into the death-struggle like the war-horse, whose arching neck is clothed with thunder.

When the Constitution fell in with the Guerriere, and it was hardly yet ascertained whether she was a ship-of-the-line or a frigate, a sturdy sailor walked aft to Commodore Hull, and said in an eager, determined tone, "Commodore, if you will lay us alongside, sir, we will do our duty." "Clear the ship for action," cried the commodore; and they *did* do their duty. They captured the enemy before his recovery from the astounding effects of their first broadside. They broke the charm of British invincibility, and filled the heart of the nation with courage and resolution.

Not only on the battling deck, heaped with the dying and the dead, is the sailor firm, but when thrown upon land he is the last to quit the unavailing battery. When others had fled at Bladensburg with a speed that might have taken them to the foot of the Rocky Mountains, if not the shores of the Pacific, one stout fellow still remained at his gun, and was found when the enemy was within a few rods of him, very coolly ramming home to give him another shot. He was a regular Jack tar, who had very little respect for the lessons of the old distich:

> "He who fights and runs away,
> May live to fight another day."

When an order reaches the ear of a sailor, he never

stops to inquire what may be the consequences to himself of carrying that order into effect. The preservation of his own limbs and life comes not into the account. The order is all-paramount with him, and he obeys it as if it possessed an irresistible power over the energies of his will. It may be one full of the extremest peril, as is often the case, still he executes it as promptly as if danger were a fiction, and death a dream.

> An order given, and he obeys of course,
>   Though 'twere to run his ship upon the rocks,
> Capture a squadron with a boat's crew force,
>   Or batter down the massive granite blocks
> Of some huge fortress with a swivel, pike,
> Or aught whereby to throw a ball, or strike.
>
> He never shrinks, whatever may betide:
>   His cutlass may be shivered in his hand,
> His last companion shot down at his side,
>   Still he maintains his firm and desperate stand;
> Bleeding and battling, with his colors fast
> As nail can bind them to his shattered mast.

CHAPTER II.

> Such men fall not unmourned: their winding-sheet
> May be the ocean's deep, unresting wave;
> But o'er that grave will wandering winds repeat
> The dirge of millions for the fallen brave;
> While each high deed survives in safer trust,
> Than those consigned to mound or marble bust.

THE SAILOR'S CHIVALRIC DEVOTION TO WOMAN—ROUGHNESS AND HONESTY IN COURTSHIP—HIS WAY OF BEARING UNREQUITED LOVE—PRODIGALITY AND ITS CAUSES—JACK AT THE BUNKER-HILL FAIR—HIS PRICE FOR A KISS—EXPLOITS OF THE CREW OF THE NORTH CAROLINA—BUYING A HOTEL FOR A BALL—GIVING IT BACK TO THE LANDLORD—SUPERSTITION OF THE SAILOR—INTOLERANCE OF THE SHARK AND THE CAT—JACK'S WAY OF GETTING A BREEZE—BELIEF IN GHOSTS AND THE SPIRIT WORLD—A MESSMATE FROM THE DEAD—INDIGNATION AT INJUSTICE—JACK'S DEFINITION OF A NONDESCRIPT—BATTLE BETWEEN THE AMERICAN ROUNDABOUTS AND THE FRENCH DRESS-COATS.

ANOTHER prominent feature in the character of the sailor is his rough, honest, heartfelt esteem for the fair sex. His devotedness has all the generosity which characterized the highest noontide of chivalry, but without any of the follies and crimes which belonged to that system of self-immolation. The exploits of the knight-errant have been the very soul of romance and song, while the death-daring love of poor Jack has been hymned only by the billow.

His love, it is true, has not that exquisite refinement which expresses itself in the delicate tints and odors of flowers, but it gushes up warm and fresh out of his strong heart.

Were he to encounter you in a nocturnal serenade, with your sentimental eyes rolled up to the lattice of your lady-love, and with guitar in hand singing,

> Love wakes and weeps, while Beauty sleeps;
> Oh! for music's softest numbers,
> To prompt a theme, for Beauty's dream,
> Soft as the pillow of her slumbers;—

were he to meet you in this interesting attitude, he would be very likely to ask you what you wanted to disturb that fair sleeper up there for, as it was not her watch on deck, and he would advise you to call upon her when she should be wide awake, and tell her like an honest man, that you loved her, and ask her to ship with you for life.

Were the gentle being whom you thus tenderly accost in these dulcet strains, in a house enveloped in flames, or amid the surge of boiling breakers, poor Jack's rough humanity would rescue her before your exquisite sentimentality had sufficiently recovered its wits to ascertain whether any thing could be done or not; for he excels all men in presence of mind and promptitude of action.

When you offer yourself to a lady and she refuses you, you would be gratified, perhaps, were she at last to wed a knave or fool, simply because she declined marrying you. Not so with poor Jack—he wishes her all happiness, and hopes to meet her again on the great ocean of life; and does he meet her there, and in destitution, she shall not want while a shot is left in the locker. Such is Jack's retaliation of unrequited love. Were there more of his frankness and generosity in such matters generally, there would be fewer unhappy marriages; for who ever heard of a sailor's troubling the courts for a divorce? If he cannot make good weather on one tack, then he tries another; but he never scuttles his ship, or throws his *mate* overboard. A world without woman in it would be to him like a garden without a flower, like a grove without a bird to sing in its branches, like an evening sky without a star to smile through its blue depths.

Another prominent trait in the character of the sailor is his prodigality. No other being earns his money through such perils and hardships as he, and yet no one spends it so freely. The wages of a long South Sea voyage, or of a three years' cruise, are spent in a few months, often in a few weeks. The reason of this is the comparatively few convivial occasions which cheer his hard lot, and a conviction that with him life at longest is short.

His maxim is, live while you live—and that, it must be confessed, by no means in the highest or best sense: he says to himself, make sure of the present: he dips of the current as it flows. I have often tried to induce the sailor to lay up his earnings, to put his money into the Savings Bank; and have told him, by way of inducement, that he would find it there with interest in his old age. "Ah!" replies the sailor, "and suppose I should die in the mean time?" This apprehension of an early death, and the novelties of the shore, make the sailor a prodigal. He never, however, throws away his money in the luxuries of the table; it is generally in some freak of fancy, some whim which would never enter the imagination of any other being, nor his own perhaps, either, unless inflamed with the boozy wine.

At the Bunker Hill Fair in Boston, among the crowds which entered the magnificent hall where it was held, there rolled in a frank Jack-tar of the deep. He moved along in his white pants, his blue roundabout, and new tarpaulin, till one of the ladies, and the most beautiful one in the hall, arrested him at her stand with a solicitation to buy some of her fancy articles. "No," said the sailor, "I don't think I want any of them 'ere spangles, but I will give you twenty dollars for a kiss." "Agreed," said the fair, when the sailor saluted her on the cheek, and, drawing out his purse, handed her twenty dollars. "Cheap enough at that," said Jack, and rolled on. Those who have never studied the sailor's character, may impute to him improper feelings. Not so: he would have perilled his life to protect that lady from indignity; and never was a thorough sea-bred sailor known to insult a virtuous woman.

When the crew of the North Carolina, on her return from the Mediterranean, were discharged at Norfolk, several hundreds of them started in company for New York. They arrived, at length, in the State of Delaware, which they crossed on foot, (for railroads were then unknown,) and, night coming on, they cast about for quarters. The keeper of the hotel in the village at which they had arrived, looking at their numbers, and recollecting that his large hall had been engaged for a ball that night, declined all attempts at accommodating them. The mention of the ball struck the imagination of the sailors at once. They asked him what he would take for his hotel; he stated the sum, which was moderate, as the building, though large, was old and somewhat decayed. Instantly they raised the amount, handed it over to the astonished keeper, and took possession of the premises.

The ladies and gentlemen soon began to arrive, and were received with great cordiality by the sailors. The old hotel was for once brilliantly illuminated, and every attention was paid to the ladies which the respectful homage of poor Jack could suggest. When the gentlemen called for their bills, they were informed by the sailors that no charge had been made, and no money would be accepted. As the company departed, three cheers were given to the ladies. The sailors remained through the following day and night enjoying their snug harbor; and, the next morning, calling for the landlord of whom they had purchased the hotel, made him a present of it, on the condition that he would never again turn away a sailor so long as a foot of unoccupied room remained.

Now, whoever heard of landsmen purchasing a hotel from a freak of fancy, and then giving it back again to its previous owner? It is that sort of business operation which belongs only to the sailor; but, after all, it is quite as safe and profitable as many of the speculations into which much sounder heads sometimes enter.

These are a few illustrations, out of a hundred that might be quoted, of the benevolent, careless prodigality of the sailor. He purchases a hotel to secure a night's lodging, gives twenty dollars for the privilege of respectfully saluting a lady, and empties his purse for a song! This trait in his character can never be made to undergo a radical change. It is blended with the very elements of his moral and social being. It can never be reached by the lessons of a cool, calculating prudence: it is above the influence of time and the force of circumstances.

You who censure this trait in the sailor, did you ever reflect that you often spend your money for that which contributes as little to your substantial comfort and happiness as he does? You spend thousands for splendid furniture in your dwellings which never yet started a pure impulse of pleasure, or relieved one pang of sorrow, but which you are vain enough to exhibit, and others weak enough to envy.

Superstition is another characteristic feature of the sailor. He will never go to sea on Friday if he can help it, and still insists that the horse-shoe be nailed to the foremast, as a protection against the visits of the Evil One. How this rim of rough iron came to be regarded as possessing such a potent charm, his own philosophy, not mine, must explain. The Evil One, in his opinion, always tries to conceal his club-foot, and this shoe would so exactly fit it, that its very sight repels the intruder.

A sailor regards the presence of a shark about a ship a most fatal omen to the sick on board. The highest exultation I ever witnessed on board a man-of-war, was occasioned by harpooning a shark that was hanging about us while a favorite sailor was sick; though I rather doubt if it was the harpoon that saved the sailor's life; and yet it may have had as much agency in it as the doctor's pills.

A sailor will never tolerate in his ship a member of the feline species, especially if she has a dark complexion. We took on board at Gibraltar a large, beautiful black cat; we were bound to Mahon, and, as it happened, encountered a tedious succession of light head-winds and dead calms. The sailors at last began to look at our new-comer as a sort of Jonas on board. The next morning the black cat was missing, and suspicions fell very justly on an old sailor, who had been heard to threaten her life. I asked this old sailor what could induce him to commit such an act of cruelty. "Sir," said he, "we have been boxing about here for two weeks without making any headway, and I determined at last to put that black cat out of the way. I didn't murder her, sir; I tied a shot to her and she sunk without a scream; and now you see, sir, we have got a fine breeze."

The sailor is also a profound believer in ghosts: one of these nocturnal visitants was supposed, at the time to which I refer, to frequent our ship. It was with the utmost difficulty that the crew could be induced to turn in quietly at night. You might have seen the most athletic, stout-hearted sailor on board, when called to take his night-watch aloft, glancing at the yards and tackling of the ship for the phantom; and square off, muttering his challenge to it to come in some honest shape, and not be skipping about there on the sky-sails and moon-raker, half the time in sight, and half the time lost in shadow. It was a long time, in the opinion of the crew, before this phantom left the ship; and no philosophy that was preached in sermons or otherwise could shake their confidence in its reality.

Now and then an occurrence takes place on board ship which seems to invest these mysterious phenomena with some reasonableness and force. A sailor in one of our ships-of-the-line had died of a slow, lingering disease. He was laid out on a plank, as is customary, and after some fifteen or twenty hours, his messmates were called to wrap him for burial, when he rose to a sitting posture, white as his linen. With eyes glassed in death, he told the crew, as they were standing in breathless awe around him, that he had been sent back into this world to warn them, and that unless they repented of their sins, and reformed their lives, they would perish forever. His language, though a common seaman, was select and forcible, and free of the technicalities which make up the dialect of the sailor.

When he had finished his admonitory appeal to the crew, which was uttered with indescribable solemnity, he sent for the commander-in-chief. This officer came to him: "Commodore," said he, "a few hours ago it was for you to command, and for me to obey; it is now for me to speak, and for you to listen. Commodore, you are tyrannical to your crew, and profane to your God. You must repent of your sins and cast yourself on the compassion of Christ, or you are undone. My mission is now accomplished, and I must return." He then sunk slowly back again on his death-pillow. The body was kept for a week or so, and then consigned to the deep.

Such was the appalling impression produced by this occurrence, that for several days scarce a loud word was heard among the crew, and the commander-in-chief carried the impression with him to the grave. I had this narrative from the surgeon of the ship, who was present and witnessed the whole.

If you ask me whether I believe this sailor had really departed to the world of spirits and reappeared among us again, I answer that I have stated the facts of the case as related to me by an eye-witness, and I leave you to draw your own inferences. I know nothing in the Bible which discredits a belief in the return of departed spirits. One shadowy visitant may be sent to startle the sinner from his fatal slumbers; and others may be commissioned to cheer the weak, to sustain the dying:

>Hark! they whisper: angels say,
>Sister spirit, come away.

The uncomplaining submission of the sailor to just punishment, and his indignation at unmerited chastisement and rebuke, form another prominent trait in his character. He seldom seeks, when guilty, to escape the penalty through prevarication and deceit. He has no lawyer to tell him to plead not guilty, and to extricate him through some technical informality in the proceedings. He acknowledges his offence, and submits to the punishment as an admonition to himself and others too. But he resents, with the full force of his moral nature, even the imputation of crime when innocent.

When Small confessed his participation in the projected mutiny on board the Somers, not the shadow of a shade of doubt respecting his guilt rested on my mind. Had he been innocent, the very keel of that ship would have trembled with his remonstrance. A sailor tamely submitting to death in expiation of a crime he never committed or purposed!—such a thing is not known in all the annals of the ocean.

He will not silently submit even to an opprobrious epithet on board a man-of-war. One of our officers in charge of the deck called a sailor a nondescript. He had scolded him for some supposed neglect of duty, and then said, "Go forward! you are such a perfect nondescript, I don't know what to do with you." Forward the sailor went, muttering to himself, "Nondescript—what does that mean? Here, Larkin, can you tell me what nondescript means?" "Why, what do you want to know what nondescript means for?" "Why, the officer of the deck called me a nondescript, and it means something bad, I know, for he was angry." "Well, I don't know what it means," said Larkin: "send for Wilkins, he can tell." Now, Wilkins was a sort of ship's dictionary; and, though ignorant as any on board, he had a reason for every thing, and a definition besides. So Wilkins came: "What is the meaning of nondescript?" inquired the aggrieved sailor. "Nondescript," said Wilkins, after a moment's pause, "nondescript means one who gets into heaven without being regularly entered on the books." "Is that all it means?" said the sailor:

"well, well, I shall be glad to get there any way, poor sinner as I am!" If there was more of that sailor's *spirit* ashore, there would be less wrangling on doctrinal points.

A prejudice against all innovations is another trait in the character of the sailor. Holding to ancient usage with the fidelity of a Turk, a habit consecrated by time has with him a sacredness which he will not lightly surrender. He is attached to a custom because it is a custom,

  And scorns to give aught other reason why.

No regular sea-bred sailor will ever go on board one of our steam frigates, except by compulsion. He detests steam even in a dead calm, though he must lie there

  " As idle as a painted ship
  Upon a painted ocean."

He thinks it fit to be used only in crawling off a lee shore; and even then, sooner than resort to it, he would risk a thump or two with the breakers. He likes an open sea, long sweeping waves, an ample spread of canvas, a stiff, steady breeze, and the foam rolling away as if in terror from his careering keel.

Some French sailors once went ashore at Mahon in dress-coats. They were encountered there by American sailors in their roundabouts, and a battle ensued, in which some bones were broken. When the matter was inquired into by the proper authorities, the reason assigned by our tars for their terrible onslaught upon the French boys was, that they wore coats with tails to them. "I don't care," said Jack, "about the tails on their coats, if the polliwogs didn't call themselves sailors; they disgrace the profession, sir." A sailor, fickle and impulsive as he may be on other subjects, is firm in his prejudices

> He is a child of mere impulse and passion,
>   Whose prejudice oft deals his hottest blows,
> And fickle as the most ephemeral fashion,
>   Save in the cut and color of his clothes
> And in a set of phrases, which or land
> The wisest head could never understand

CHAPTER III.

> He thinks his dialect the very best
>   That ever flowed from any human lip,
> And whether in his prayers, or at a jest,
>   Uses the terms for managing a ship;
> And even in death would order up the helm,
> In hope to clear the "undiscovered realm."

HUMANITY OF THE SAILOR—EMOTIONS IN VIEW OF THE DYING DOLPHIN—JACK AND THE PORCUPINE—HIS FONDNESS FOR EXCITEMENT—ADDICTEDNESS TO THE CUP—TEMPTATIONS OFFERED HIM—GOVERNMENT TO BLAME—ABOLITION OF THE WHISKY RATION ARGUED—FACTS IN POINT—CONGRESS BOUND TO SUPPLY A SUBSTITUTE—TEETOTALISM THE ONLY SAFETY FOR ARMY AND NAVY—THE SAILOR'S SUSCEPTIBILITY TO RELIGION—PRIVATION OF CHRISTIAN PRIVILEGES—ERROR CORRECTED—THE SAILOR REMEMBERED ON THE CROSS—HIS DIALECT THE WING OF PRAYER—SHAKING IN THE WIND.

ANOTHER feature in the character of the sailor is his humanity to dumb animals. Though he may knock down a French sailor for wearing a coat with a tail to it, he will never turn out a poor old faithful horse on a public common to die. He leaves such accursed inhumanity to those who surfeit the guest, and starve his steed.

When pushed hard for fresh provisions on a cruise in the West Indies, we took our lines and angled for the dolphin. One was at last hooked and brought on board. As this most beautiful fish of the ocean was dying, I observed an old sailor leaning over it and watching its spasms. As its complexion trembled through the successive colors of the rainbow to the last one, when death set its seal, a big tear floated in the eye of the old tar, while his lips half unconsciously murmured, "That's hard—that's hard." He believes with Shakspeare,

> "The poor beetle that we tread upon,
> In corporal suffering feels a pang
> As great as when a giant dies."

We had on board the Constellation a lamb, which became quite a pet with our crew, but from a fracture of one of its limbs by the falling of a belaying-pin, it became necessary to kill it; but not a sailor who had played with it would touch a morsel of its meat. "Eat Tommy!" said Jack; "I would as soon eat my own child."

We had also many pets on board, among them the greyhound, the gazelle, the falcon, and that most endeared of all pets, the carrier pigeon; but the favorite with the sailors was the fretful porcupine. They respected him, for they said he could take care of himself; and indeed he did, as there was scarce a nook or corner of the ship where the rogue did not commit his depredations. Our Newfoundland dog was trained by the sailors to take his station regularly when all hands were called, and he always led off when the main-tack was manned. Our sailors could manage every thing but the monkey; they could never make any thing out of that mischievous caricature of man!

Another feature of character impressed on the sailor by his ocean life, is a passionate fondness for excitement. The great element on which he moves is never at rest. If it be quiet at one point, storms are howling and breakers lifting their voices in thunder at another. Here, an iceberg, in mountain majesty, tumbles on its terrific way; there, a roaring waterspout seems as if emptying another ocean from the clouds; and yonder, the vast maelstrom draws whole navies down its whirling centre. Reared amid these stirring wonders. the sailor becomes impatient of repose.

> It is his life's first pulse to be in motion,
>   Roaming about, he scarce knows where or why;
> He looks upon the dim and shadowy ocean
>   As his home, abhors the land, and e'en the sky,
> Boundless and beautiful, has naught to please,
> Except some clouds which promise him a breeze.
>
> He looks up to the sky to watch that cloud,
>   As it displays its faint and fleeting form;
> Then o'er the calm begins to mutter loud,
>   And vows he would exchange it for a storm,
> Tornado, any thing, to put a close
> To this most dead, monotonous repose.

This love of excitement in the sailor leads him to the cup—his flattering, false friend; his companion in moments of conviviality; his refuge in hours of gloom. He sees not the serpent which lurks in the fatal bowl, and wakes up to his peril only in the death-horrors inflicted by its fang. And yet the Government, the kind, paternal Government, puts this poisoned chalice to his lips! If you would reform him, strike the fire-whisky out of his ration. Let the moral power of your disapprobation be felt in your acts, not proclaimed in your theories. But, instead of this, you go to him with a cup of whisky in one hand, and a temperance tract in the other! The wonder is, that he ever dashes the whisky aside, and listens to the total abstinent lessons of the tract. And yet, not one-third of the sailors afloat in our national ships touch the whisky ration thus presented to their lips by the Government.

If Congress would forego President-making for the people, and give more time to those whose lives are at issue upon their legislative acts, they would better consult their own duty and the interests of humanity. Nor can any man make a better use of the influence of his name than by appending it to a memorial to Congress to abolish at once this whisky ration in the Navy. There was a time when most of those connected with the Navy were in favor of the whisky ration. It was regarded as an element which the habits of the sailor, if not the hardships of his condition, had rendered expedient. We were once of this opinion ourselves; but experience, that great and final test of all things, has produced a different conviction.

It has been shown, with a conclusiveness that admits of no cavil, that the hardest sea service is best performed by those who use no alcoholic drinks. We adduce, in evidence of this, the health and strength found in our whaling vessels, where no spirituous liquors are used, and where the hardships are unequalled in any other branch of our marine. We have, also, hundreds of merchantmen afloat, where the utmost enterprise and vigor prevail, and where no artificial stimulants are used.

But our evidence stops not here: we have men-of-war in service, where, among a large proportion of the crews, the whisky ration has been voluntarily commuted for other articles, and where still the highest degree of alacrity and strength prevails. And, further, we have one frigate, at least, afloat, where, as we are informed, every soul on board, from the commander down to the loblolly-boy, is a teetotaller; and where order, discipline, and energy are unsurpassed. With these facts before us—facts founded in experience—we are prepared to say that the whisky ration in the Navy can well be dispensed with.

The law, as it now stands, makes it a part of the sailor's ration; and no commander, not the Secretary of the Navy himself, can withhold it. A large proportion of the crews of our public ships voluntarily relinquish it. A few, from the force of habit, or ignorance of the benefits of giving it up, continue its use. This comparatively small number are called on deck twice or thrice a day, where, in the presence of all the rest of the crew, the whisky is dealt out to them, and where their faces are lighted up for the moment with the delirious excitement imparted.

Now what must be the effect of such an example? What its effect on the youth of the crew, and on that sailor whose abstinent purpose sometimes wavers? Temptations out of sight lose half their power. It is our eyes that give the forbidden fruit its charm. And yet no commander, under our present law, can refuse to present this pernicious, infectious example to his crew every day. He cannot have this insidious poison administered in secret; he has no right to order the men down into the hold for the purpose; nor can he cast upon the indulgence any stigma or rebuke. It is honored and protected by law, and he is obliged to respect that law.

What, then, in view of all these facts, is the duty of that body which made this law, but to repeal it? Can any man face this evidence and protect it? Can he look at the evils which it inflicts, and plead for it? Can he stand over the ruins of soul, mind, and body which it entails, and defend it? No, no; not for one moment. It ought to be abolished at once, utterly and forever. It ought never to have been incorporated with the provisions of the service. But ignorance of its destructive nature allowed its enactment.

That ignorance, however, now no longer exists, and there is no apology left for its continuance. Let Congress, then, strike it from our Naval statutes, and substitute for its poison what will promote the comfort, health, and strength of our seamen.

Most of the evils, also, which exist in the Army, result from the use of ardent spirits. The gill *per diem* which Government allows to each soldier would not of itself produce these ruinous effects; but this allowance only creates a craving appetite for more, and the means of indulging it to a fatal excess is presented by the sutler. Thus hundreds who entered the Army with habits of temperance are led on, step by step, in this ruinous course, till they sink into an untimely grave, or are cast into hospitals, the mere relics of what they once were; while hundreds more drag out a miserable existence between the tempting cup and the pangs of a relentless chastisement.

Such were not the men who achieved our independence; nor are they those upon whom this country could place much reliance in the hour of peril. They are a mere apology for a defence, and, so far from being fitted for active service, they could scarcely make even a *reeling demonstration*.

Now all this wretchedness, misery, and death have not the slightest necessity to plead as an apology. It is in the power of Congress to banish intoxicating liquors from the camp; and the voluntary surrender of their allowance by the garrisons at Fort M'Henry and Sackett's Harbor, show that no great violence would be done to the feelings of the more reputable part of our soldiers if the sutler's license to deal in spirits should be withdrawn, and the whisky ration be commuted for articles that cannot injure the health or morals of the soldier.

It is the opinion of General Macomb (than whom no man in the country has a better opportunity of knowing) that ardent spirits can be dispensed with in the Army, and that incalculable good would flow to the troops from a vigorous prosecution of measures calculated to secure this object.

But another feature in the character of the sailor, whom I may seem for a moment to have forgotten, is his susceptibility to religious impressions. A great affecting truth connected with the destiny of the human soul, finds a ready access to his feelings. It has no prejudices to break down, no skeptical doubts to overthrow: it is unresisted by his intellect; it falls at once, with its full force, on his heart.

It is well for him that it is so: if truth reached his heart by the same slow degrees that it generally does that of other men; if it had first to be filtered through the alembic of his intellect, it would rarely, if ever, accomplish the errand upon which it was sent. He has incomparably less time and fewer opportunities than other men. His home is on the ocean; he is rarely in a vessel that has a religious commander;

and still more rarely in a ship where there is one whose duty it is to instruct him in the great truths of Revelation.

He starts on a voyage across the Atlantic, or into the South Seas, or to the East Indies, and during his long absence never, perhaps, once hears a chapter read from the Bible, or a prayer offered to his God. He returns, and is on shore for a few weeks; he has no sacred and endeared home of his own to go to; and he seeks those scenes of amusement, excitement, and conviviality which are congenial to his roving habits, and for which his long deprivations have given him a keen zest. Before the land has become stable around him, and the buildings have ceased to rock as the masts of his vessel, his money has been spent, and he is off to sea again.

And now, is it strange that you cannot catch him in this whirl of enjoyment, and make a sober Christian of him? Catch a wild Mohawk, and make a Cincinnatus of him as well! There are thousands who live ashore in the midst of a praying community, have faithful evangelical preachings on the Sabbath, two or three lectures a week, precept upon precept, line upon line, here a little and there a little—and, after all, exhibit but faint traces of piety; and then affect to wonder that poor Jack, thrown ashore for a few weeks among our grog-shops and stews, does not at once become religious!

The wonder is, that he becomes religious at all:

3

indeed, he never would, did he not possess ten times the susceptibility which some of those evince who affect to wonder at him. Truth has to do its work with him at once: its sacred image must strike his soul with the suddenness and fidelity of the daguerreotype impression.

It is no small obstacle to the success of religious efforts with sailors, that they are generally considered as the least likely of any class in the community to be brought under the saving influences of grace; and the clergyman who attempts it, is regarded by many as leading a forlorn hope. When I entered the Navy, a staid clergyman of New England asked me, "Is it possible that you are going to throw away your talents and education on sailors?"

I said to him what I would say to all such inquirers now, the sailor was remembered on the Cross, and if worthy of the dying agonies of the Son of God, he certainly is of the efforts of a poor fellow-mortal. The fact that the Saviour died for him is sufficient evidence that he may be, and in some instances will be, a trophy of redeeming love and grace.

The dialect of the sailor, again, prejudices the seriousness of his Christian character with the community. You can hardly associate the solemnity of religion with the queerness of his nautical phrases. And yet, his dialect is the most concise and expressive known to human speech; and it will wing a prayer to heaven as fast as that conveyed in more polished terms.

Among the sailors in one of our navy-yards, one winter that I was connected with it, there was unusual religious feeling. Of the little crew attached to the receiving ship, almost all became hopefully pious. I asked one of those sailors, as I met him in the yard, how they were getting on as to religion. "Oh," said he, "we have all got on the right tack now, except one, and he is *shaking in the wind.*" Now find me, in all the compass of the English tongue, a phrase so significant and expressive as this of the situation of one hesitating between inclination and duty.

CHAPTER IV.

> Oh, wad some power the giftie gie us,
> To see oursels as others see us,
> It wad frae mony a blunder free us,
> And foolish notion !
>
> — BURNS.

NAVY CHAPLAINS—A REFORMER IN WORD AND ONE IN DEED—THE CAPSTAN AS A PULPIT—THE SAILOR IN VIEW OF DEATH—SICKNESS AT SEA AND ON SHORE COMPARED—BURIAL IN THE DEEP AND UNDER THE SOD—THE WORLD'S DEBT TO THE SAILOR—CHRISTIANITY HIS CREDITOR—HIS LIFE AND CHARACTER LITTLE KNOWN—HIS NATURE IN RUINS—HOW TO BE BUILT AGAIN—HOMES VERSUS BOARDING-HOUSES—THE PLEA OF PHILANTHROPY—AN APPEAL TO THE POCKET—SOURCES OF ENCOURAGEMENT—CHRISTIAN PHILANTHROPY MIGHTY.

WE have been told, through one of our religious journals, that the sailors connected with our national service would be much better men, if their chaplains were better ministers. This indiscriminate reproach was penned by one who had just entered the service as a sort of moral reformer. His rebuke, however, was confined to his language; it derived no force from his own example; for when ordered to sea, he threw up his commission. This was *his* way of showing his interest in sailors.

I have nothing to say in eulogy of the chaplains: many of them are well qualified for their duties, and are faithful in discharging them; while a few owe their appointments to political influence, and are a moral incubus on the corps. But a bishop inditing a party pasquinade, and a politician consecrating a priest, are both very much out of their calling.

So far are sailors themselves from being removed by their habits beyond the influences of religious truth, that could I at all times select my pulpit, place of worship, and auditory, I would take the capstan of a ship-of-the-line, with her thousand sailors on her spar-deck, and if I failed of making an impression there, I should despair of making it anywhere.

It is true, however, that these impressions are less permanent than those made on other men, for an impression, the more easily it is made, is the more easily obliterated. An inscription in wax perishes almost under your style, but engraved on marble it remains, and will be read long after the hand that traced it hath forgot its cunning. Yet, without doubt, many a sailor will retain the images of truth impressed on his soul, and will be graciously remembered in that day when God shall number up his jewels.

Another feature in the character of the sailor is his resignation in death. He looks upon this dread event, come at what time and in what shape it may, as a fixed dispensation of Providence which he cannot alter. He regards it as the decision of a power which it would be idle to resist; as the appointment of a wisdom which it would be impiety to arraign. Hence he submits himself calmly, and without a murmur, to the fearful issue.

>One call on his forgotten God to save,
> One thought of those he never more may see,
>A desperate struggle with the conquering wave,
> A wild farewell, a gasping agony,
>A bubbling groan, and all with him is o'er;—
>Nor friends nor home will see the sailor more.
>
>Oh, there is something in this hurried form
> Of leaving life and all its lovely things,
>Which fills the heart with dread—'tis not the storm,
> The rock, or wave, that gives to death these stings:
>It is the sudden, unexpected stroke
>By which our last link to the world is broke.
>
>Death is a serious thing, come how it may;
> Fearful though it appear in our repose,
>When this our breath and being ebb away,
> As music to its mild, melodious close;
>And where no parting pangs a shadow cast
>On that sweet look—the loveliest and the last.
>
>But 'tis not thus the shipwrecked sailor dies—
> A sudden tempest or a hidden rock,
>And on the gale his fluttering canvas flies,
> And down he sinks, with one engulfing shock!
>While 'mid the dashing waves is heard his prayer,
>As now he strikes his strong arms in despair!

It has been my melancholy lot to see many sailors die. In the West Indies we were swept to the sepulchre of the wave by the yellow fever, and in the Mediterranean by the cholera. These diseases, sufficiently terrific on land, are inexpressibly more so within the confined inclosures of a man-of-war. Our sailors fell like the first drops of a thunder-shower: but not a word of fear or complaint escaped the lips of any. As death approached, the sufferer, confessing his manifold transgressions, threw himself on the compassion of Christ. As objects grew dark around him, as his breath ebbed away, and the pulses in his frame stood still, I have seen that eye lit with a transport over which death and the grave have no power.

We die at home in the Sabbath calm of our hushed chamber; the poor sailor dies at sea, between the narrow decks of his rolling vessel. The last accents which greet our ears are the tenderest expressions of sympathy and affection, such as flow from a mother's devotedness, a sister's truth, a husband's solicitude, or a brother's cares. The last sounds heard by the dying sailor are the hoarse murmurings of that remorseless wave, which seems to complain at the delay of its victim.

We are buried beneath the green tree, where love and grief may go to plant their flowers, and number over our virtues; the poor sailor is hearsed in the dark depths of the ocean, there to drift about in its under-currents, without a memorial, and without rest, till the great judgment-day. Always the child of misfortune, impulse, and error—his brief life filled with privations, hardships, and perils—his grave in the foaming deep! Though man pity him not, God will remember his weaknesses and trials in the day of his last account.

It should be remembered and noted here, that the most of what is endured by the sailor inures to the benefit of his species. The whole world shares in the fruits of his sufferings. The light of the sun is scarcely more universal than the benefits which flow from his enterprise. To his hardships we are indebted for most of the elegancies, and for many of the substantial comforts of life. He is the only being who puts his life at peril to bring to our hearth the products of other climes, the fabrics of other lands.

But for the courage and hardships of the sailor, what would have been the condition of this continent of North America, now the fairest abode of humanity and freedom on the face of the earth? Would golden harvests wave over its hills, and the sound of its manufactories overpower the roar of its waterfalls? Would the sacred temple heave its spire above a hundred swelling cities and ten thousand romantic villages? Would the triumphs of philosophy and art adorn the portico and grove? Rather, would not the primeval forest still gloom over these hills and valleys; their thick shadows be broken only by the wigwam and watch-fires of the naked savage?

And but for the same daring enterprise of the sailor, we, who sit safely under the shadow of the American tree of liberty, might be slavishly picking the crumbs of a miserable subsistence, under the crushing weight of the aristocratic institutions of Europe. Under God, it may be that we owe our very existence to the sailor, certainly much that dignifies and adorns it.

But for the sailor, all intercourse with foreign lands would at once cease; every ocean would be as impassable as the fabled waves of that sea over which even the adventurous bird never winged its way; our very position on the globe, central as it now is, would be as isolated as the Egyptian pyramid towering above its desert of sand, or Mohammed's coffin, suspended between heaven and earth.

But for the sailor, the breaking light of Christianity might have lingered for centuries on the eastern shores of the Mediterranean; and never, perhaps, have reached the magnificent throne of the Cæsars, till that throne had crumbled under the iron heel of the Vandal. And now, who but the sailor carries the missionary to his field of labor, and the Bible to the hearth of the pagan—that blessed book whose holy light is kindling along the icy cliffs of Greenland, throwing its radiance over the benighted bosom of Africa, and pouring the splendors of a fresh morn along the darkened banks of the Ganges? In the last great jubilee of nations, redeemed by the love of Christ, millions on every shore will hymn the obligations of the WORLD to the SAILOR.

We have thus attempted to trace a few of the more marked features in the character of the sailor, as they are impressed upon him by his ocean-life. I have sketched his generosity, his courage, his improvidence, his prejudices, his superstition, his submission to just punishment, his love of excitement, his respect for female excellence, his humanity to dumb animals, his frankness and honesty, his susceptibility to religious impression, his resignation in death. Those who have followed me through these traits of his character, with the veritable illustrations which have been given, have arrived, I doubt not, at this conclusion,—that the character of the sailor is but imperfectly understood by those whose occupations confine them to the land.

Another conviction must also have anchored itself in our minds, and that is, that the character of the sailor, in many of its features, is peculiar to himself; and that the ordinary rules of moral judgment, applied to him, would do a serious injustice. We have found, in the analysis of his character, some traits which call for our stern reprehension; but many more which claim our admiration and tears. The sailor is the most affecting illustration that can be found on our globe of the magnificent ruins in which our nature lies. The massive wall and majestic column, the sculptured architrave and glowing frieze of this moral temple, are blended together in one common wreck.

Such are the habits, tastes, and associations of the sailor in his wild, rude, ocean-life, that they quite unfit him for the elegancies, and even the sober realities of the shore. When he lands among us, seeking rest and diversion from the fatigues of his long voyage, where shall he go? Friendless and kinless as he often is, he finds none to take him to a genial home, and

> Question him the story of his life;
> Of moving accidents by flood and field;
> Of hair-breadth 'scapes i' the imminent, deadly breach.
> And love him for the dangers he has passed,
> As he would you, that you did pity them.

Oh, no, our Desdemonas are all dead; though the tragic tales of Othello still survive in the disastrous lot of the sailor.

Where, then, shall the homeless mariner moor his ship, and find snug-harbor? Save in the establishment of Sailors' Homes, there is but one anchorage left him, and that is those grog-shops under the name of sailor boarding-houses, on every portal of which should be written, THIS IS THE WAY TO HELL, LEADING DOWN TO THE GATES OF THE GRAVE. For what is the fate of the poor sailor in these receptacles of drunkenness and crime? Just what might be expected: he is made delirious with drugged liquors, robbed, and turned half naked into the streets. If it be possible for Satan to be disgusted with any of the miserable wretches driven into his realm, it must be with the monsters who keep these dens!

From such monsters, less merciful than cannibals— for they devour their victims and end their misery— the sailor has but ONE refuge, and that is in the provisions of philanthropy—in those HOMES which Humanity and Christian Benevolence are solicited to provide for him. In such a home only is he safe. In any other place he will inevitably be the dupe and victim of avarice and crime.

I have no confidence in those sailor boarding-houses which have reformed themselves for the sake of custom. The motive stamps the whole establishment with just suspicion. They have always two systems of accommodation, as they have two sets of customers. They have cold water for those who dislike rum, and rum for those who dislike cold water; and little is the difference to them, provided only they can keep their man till they have gone to the bottom of his pocket.

If it be asked where is the necessity for taxing the benevolence of the community for the support of the SAILORS' HOME, since he returns with the wages of his voyage in his pocket, I answer with another question, What are you going to do with him, who, before he has reached this Home, has fallen into the teeth of those land-sharks, and been devoured of all his means? Where shall *he* go? Where shall he find a Good Samaritan and a hospitable inn? Where, but in that happy resource of Christian Philanthropy—a well-organized and authorized Sailors' Home?—a home where he can rest from the weariness and fatigue of his voyages.

These intervals in a sea-life are dearer to the sailor

than landsmen know. Into them are thrown the few hours of rest and enjoyment which relieve his hard lot. His sea-attire excludes him, on coming to land, from our large, well-regulated hotels. Nor could he, if admitted into one of them, endure the expense. Shall he be forced, then, into those abodes of vagrancy and guilt, which jeopard the peace and pollute the moral atmosphere of our large cities? Long enough have these infamous haunts of dissipation and crime been the resort of the sailor. In them he has left the earnings of his best years, his peace of conscience, and his hope of heaven! They have been the grave of his soul.

We must, then, provide him with something deserving the name of home on a scale of keeping with his better taste, and commensurate with his wants. It should be furnished with agreeable apartments, a wholesome, attractive table, and a reading-room, supplied with the papers and periodicals of the day. It should contain within itself sources of innocent recreation and amusement; all intoxicating drinks should be excluded, and the whole should be under the care of a family who love the sailor, who will sympathize with his bereavements, watch over him when sick, restrain his improvidence, take a heartfelt pleasure in ministering to his wants, and be to him father, mother, and sister.

Let such a home as this be furnished the sailor in reality and not merely in name, and you have laid the foundation of his respectability and usefulness here, and his happiness hereafter. But without this primary provision, all our efforts to elevate him, to establish him in habits of sobriety and virtue, will be in vain. Our house will be built on the sand; and we shall find that we have but curbed and graded the stream of his depravity, while the fountain boils as high as ever. Here, then, is a tangible object which all who read can reach. If you cannot build entire a sailors' home, you can each put a stone into its foundation, and a brick into its walls. It was such contributions as these that pillared the magnificence of the Ephesian temple, and reared over the august shrine of St. Peter's the splendors of the heaven-suspended dome.

In such a home only as we argue for can the sailor enjoy religious instructions, or be brought under moral restraints. He is on shore but a few weeks, or months, at longest; and it is of infinite moment to him, as an accountable being, that divine truth and the elevating influences of correct social life should reach him in every shape possible. Even *with* these brief advantages, he must be almost a miracle of susceptibility, if he do not go to sea again without any radical transformation of character. *Without* them, what then can be hoped for?

The moral results of this exclusion from the light of truth and the humanizing influences of society are fatal to any class of men, but fearful especially to the sailor. It is this social neglect and Christian abandonment that makes the pirate. Cast any class of men, whose hearts the restraints of religion have not reached, upon the ocean, and cut off all intercourse with the social influences of the shore, and they will become a reckless crew of roving corsairs.

Even in a three years' cruise in a man-of-war, though frequently in contact with the shore, there is often a perceptible DEGENERACY in those on board. Let this deprivation of moral and social influence be continued, and the Somers' tragedy would be but a prelude to the bloody drama of horrors that would invest the ocean. So that the lives of the defenceless thousands who traverse the deep, and all the great maritime interests of the world, are at issue on the moral influences which you throw around the sailor while on land.

It is proper to remark here, that there is nothing in the alleged failures of past experience to discourage such benign efforts in behalf of seamen, especially when these efforts are contrasted with results in other departments of Christian philanthropy. Twenty, and, I may say, forty sailors, have been converted to Christ to one Mohammedan or intelligent Hindoo, though the efforts and sacrifices for the latter would outweigh, ten to one, those made for the former. Yet, who thinks of abandoning the Mussulman and Gentoo to their fatal superstitions? No one. We pursue our labor of love; we exercise our FAITH; we hold on to the PROMISES; and the Church will continue to do the same, unless her hopes shall have been realized, when centuries have rolled over our graves.

CHAPTER V.

> Look to the weather-bow,
>   Breakers are 'round thee;
> Let fall the plummet now—
>   Shallows may ground thee;—
> Reef in the foresail, there!
>   Hold the helm fast!
> So! let the vessel wear,—
>   There swept the blast!
>
> Mrs. Southey.

THE RELATION OF THE CHURCH TO THE SAILOR—THE POETRY AND THE PROSE OF HIS LOT—HIS PRIVATIONS AND HARDSHIPS—HIS WEAR, TEAR, AND FARE—NOW REEFING ON THE YARD-ARM—NOW BUFFETING THE BILLOWS—NOW A PALE CORSE IN THE DEEP SEA—THE LAZARETTO AT SEA AND THE EPIDEMIC ASHORE—HOME UNKNOWN TO THE SEA—WHERE TO FIND SOLITUDE—THE SOCIAL CONDITION AT SEA NECESSARILY A DESPOTISM—THE SABBATH PRACTICALLY UNKNOWN—EFFECT OF THIS MORAL BEREAVEMENT.

WE have sent our missionaries to the icy cabins of the Greenlander, the scorching huts of the Hottentot, the squalid tents of the Arab, the desolate shrines of the Greek, and the funeral pyres of the Hindoo. Nor would I recall one of these heralds of the Cross from his field of labor, or divert from their present object his messages of love. I would swell their numbers, and animate and sustain their efforts, till every nation, enlightened by the truths which they convey, should exclaim—How beautiful are the feet of them who preach the Gospel of peace, and bring glad tidings of good things! But I would say, also, "Go up, and look towards the sea."

Those ships moving to and fro are freighted with human life. Those veering sails obey the will of men, who sway the strong ship to their purpose, as the rider his steed—of men whose graves may be in the depths of ocean, but over whose immortal natures the gale and wreck have no power. Could they perish, could the wave which sepulchres their forms be the winding-sheet of their souls, we might withhold our sympathy and concern. But they have spirits that will sing in worlds of light, or wail in regions of woe, when the dirge of the deep sea is over.

It is this after state of being that gives the sailor's lot its strongest claim upon our Christian solicitude, and makes it meet that we should endeavor to mitigate its physical evils, in order that we may secure its future and everlasting good. His life at sea, at the best, is full of hardship and peril. It can never be any thing else, so long as the winds and the waves remain.

The poet may roll through it the melodies of his verse, and the painter throw around it the enchantments of his pencil; but its stern realities will still remain, and still assert themselves in the tragic horrors of the gale and the wreck. The ocean's harp plays only anthems for the dead.

That they whose life is on the deep may, at times, little reck of the perils that environ them, is true; but this is the result of being inured to the danger, even as the peasant, rocked by the earthquake at the shaking base of Etna and Vesuvius, sleeps soundly, although that sleep may be his last, and day may dawn over the tomb of another Herculaneum! The caverns of the deep are full of corpses which will start from their abysses at the summons of the last trump; and millions will wake to an endless life of bliss or woe—

> "That sank into the wave with bubbling groan,
> Unknelled, uncoffined, and unknown."

But when these last disasters of the sea are escaped, the life of the sailor is full of hardship. Of all the quiet comforts and fresh luxuries of the shore he is utterly bereft. The products of the garden, the fruits of the vine—all that give variety and attraction to our tables, never relieve his hard fare. His meals are made from bread which often the hammer can scarcely break, and from meat as dry and juiceless as the bones which it feebly covers. A flowing bowl of milk, which the child of the poorest cottager may bring to its lips, is as much beyond his reach as the nectar which sparkled in the goblets of the fabled divinities on Ida.

When Adam, under the rebuke of God, went forth from his lost Eden, he still found some flowers springing up amid the briers and brambles that infested his path, and he still had a confiding companion at his side to share the sorrows of his lot; but the sailor finds no flowers springing along the pathway of the sea, and no soothing companion there, except in his dreams of some far-off shore.

When the night-storm pelts our secure abode on the land, we can close our shutters, and quietly forget its violence in the arms of slumber. Not so with the sailor; it summons him from his hammock to the yard-arm; there, on that giddy elevation, while his masts reel to the sea, while the tempest is roaring through his shrouds, the waves howling in tumult and terror beneath, the thunder bursting overhead, and the quick lightning scorching the eyeballs that meet its glare, the sailor attempts to reef sail!

One false balance, one parting of the life-line, and he is precipitated into the rushing sea. A shriek is heard! but who, in such a night of storm and terror, can save! A bubbling groan ascends—the eddying wave closes over its victim—and he sinks to his deep watery bier. His poor mother will long wait and watch for his return, and his infant sister, unacquainted with death, will still lisp his name in gladness. But they will see his face no more. He has gone to

> That dim shore, from which nor wave, nor sail,
> Nor mariner has e'er returned—nor one
> Fond farewell word traversed the waters back.

These are not perils which overtake him merely

once in his life, or once in the progress of a voyage. They come at all times, in every clime, and in every sea. They are constantly occurring links in the chain of his strange experience; they are his life's history; they belong to the sailor's universal lot. They are the first as well as the last act in the great tragedy of the sea.

When disease assails us on land, when a fatal epidemic strikes our cities, filling all hearts with dread, overpowering the timid, and reducing the brave to despair; when only the hearse is heard in the streets, and they that look out at their windows are darkened, we have an escape left, at least a temporary refuge in the surrounding country. But when this fatal malady reaches a man-of-war, it comes like the executioner to a prisoner in his cell. Beyond the wall of that floating prison there is no escape but into the depths of ocean. Each must stand in his place under this cloud charged with death. He may not move, or even tremble, though the next bolt is to strike himself.

Confined as all are to their floating lazaretto, they only can go over the ship's side, who move in silence and in canvas cerements to the sepulchre of the sea. That hollow sound—that plunge of the hammocked dead into the deep, can be imagined, perhaps, by those who have heard the coffin of a loved companion mournfully rumbling into its untimely grave. But the putrid corpses of the buried coming up through the stagnant surface of the sea, and floating in spectral terror around the devoted ship, constitute an appalling climax of horror which landsmen can never know.

No carnage that war ever yet made on the decks of a man-of-war, can rival in terrors the helplessness and despair caused by the pestilence. Phrensy may fill churches when the earthquake rocks, but it is necessity that dooms mariners to die in masses on a man-of-war, when the cholera, or yellow fever, or East India dysentery have invaded her.

The battle and the breeze have exciting charms for the robust sailor, that reconcile him to many of the evils of his lot. But in scenes like those of sickness and death, he sighs for the shore, and the stoutest heart quails and feels, if it does not say with the poet,

> "Ah! let me live on land, where rivers run,
>   Where shady trees may screen me from the sun;
>   Where I may feel, secure, the fragrant air;
>   Where, whate'er toil or wearying pains I bear,
>   Those eyes which look away all human ill
>   May shed on me their still, sweet, constant light,
>   And the hearts I love may, day and night,
>   Be found beside me safe and clustering still."

But how little is the sailor conversant with delights like these! That word HOME, with the thousand quiet thoughts and endearing associations which it brings with it, is not known to the vocabulary of the sea. Were strangers to enter our dwelling, turn our wife and children out of it, throw the furniture into the streets, swing hammocks in the chambers, fill the parlors with the arms and munitions of war, narrow the foundations to a keel, unroof the walls, and set the whole rocking as if an earthquake were under it, we should have some conception of a SAILOR's home. We might possibly endure such a home, could wife or children share it with us; but without them, it would be like a ruined altar where the vestal flame had gone out, or a trampled shrine from which the divinity had fled.

There is nothing at sea like home. The sympathy which sanctifies the domestic hearth is all unknown to the sailor. Those tender assiduities which flow from hearts allied, relieve not his rough experience. There *are* no hearts around him into which he can pour the sorrows that oppress his own. Although the fountain may be there, and swelling up to its marble curb, tears may not channel his rough cheeks. His grief is confined within him, as lightning in the isolated cloud.

It is this sense of loneliness, this excision from social love and sympathy, that gives to the sailor's lot its most dreary features. It throws a desert around him, barren as that on which the solitary palm of the Arabian desert casts its shade. Would you know what real solitude is, wake up on board a man-of-war, or in the heart of London or Paris, where, among the swarming multitudes of the mighty metropolis, there is not one that has ever heard of your existence; and where your death would be as little noticed as the falling of a leaf in the great forest.

The social condition and government of a ship is, necessarily, perhaps, a despotism. There must be some one there whose authority shall be supreme. Emergencies are constantly occurring which forbid all consultation. The slightest delay in giving the orders would put in peril the lives of all on board. The ship's safety lies in instant action. This makes it necessary that her commander should have absolute sway. This authority, too, he must possess at all times. If emergencies only can confer it, who shall judge of the necessity? A disagreement on that point might result in mutiny.

The sailor is, therefore, necessarily under a despotism, and is exposed to all the ill-treatment and cruelties which an abuse of this absolute authority can inflict. To question this authority is a crime; to resist it is death. He has no alternative but in submission; and he *does* submit, though his wrongs lay in ruins his strong heart.

Nor do the hardships and cruelties which the sailor endures stop with those which result from oppression and tyranny in his commander; the ocean has been incarnadined with his blood, to gratify the animosity or ambition of princes. The terrible triumphs of Trafalgar and the Nile filled the English Isle with exultation; but it filled the ocean with her dead. And never was the naval battle fought, or victory won, which the life-blood of the sailor did not pay for.

Could the sea reveal its secrets, could the wrongs endured on that element find a tongue, there would be louder thunders there than those which roll from the breaker and the cloud.

If the spirits of those whom Moslem jealousy has murdered and sunk in the Bosphorus still float that stream in the form of complaining birds, which never rest, the ocean might be covered with these shrieking symbols of outrage and crime. It is no wonder that the organ tones of the sea are so full of plaintive melancholy and grief; nor is it surprising that all the minstrelsy of the mariner partakes of the same sadness. Any other notes with him are like jocund airs under the cypress that droops over the dead.

Were there now an offset to all the sailor's disabilities in his improved moral condition when at sea, neither himself nor his friends would remonstrate or complain in his behalf. But so far from this, the institution which is at the foundation of all true morality and religion, is almost unknown at sea, as to the observance required of it in the law of God.

If the Sabbath bring with it a cessation from labor in some extraneous departments, still the great business of managing the ship in the midst of fickle and violent elements must go on. The sailor is, therefore, deprived of the greater part of the benefits which result from a regular observance of the Lord's day.

This is a moral bereavement which no Christian community on land could long survive. To take the Sabbath from the heart and habits of man, is like taking the dew of heaven from the plant. The last weapon which Atheism has resorted to has always been its extinction. The little religion which the sailor possesses must take root then without such nourishment; and it grows as do violets and myrtles on the verge of the avalanche.

CHAPTER VI.

> May pleasant breezes waft them home
> That plough with their keels the driving foam:
> Heaven be their hope, and Truth their law;
> And Conscience keep their souls in awe!

PECULIAR POSITION OF A SHIP AT SEA—A QUESTION FOR PHILANTHROPY—PHYSICAL AND MORAL DISABILITIES CAN BE RELIEVED—THE RESPONSIBILITY OF MERCHANTS—INADEQUATE MEDICAL RELIEF FOR SEAMEN—PUBLIC OPINION EMBODIED IN LAW—THE DUTY OF MEN ASHORE—HOW TO IMPRESS THE SAILOR—CAPTURING THE CITADEL OF HIS HEART—HINTS FOR A SAILOR'S PREACHER—WHAT WE CAN DO—HOPE FOR THE MARINER—THE CHURCH HIS PATRON AND FRIEND—PLEA IN HIS BEHALF.

THE moral condition of the sailor receives little or no advantage from the ordinance of the gospel ministry. Not one ship in a thousand that floats the deep has a person on board whose sacred office it is to inculcate on those around him the precepts of religion; and by too many even the Bible has been considered as almost out of its element, and useless if sent among sailors. It reached the watch-fires of the savage long before it found the capstan of the mariner. It threw its light around the solitary steps of the Arab, when Egyptian night hung on the great highway of nations.

Prayers may have been offered for those who go

down to the sea in ships, and who do business on the great waters, but they have been often passionless as purchased masses performed for the dead. The relative position of a ship at sea to the rest of the Christian world, has, until recently, been like that of a ball suspended in the centre of a hollow sphere. It is this isolation that has placed it beyond the reach, and seemingly beyond the sympathies of those who dwell on the land. Too many have regarded it as a thing with which they had no community of interest or feeling, no common bond of brotherhood; and they have abandoned it to its calamities and its crimes.

When guilt and misery have done their worst, when the pirate-flag has been unfurled where the insignia of commerce streamed before, instead of accusing their own moral negligence and apathy, they have seemed to regard the terrible spectacle as an exemplification of human depravity, in respect to which they had neither responsibility nor control.

But the practical question now arises in a philanthropic age like this—What can we do to relieve the physical and moral disabilities of the sailor, and what ought to be done by mercantile and Christian communities in his behalf?

We cannot, it is true, lay the storms which reduce his vessel to a wreck; but we can provide him with something better than a naked plank on which to escape from a watery grave. No vessel ought to be allowed to leave a Christian port where there is not ample provision in the shape of life-boats for the preservation of all on board.

The practice of shipping passengers without such a provision, is cruelty to them and treachery to the crew. In the extremities of a disaster at sea, there is no possibility of escape, except for the few who take possession of the boats. The rest must sink with the ingulfed wreck; and the owners of such a ship unprovided with life-boats, have a responsibility which they must carry to the bar of God for the human life sacrificed through their culpable neglect. Christian benevolence cannot, indeed, of itself furnish our packets and merchantmen with boats for such emergencies; but it can expostulate with their owners, and through public opinion it has power to make that remonstrance felt.

We can relieve the physical condition of the sailor in other respects: we can insist upon it that, first and foremost of all, his health and comfort shall be consulted in the quarters he is to occupy. To make room for an additional quantity of freight, he is now often obliged to swing his hammock where he has no wholesome air, or where he is exposed to the elements.

His hours of rest are always precarious; and when they do occur, it is barbarous that he should not be allowed the few poor comforts which his hard lot permits. We cannot reprobate too sternly that avarice and inhumanity which are more anxious for the preservation of a bale of goods than the life of a human being. The horrors of the Middle Passage are not confined to the African slaver: they are found in other departments of the marine service; and it is the duty of Christian communities to look to these wanton cruelties, and bring their authors to merited chastisement.

We can also relieve the physical condition of the sailor in reference to his food. We cannot furnish him with the fruits of the garden and the fresh products of the field; but we can insist upon it, that the provisions which he does have shall be wholesome and sound, and that they shall have all the variety compatible with a sea life. This variety is meager enough at best; for there is not an almshouse in the country where the inmates are not better fed than the sailor.

If he complains of his fare, he is met with reproaches, and sent back to his work with abuse and menace. It is for us to come to his relief, and to bring the weight of public opinion to bear upon his wrongs. He cannot redress his own grievances; but *we* can redress them, we *ought* to redress them, and we SHALL redress them, unless the instincts of humanity within us are dead.

We can relieve the physical condition of the sailor, also, in reference to disease. No provision, worthy of the name, is now made for his relief in sickness. The pharmacopia of a merchantman or whale-ship that may have a large crew on board, is confined to a vial of laudanum, an ounce of mercury or blue pill, and a few pounds of Epsom salts. Nor is there ordinarily a person on board that knows when or how even these should be administered. And if the use of the lancet be attempted, it is just as likely to strike an artery as a vein!

Yet, with these inadequate medical provisions, to which we would hardly commit the life of a pet dog, the sailor is obliged to traverse every ocean, and be exposed to the maladies of every clime. Is it to be wondered at that he does not live out half his days, or that the average life of American seamen is but thirty-six years?

Now it is for religious and humane communities to require that every vessel shall have attached to her, in the capacity of captain, mate, seaman, supercargo, or loblolly-boy, a person who shall have some knowledge of medicine. The presence of such a person should be made indispensable to her clearance at the custom-house. If she attempted to leave port without one, heavy penalties should fall on her owners.

Public opinion must be made to embody itself in the shape of law; and that law must be enforced, not by the occasional spasms of humanity, but by a consistent and profound sense of duty. It is the certainty of its execution that gives a law its moral power. The Ottoman throne, with all its political deformities, stands, because the cimiter of the headsman is sure to follow the evidences of guilt.

I inquire now, What can we do, and what ought we to do, to relieve the moral condition of the sailor which we have already surveyed? We cannot, it is clear, gather these sons of the ocean into our churches on the Sabbath; but we can run up the Bethel flag over their own decks. They have no aversions to that flag, as a class: it is to them the symbol of peace and love, and the harbinger of that haven where the tumults of life's ocean cease, and the weary are at rest. It is a messenger-bird, come through night and storm from the spirit-land.

Yet, let no one think that mere sentiment can mold the character of the sailor. The beings who compose that mass of life which stirs from keel to mast-head on board ship, are like rocks from nature's quarry—feeble blows will not shape them for the great Builder's use. Long before they could be fashioned by such a process, the hand that should attempt it would have forgotten its cunning.

Occasion is every thing in making an impression on the sailor. There are pauses in the storming passions which sweep our earth when the gentle accents of truth can be heard. There are periods of repose in the conflicts of the moral elements when celestial influences can reach the human heart. The dew falls when the winds are laid. These intervals of calmness and reflection are ever occurring in a sea life: and it is in these that the silent messages of truth will exert their greatest force, and produce their most decisive results. When the wind, the fire, and the earthquake had passed, that still, small voice became audible, in which the prophet recognized the whisper of his God.

These messages of truth must be addressed directly to the *heart* of the sailor. Their power should be exerted, not on those phantoms of skepticism which flit through his mental twilight, but on their source,— not on those bubbles of frivolity which brim the fountain of his gushing heart, but on the fountain itself, and the secret springs in which it takes its rise.

Of all beings, the sailor is most the creature of feeling. Impulse is with him the prime source of action. His heart is the bow from which the arrow of his life takes its flight and direction. It is his heart, therefore, that we are to move upon with our undivided strength: it is this that we are to beleaguer with all our forces, and press upon it at all points, as the encircling wave embraces and encroaches upon the diminishing isle.

The heart of a sailor once captured, the citadel taken—the outposts fall. Even the last poor picket-guard of doubt and desperation lays down its arms. The surrender is entire: nor will that captive to Christ ever seek a ransom, or ever forgive himself that he held out so long before he struck his black flag to the banner which streams in light and love from the Cross. But this conquest is not easy: untutored and impulsive as the heart of the sailor may be, it is yet too gigantic in its strength to be easily overcome. Cradled on the deep, and reared amid the exhibitions of its gloomy grandeur and strength, moral realities must be made to take to his mind a corresponding vastness, solemnity, and power. The sailor must be made to

> Feel his immortality o'erleap
> All space, all time, all pains, all fears, and peal,
> Like the eternal thunders of the deep,
> This truth into his ears—THOU LIVEST FOREVER!

It is also of the last importance to know how to approach the sailor, and in what shape to exert your moral strength. You should not waste your energies in attacking the phantoms of his superstition. You should not attempt to drive away the spectre, but to pour light into its grave. Let the response of the oracle go, but dash in pieces the oracle itself. There is an altar in the heart of the sailor inscribed to the unknown God. Him whom he thus ignorantly worships, aim to enthrone there in the majesty of supreme intelligence, rectitude, and love. Exhibit truth to him in its real character. Throw the practical into prominent relief: let metaphysical distinctions lie where they belong—in shadow. But man's guilt, the cross of Christ, and the judgment-bar bring out from the canvas, as if there were only eternity beyond.

The sailor prefers to meet the dread truths of Revelation as he would meet the rocks of ocean, not beneath the wave but above it, where he may be apprised of the danger before he is wrecked. He is open to these truths: he is not a philosopher to be reached only through his intellect. All the sensibilities of his ardent nature are so many avenues of approach.

Through these, we can cast pure or adulterated metals into the flaming alembic of his soul. There are with him, as with all men, moments when moral repulsion seems suspended, and when truth may reach his heart with the suddenness of the flashing sun's daguerreotype impression. That image, if you can but seize the favorable moment, though momentary in its production, will remain, and all its lines will be found distinct and legible, when the light of eternity shall play upon the tablet.

Such are some of the methods by which we can benefit the sailor, physically and morally. If we cannot pour milk and honey into his cup, we can pour truth into his mind; if we cannot quench the thirst which parches his lips, we can relieve the drought which withers his soul; if we cannot calm the storms around him, we can lay the tempest within; if we cannot secure him the sympathy and protection of man, we can offer him the guardianship of God; if we cannot lift him into authority, we can make him cheerful in a state of obedience; if we cannot take the intoxicating aliment from his sea allowance, we can make him refuse to drink it.

If we cannot ward off from him disease, we can lift him above the fear of death; if we cannot make him a philosopher, we can help to make him a Christian; if we cannot confer upon him a possession on earth, we can offer him an inheritance in heaven; if we cannot make him the associate of princes, we can make him a companion of the saints in light. All this, through the divine assistance, we *can* do; and, if there be joy in heaven over one sinner that repenteth, this is enough.

Our duty and responsibility, therefore, in reference to the sailor, reach to the joys of heaven and to the agonies of hell. The disasters of unfaithfulness are irretrievable. If Christian philanthropy abandon him, his ruin is inevitable. There are no other influences but those of the Gospel that can save him. If he falls into the sea, he may clasp the life-buoy and be rescued; but there is a deep to which no such provision of humanity extends — a deep where the signals of distress are all unseen, and where eternity only answers back the minute-gun of despair.

Shall this be the portion of the poor sailor? Shall he, after all the neglects, hardships, and perils which he has endured here, lie down at last in sorrow? Shall he have lived in exile from our Christian communities, to be exiled at last from heaven? Shall he escape from his last wreck here, to be wrecked again and forever, when heaven's last thunder shakes the sea?

Oh! if wrongs could fit the soul for the presence of its Maker; if cruelties endured here could win happiness hereafter, the sailor need not be without hope! But the laws of our moral being cannot be changed, or the requirements of infinite rectitude set aside. The pure in heart only can see God; and that moral purity is never the natural consequence of moral wrong. Oppression drives even the wise man mad; how much more the fool, which all men are until regenerated by grace!

The Church must, therefore, be the friend of the sailor, the advocate of his rights, his patron under injuries, the stern rebuker of his wrongs. She must pity him when others reproach, pray for him when others denounce, cling to him when others forsake, and never abandon him, even though he should abandon himself. That love which never wearies, that affection which never forsakes, have rescued thousands whom retributive justice would have delivered over to hopeless misery and crime. Many a sainted spirit, ere it winged its way to heaven, has cast on erring youth a chain of light and love which has brought its footsteps back to the paths of life and peace. The ocean, as well as earth, has its moral gems, which will one day sparkle in the diadem of him who has saved a soul from death

There is a loss, compared with which that of life is not worthy of being named. From this fearful loss we can all do something to save the sailor. We have seen the moral perils and hardships of his lot. We know his uncomplaining fortitude, and his generous disregard of danger; we know his weaknesses, his sins, and his sorrows. He is a noble being, but in ruins. It is for us to recover him, to strengthen him in the right, and to guard him against the wrong. He is the child of impulse, the creature of circumstance; and it is our duty to see that these eventful influences are not fatal. He will repay this care in his gratitude, his reformation, and his prayers. Then give him a helping hand. He would spring from deck or rock, amid sweeping sea or breaker's foam, to save *you;* save HIM, then, from perils worse than those of a watery grave.

A TALE OF THE SEA.

I.

We dropped our loaded net in quest of shells
    Among the tideless caverns of the sea—
Those coral grottoes, where the mermaid dwells
    And charms the naiads with her minstrelsy—
And " lifting in," found on its dripping comb,
What brought to all the sweetest thoughts of home:

II.

A golden ringlet!—fair, and soft, and flowing
    As on a living brow—once near an eye
That flashed with light and love—nor faintly showing
    Dimness or stain upon its glossy dye.
It seemed as if it had by stealth been taken
From one who slept, and in a breath might waken.

III.

Would that she might awake! but no, the seal
    Which death has dimly set, may not be broken,
Nor can a look or line henceforth reveal
    Of all once worshipped there one tender token.
And yet we linger near—and half believe
'Tis some delusive dream o'er which we grieve.

IV.

Oh that this fair-haired tenant of the grave
   Could but one moment reappear to light;
And bless the living with the look she gave
   E'er death had thrown its still and starless night
Upon her radiant features—but, alas!
She sleeps beyond that boundary none repass.

V.

No more on her will beam the smile of love,
   Nor voice of parent, brother, sister, friend,
Or aught of all the accents wont to move
   Her heart to gladness, on her dream descend·
No more the breaking morn or purpling eve,
Or thought of home her spirit glad or grieve.

VI.

Still at her father's hearth the lisping child
   Will oft repeat in free, unconscious gladness,
His sister's name—wondering that those who smiled
   At that loved sound, now look in silent sadness,
Giving his artless questions no reply,
Except a starting tear or deep-drawn sigh.

VII.

How came she to her solitary grave?
   By treachery's wile, or grief, or wan disease?
By gale, or wreck, or pirate's flashing glave?
   Where was her home—and who her kindred?—these
Quick, melancholy questions, ne'er will be
Solved by the incommunicable sea.

VIII.

A pirate once, while in his dungeon lying,
   To him who shrived his guilty soul, confessed,
That on the wave o'er which our flag was flying,
   Those deeds were done which now his conscience pressed;
And 'mid the many then consigned to slaughter,
Were two—an old man and his only daughter.

IX.

The latter was so young, so sweetly fair,
   The pirate-crew, in melting mood, agreed
Her tender years should not thus early share
   The death to which her father was decreed.
This sentence passed—the parent bade a wild
And last adieu to his despairing child.

X.

His eye was cast to Heaven in silent prayer,
   Then to his daughter, as he walked the plank;
No word of weakness broke from his despair,
   As through the parted waves his white locks sank,
And far above the circling eddies' close,
One low, deep moan in bubbling anguish rose.

XI.

But fear is ever with the guilty—they
   Who sought to save, saw in that timid child
Their strong accusing angel—they could slay,
   And wade in blood—but one so undefiled,
So free of all that virtue ever feared,
With every glance their throbbing eyeballs seared.

XII.

She read her fate in that dejected air,
    That meditative, melancholy cast
Of countenance which men will sometimes wear,
    When they perceive their destiny has passed
To deeds which all their sympathies disown—
'Tis nature, speaking in an under-tone!

XIII.

As round their victim closed the pirate ring,
    A sudden tremor shook her airy frame;
Sorrow for her had no new pang to bring,
    But when a whisper breathed her father's name,
Quick o'er her soft, transparent features spread
The pale and pulseless aspect of the dead.

XIV.

And to the deck she fell—as falls a bird
    Smitten on high by some electric stroke;
While through the savage crew no whispered word,
    Or hurried step, the breathless silence broke:
But each, with shrinking aspect, eyed the rest,
As if some secret sin his soul oppressed.

XV.

But he to whom the headsman's evil lot
    Had fallen, still his fearful work delayed,
And stood as one arrested near the spot
    Where he had some confiding friend betrayed,—
One whose unquiet ghost in piteous plight
Now slowly rose to his bewildered sight.

XVI.

Amid the ring, he whose commanding air
  And eye of sternness well bespoke him chief,
Rushed to the child so statue-like and fair—
  'Twas not to save or proffer short relief,
But cast into the sea, ere conscious breath
Might break this swoon, and give a pang to death

XVII.

An idle pity!—her pure soul had fled;
  And as he, bending, raised her nerveless form
Pale o'er his brawny arm, the drooping head
  Lay as a lily bowed beneath the storm;
While o'er her features fell the corsair's tear,
As he consigned her to a watery bier.

XVIII.

Perchance the glossy ringlet which the sea
  Yielded to our deep search, once lightly rolled
O'er that fair brow—but this deep mystery
  Nor breeze, nor breaking wave, will e'er unfold:
Yet fancy still the flowing lock will trace
To that once known and long-remembered face.

XIX.

And when the last great trump shall thrill the grave,
  And earth's unnumbered myriads reappear,
She, too, will hear the summons, 'neath the wave
  That now in silence wraps her sunless bier;
And, coming forth, in timid meekness bowed,
Unfold the tongueless secrets of her shroud.

XX.

How darkly changed this world since that first hour
    When o'er its brightness sung the morning stars!
Time, care, and death's dark footsteps had no power
    Upon its beauty: man, who madly mars
His Maker's works, has swept it with a flood
Of orphans' tears, and deluged it with blood.

XXI.

It has become a Golgotha, where lie
    The bleaching bones of nations;—every wave
Breaks on a shore of skulls—and every sigh
    The low wind murmurs forth, seems as it gave
This mournful tribute, unconfined and deep
To millions, for whom man has ceased to weep.

XXII.

It is a dim and shadowy sepulchre,
    In which the living and the dead become
One common brotherhood—and yet the stir
    And sting of serpent-passion, and the hum
Of jocund life, survive with but a breath
Between this reckless revelry and death.

XXIII.

It is a rolling tomb, rumbling along
    In gloom and darkness through the shud'ring spheres,
And filled with death and life, and wail and song,
    Laughter and agony, and jests and tears;
And—save its heartless mirth and ceaseless knell—
Wearing a ghastly, glimmering type of hell!

XXIV.

When woman dies, 'tis as the silent leaf
   The forests drop—the boughs wave on the same—
The dew-drops, nature's seeming tears of grief,
   The young Aurora dries with her first flame;
While that poor leaf, where'er its grave may be,
Lies unremembered in the wild-wood's glee.

XXV.

Thus perish all—except the honored few—
   The great in Arms, Religion, Letters, Art—
The urns of those the tears of crowds bedew;
   And yet that worth which fires the nation's heart,
Beneath a MOTHER's faithful culture grew—
She held the bow from which the arrow new.

www.ingramcontent.com/pod-product-compliance
Lightning Source LLC
Chambersburg PA
CBHW030425300426
44112CB00009B/849